STARS

DON'T STAND STILL

IN THE SKY

Music AND *Myth*

Edited by Karen Kelly and Evelyn McDonnell

Introduction by Greil Marcus

ROUTLEDGE

London

Published in collaboration with Dia Center for the Arts, New York

First published in Great Britain, 1999 by ROUTLEDGE
11 New Fetter Lane, London EC4P 4EE

ISBN 0-415-19869-0 (hbk)
ISBN 0-415-19870-4 (pbk)

Manufactured in the United States of America

10 9 8 7 6 5 4 3 2 1

STARS

DON'T STAND STILL

IN THE SKY

Music ^AND *Myth*

Contents

History and Memory

A Note on the Series

Dia's series of Discussions in Contemporary Culture has become an influential component of our ongoing programs, particularly through the books that document them. This twelfth conference and book in the series extends the cultural inquiry into the realm of music, specifically rock 'n' roll. Participants in the event and contributors to the book include, not only music scholars and critics, but artists and producers, discussing theory as well as practice.

The conference and publication were organized and edited by Karen Kelly, Dia's Director of Publications and Special Programs, and consultant Evelyn McDonnell. Both deserve special thanks for their dedication over three years of planning and working.

We'd also like to thank the numerous friends and colleagues that contributed to shaping the conference and the resulting book. First, we acknowledge Lawrence Weiner for the inspirational title of the conference and this book, which is borrowed from the work *Stars Don't Stand Still in the Sky*, pictured on page 30. Lynne Cooke, Neil Benezra, Laura Fields, Phil Mariani, and Franklin Sirmans were especially encouraging in the planning of the event. By introducing Karen Kelly to Evelyn McDonnell, Katherine Dieckmann was also exceedingly instrumental in making this project happen.

For their support, enthusiasm, and guidance while getting this book to press, we'd like to thank Greil Marcus and Eric Zinner at NYU Press. Diana Stoll made useful editorial comments on the manuscripts. Numerous photographers, artists, and photo archives were remarkably helpful in putting together the visuals that accompany the essays. We'd especially like to thank Mark Kemp and Ingrid Johnson at MTV for their help.

Bethany Johns, as always, and her assistant Jackie Goldberg worked them into a complementary design, and, in the process, were a joy to work with.

Most importantly, we'd like to thank the participants and contributors for sharing their ideas here.

Generous sponsorship was provided by AT&T and Wenner Media.

Michael Govan
Director
Dia Center for the Arts

Preface

John, Paul, George, Ringo, and I were camping at Yosemite. I had met them at a concert where my press pass gave me backstage access and, having hit it off, was helping them experience the wilderness side of America, a side they never saw in their travels from airports to skyscraper offices, from hotel rooms to stadiums. We were hanging out inside a camper van surrounded by the great outdoors, talking, playing cards, and having a good time. I was particularly friendly with John Lennon, but, since I was way jailbait (my parents must have been camping nearby), the bond was romantic in an innocent, Platonic way. We were all mates, peers—in fact, I might as well have been a member of the band.

It was 1975. The Beatles had broken up five years earlier, and I, at eleven years old, had recently discovered their music. Obviously, the camping scene is fictitious, a myth. In fact, it was a dream, the first dream I remember ever having about rock 'n' roll. Before the dream, I liked a few of their songs; after it, I was a Beatlemaniac. I even wrote a paper for some junior-high class about the Beatles—my first venture into writing about music.

This dream is also a myth in what I have come to think of, while editing this book, the "good way"—it's what Greil Marcus in "All This Useless Beauty" calls "a big story." Or, more precisely, it partakes of several myths, as channeled into the nighttime fantasies of a just-pubescent girl. Some of these are non-pop-cultural and reflect my childhood experience of touring the country in a trailer; the American dreams of nature, mobility, and expansion embodied in those KOA summers could fill an essay themselves. What's interesting for the current purpose is how those American dreams dovetailed with the pop myth of the band as a miniature democratic utopia—a place where I could hang out, escape my parents, be myself, and be cool. I'm not sure where my belief in rock-star access and amiability came from. I don't think the Beatles qualify as a Jungian archetype, but I must have been tapping into the Zeitgeist in some way, there must have been something ambient about this myth; I mean, I hadn't even seen *A Hard Day's Night*. I do remember, as a young bookworm, reading some pulp novel about a *Teen Beat*–ish girl reporter who got to meet heartthrobs and, Nancy Drew–style, have adventures with them. With the hindsight of a couple decades and several hundred bylines, I can safely say that book was a myth in the "bad way": a lie told to obfuscate reality for wicked purposes—in this case, to feed young girls romantic folderol. All the same, here I am, girl reporter.

My life as a rock critic has scarcely been as glamorous or exciting as depicted in that paperback (though it's had its moments), for several reasons. A: Reality never lives up to romantic myth; i.e., most bands treat journalists and girls similarly—as, at worst, dirt beneath their platform shoes or, more diplomatically, a necessary evil. Backstage access has more often provided a gateway to an endless wait and hangers-on than to great adventures and heartthrobs. B: My swinging seventies dreams smashed into the just-say-no eighties. C: I've found rock critics to be a surprisingly uptight bunch, more concerned with proving their field's legitimacy, preserving their objectivity, and generally being moralistic and aesthetic gatekeepers (assholes) than with chasing good times. This is probably a particularly American earnestness: English journalists Nick Kent, Vivien Goldman, and Everett True have a lot more fabulous stories to tell. So did Lester Bangs, but he died in 1982; Bangs may be rock criticism's great lost icon, but no one has successfully followed his lead.

I tell you all this not because I have any delusions that my dreams are so important, that my story is that big, but because, to quote Thoreau, "I should not talk so much about myself if there were anybody else whom I knew as well." When Karen Kelly and I were editing the essays for this book, we were surprised by how many people used personal experience— as opposed to, say, scholarly research or musical analysis—to make their points. Having fallen prey to this trope myself, I now understand it better. One of the purposes of the conference at which most of these papers were first presented was to bring together critics, scholars, and musicians.

Coming from various terrains in an effort to find common ground, many of us sampled the catchy if overplayed melody of the testimonial in order to show our roots—to earn trust through openness, since we don't share methodologies. It's similar to what's been happening in the literary culture at large, where the narrative has become subject to the confessional. Or maybe it's like telling each other who our favorite bands are, so we know what kind of people we are.

Karen and I assembled these diverse thinkers—bookish theoreticians, punk-rock singers, glossy magazine editors—for a state-of-the-art forum on "music and myth," or, more exactly, what the myths promulgated by and surrounding contemporary popular music are and how they came to be. Obviously some self-examination was in order—hence all the confessionals—since many participants are in mythmaking, as well as taking, positions. But we also hoped that the disciplines would examine each other, critiquing and learning from their various positions inside and outside music and myth. Several years ago I attended a similar conference at the University of Missouri where there was simmering tension between journalists and academics. One panel got ugly when critic Gina Arnold attacked professorial types for hiding behind theoretical jargon, and an academic responded, in turn, by lampooning the jargon of critics— "blistering guitar," "intricate riffs," etc. At the Dia conference, Karen and I hoped for a more convivial gathering of university-based and media-based writers under the big tent of cultural criticism—with artists keeping us anchored in the reality of show and biz.

You can lead critics to a conference table but you can't make them behave. At "Stars Don't Stand Still in the Sky," held in New York in February 1997, the panels and audience were studded with cultural studies and music journalism stars (such as they are). Greil Marcus, the freelance thinker whose 1975 study *Mystery Train: Images of America in Rock 'n' Roll Music* was the first scholarly book about rock, and the first to articulate how pop songs embody larger cultural myths, set the tone with his keynote presentation, "All This Useless Beauty," a useful and beautiful musing on the collision of legends and history. Most of the subsequent presentations followed Marcus's lead: they were provocative enough to stimulate debate but not so cantankerous to squelch it. Sadly, the discussions afterward did not always maintain the same level of, shall we say, sophistication. The squabbling was as much intra- as inter-disciplinary, as ideological debates turned into rock-critic ego wars—a room full of bespectacled men muttering to themselves, it's not a pretty sight. The high low point may have come early in the weekend, when one writer responded to another with the trenchant witticism "fuck you."

I remember looking around the hall and wondering how I ever expected collegial dialogue from such a bunch of misfits, misanthropes, cranks, and curmudgeons. I learned long ago that rock criticism is a petty and competitive field, that there's no one we like to dis as much as each other—and the academics were failing to lead us to higher ground (until Paul Gilroy's affecting tribute to unsung heroes, that is). These are people who have made their failure to fit into "normal" society a moral crusade, who can turn the pleasures of pop into taxonomies of categories and ratings, who can make a matter of personal taste a criminal judgment. And I expected them to share in the give and take of debate, then drink a beer afterwards?!

Not to overpartake in critic-bashing myself, I should concede that many of my peers were right to be worried about the very existence of such a conference, to resist the staid pretentiousness of mixing with collegiate types at an art-museum event. I mean, how un-rock 'n' roll! That is, if you still believe in the myth of rock 'n' roll as a medium of rebellion, a belief that at this point in time seems at best somewhat quaint, at worst, precisely the sort of dangerous mystification that's due for rigorous cross-disciplinary analysis—a good whipping!—if for nothing else, to get it in shape so we can believe in it some more. I mean, yeah, I'd rather go to a concert than a conference, or listen to CDs than read a book about them. But four decades into rock criticism's existence, and two decades since Simon Frith's *Sound Effects* offered the first book-length academic analysis of pop, we can't deny that we are participating in established fields, where the challenges to precedents are in turn being challenged themselves. It's time to clean up our own houses—to acknowledge the myths that feed and restrict our fields—in the same way we critique others.

Besides, even if you have no interest in writing about music yourself, reading about it can be fun. Really. In the bibliography for *Sound Effects*, Frith wrote, "People write about rock for love not degrees . . . rock analysis is not bogged down in academic cross-references and methodological paranoia. In short, rock books are hard to find but fun to read." As the field becomes legitimated, as books like this one are published by university presses, it's important not to lose sight of the literary standards set by our predecessors; this was the basis for Gina Arnold's Missouri attack on theory-heads. It's a snobbism to think that people who rock don't think; it's anti-intellectual to believe people who think don't rock. I'm only anti-pseudointellectual: against the virtuosic use of language to bewilder meaning.

There are several essays in this book that are explicitly clarion calls to historians, scholars, journalists, or all of the above to check their shit, so to speak. In the academic world, sociologist Angela McRobbie admonishes her colleagues for ignoring the changing economic realities of artistic production. Cultural studies dude Lawrence Grossberg challenges his peers to come up with new apparatuses for analyzing pop, then proposes a few apparatuses of his own. While both these essays specifically address the authors' field of expertise, their ideas are applicable elsewhere. They also show how academics' distance from their subject, particularly from the music-industry hype machine, can give them a fresh point of view; though much of McRobbie's analysis is based on reportage from journalists, nowhere in scores of magazine articles have I seen insights into the financial realities of electronic dance music like hers.

Meanwhile, Chuck Eddy takes his fellow critics to task for their elitist tastes and, like McRobbie, injects the too frequently glossed-over issue of class into the pop debate. Throughout this book, the coveted critical notion of authenticity gets a thorough interrogation, from outsiders like sociologist Deena Weinstein and art critic Ralph Rugoff, to journalists Eddy and Anthony DeCurtis, to DJ and critic Paul D. Miller. Then again, in one of the most eloquent pieces of writing in this collection, Gilroy chides us for losing that very sense of authenticity, "a long-vanished ontological depth," and sides with singer Kathleen Hanna in her praise of the value of a real, live musician.

Not all the pieces in this collection are so "meta." Other essays speak about specific manifestations of myths in music, or myths about music, or to their production—essays about goth, MTV, love songs, freedom songs, techno, Velvet Elvises, the Rock and Roll Hall of Fame. What isn't here is a single reference to Zeus, Shiva, or Joseph Campbell—the figures you might expect to find in a book about myth. For all our excoriation of "realness," I think critics are still wary of the inauthenticity of myth; myth is still a dirty word. Journalists and scholars are truth-seekers, after all, and a myth is a story told about something, not the thing itself. Critics tend to be boringly, numbingly, obsessed with facts, and, strangely for people who have to write them, suspicious of stories. But the truth is, we're all driven by myths, and we all reconstruct them. Myths fueled my eleven-year-old dream that turned into my thirty-three-year-old reality; retelling that dream, I make myth myself, manufacturing the details I don't really remember, like we all do when we tell our dreams.

Because the market is so adept at turning our beliefs, our dreams, our myths into ad campaigns, it's easy, even necessary, to become cynical about them. It's up to reporters and scholars to counter fantasy with fact—without forgetting that fantasies help us imagine the futures we try to create. A myth is a story, but it's a fiction aiming for truths. Sometimes, saturated by the stream of products arriving in our mailboxes, critics forget how much music can mean to people—how it can speak past language barriers, how people form identities around musical styles, how a song can change a person's life. Music permeates the modern world for a reason: not to deafen us, but to make us better listeners.

Introduction:

All This Useless Beauty

When Elvis Costello released "All This Useless Beauty," the title song of his 1996 album, the song went right past me; I didn't really hear it. It wasn't until Costello put the song out again, in a live version recorded in May 1997, when he was doing dates around the country accompanied only by his pianist, and then in a version he'd asked the band Lush to record, that I really began to hear the song. I was hearing it—particularly the Lush version—as the theme song for this book, or the antitheme song, because in this song, stars do stand still. Time stops.

According to "All This Useless Beauty," time stopped a long time ago. The song begins in a museum. "This is a song about a woman who's walking in a beautiful gallery," Costello said when he introduced the tune in San Francisco last May. "It's full of pictures of classical antiquity and idealized beauty. And she looks across to her less than fabulous, late-twentieth-century lover—and she goes, 'awwwwwwww . . . '" Costello sings the song full-throated, the words all rounded. I ran into him a few years ago in the Academy Gallery in Florence, both of us staring at Michelangelo's *David*—I can't hear Costello sing this song, this song about all this useless beauty piled up in a museum, without picturing a setting that perfect, that marbled. In the San Francisco performance, Costello even sang a chorus in Italian. You can imagine for yourself what paintings the woman in Costello's gallery might be looking at—I imagine Pre-Raphaelite scenes, like Edward Burne-Jones's *The Golden Stairs*, with a score of Hellenic maidens descending toward some unseen ceremony, or his *Tree of Forgiveness*, with Eve clutching Adam and Adam desperately trying to escape from her embrace. Whatever she's looking at, in the sing-songy, up-and-down-the-stairs cadence of "All This Useless Beauty," the woman in the gallery, Costello says, "imagines how she might have lived/ Back when legends and history collide."

Yasumasa Morimura, *Angels Descending the Stairs*, 1991, from the series Self-Portrait as Art History.   17

It's a striking line, thrown away in the song—Costello just lets it drift out of the story he's barely telling—and the sense of wonder in the words, their sense of loss and surrender, matches Bob Dylan's comment on Peter Guralnick's biography of Elvis Presley. "Elvis as he walks the path between heaven and nature," Dylan said, and those words are as good as any he's written in two decades. Those words are so balanced and explosive, they turn the next phrases of his comment, which aren't bad, into clichés: "in an America that was wide open, when anything was possible."

This is what stopped time for me. "When legends and history collide," when what we believe to be hard facts and what we know to be dimly remembered, barely describable ideals go to war against each other, or turn into each other—I think that's what both Costello and Dylan were talking about, history turning into legend, heaven turning into nature, and vice versa, in a painting of an ancient forest or in a new kind of rhythm-and-blues record. But the promise is there only to be taken away. In this song, the time "when history and legends collide," that time of all-things-are-possible, is gone, if it ever was. "Those days are recalled on the gallery wall," the song goes on, but the woman in the gallery was born too late; she missed those days. She missed it—that's exactly the word Costello uses, just like some sixties person telling someone about Woodstock: "I was there, man, and you *missed* it." Now all the woman has is a fact, a hard fact in the form of a soft fact, her lump of a boyfriend slumped at her side with all the ideals of the past, those days recalled on the gallery wall, mocking her. She waits, the singer says, "for passion or humor to strike," and nothing happens. It's the collision of history and legend that produced all the useless beauty on the walls—useless because now its only function is to remind whoever looks at it of what's no longer possible, if you're stupid enough to believe that anything, or rather every-thing, ever was.

Costello sings this song as a tragedy: a beautiful tragedy. The irony burns off as he goes on; the words, taken slowly, carefully, as if something in them, or him, might break, seem to shake in his throat on the choruses. It's painful. But as Lush does the song, it's altogether different. Over twenty years, a whole constellation of singer's singers has taken up residence in

Elvis Costello's voice: Billie Holiday, Frank Sinatra, Tony Bennett, George Jones, Patsy Cline, Sarah Vaughan, Dusty Springfield, Lotte Lenya. When he goes all the way into a piece of music, it lifts off the ground; in a way, it goes onto that gallery wall, keeping good company with whatever useless beauty is up there at any given time. As a punk he was always a classicist; he was always too much of a record fan to let the world get in the way of his sound for too long. Lush is a much younger band, guitarists and singers Emma Anderson and Miki Berenyi leading a two-man rhythm section. As a pop group they've always looked for the punk in their sound, and on "All This Useless Beauty" they find it. There's no pose, no preening; what they do with the song makes Costello seem like an actor. Like that moment in Human League's "Don't You Want Me" when the female singer comes in, earnestly telling her story in a manner so naturalistic it's an effort to remind yourself that she's singing, what Lush create with "All This Useless Beauty" is the shock of realism.

The tragic cast Costello gives his tale of the worlds that are now behind us is what lifts, what beautifies, his own tale of useless beauty. But Anderson and Berenyi take their places in the gallery like schoolgirls who've been brought in on a class trip—for the tenth time. They're too smart for their own good; that's what's always getting them into trouble on trips like this. They're suspicious, they think too much, they just don't go with it, they're always asking questions—and so what was tragic in Costello's original is now just bitter. These girls, acting out the most ordinary, everyday events in this gallery, in this song, know what the idealized images of classical antiquity are for. Where Costello feels loss, Anderson and Berenyi see a trick—and their thin, reedy, determined voices pressing through the tune word by word, nothing at all taken for granted, say one thing: This stuff on the wall—you think you can fool us with that?

A whole world of mystification opens up out of this performance, a whole social con, or a quick, frozen glimpse of an entire society organized around a con: the con of beauty, of idealism, the con that takes reality away from the life you actually live, every day, and delivers that reality up onto a wall, or into the past, for safekeeping. There are moments of coyness in Costello's performance; there are none in Lush's. Listen to it more than a few times, and in its restraint, in the way it makes ordinary talk out of Costello's elegant chorus, Lush's "All This Useless Beauty" is as hard, as resistant, as betrayed, as anything in "Anarchy in the U.K." And yet—when you're sitting around in the limbo of the present age, dreaming of times when history and legend collided, waiting for passion or humor to strike, one of the things you're waiting for is a song like this, a song that can change shape and color according to who's singing it, a song that is like a magic lamp. Here Costello's version and Lush's version collide, so do the past and the present, the tragic and the commonplace, beauty as a useless rebuke and beauty as an inevitable by-product of pressing down on some stray incident or emotion until it seems it can contain the whole of life. Pressing down—that's all the woman in the gallery does with her disappointment over her boyfriend. With Emma Anderson's disembodied contralto floating behind Miki Berenyi's gritty, plain-speech lead on the choruses—with idealism, a legend of how things should or could be, floating behind hard facts, behind anyone's history of everyday defeats, insults, humiliations—the song is beautiful, and only as useless as your life. It reveals itself as a song about what's missing when a mythic dimension is missing from life—and what's missing is the sense of being part of a story that's bigger than yourself, being part of a story that can take you out of yourself, that can take you outside of the pettiness and repetition of your life, circumscribed as it might be by whatever city or town you live in. The fact is, though, that history and legends collide every day, and we are always part of that collision.

Take what's perhaps the greatest and most pervasive of pop myths: the myth of rock 'n' roll as an agent of social or even revolutionary transformation. Now, when I call this a myth, I don't mean that it's necessarily a false story, only that it's a big story, a grand story, a story with room in it—room for whoever might want to join the story, room for whatever beginning or ending one might want to try to put on it. This story has been told many times; depending on intellectual or political fashion, it's told with aggression or apology, hubris or embarrassment, presented as a testament of ambition or naïveté. Recently I came across the most extreme version of this story I'd ever seen, in an unpublished memoir by the historian Robert Cantwell, author most recently of *When We Were Good*, a wonderful book about the folk revival of the fifties and sixties. His memoir is called *The Twigs of Folly*, and one of its themes is that of a type he names "the remorseless spitting American." Cantwell takes the phrase from Fanny Trollope, an Englishwoman who, visiting the new United States in 1830, found herself amazed by the new democratic race she found: rounders and roughnecks and women who lived in dugout houses—people who, in Cantwell's description, had made the leap from "all men are created equal" to "all men are equal."

For Cantwell, these are the true carriers of the myth of equality, down through the decades: not lawbreakers, exactly, but surely a line of moral outlaws, all of them in some final manner uncivilizable. They scorn all differences and all claims to superiority; they are the romantic, the resentful, the heroic or petty outsider Americans who are nevertheless the only real Americans: the likes of Abraham Lincoln and Lyndon Johnson, John Henry and Calamity Jane, Mike Fink and Jack Johnson, Louise Brooks and James Dean. To give the story over to Cantwell:

If the remorseless spitting American was a flatboatman, or a trapper, or a trader in the 1830s, a blackface minstrel in the 1850s, a Confederate soldier in the 1860s, a western cowboy in the 1880s, a dustbowl refugee in the 1930s, by the 1950s he was singing to us from every jukebox, radio, and record player. Who were Buddy Holly, Jerry Lee Lewis, the Everly Brothers, Carl Perkins, Eddie Cochran, Gene Vincent, Sanford Clark, George Hamilton IV, Roy Orbison, if not remorseless spitting Americans all—and, ahead of the rest, Elvis Presley.

The remorseless spitting American had become a rockabilly star.

The opening strains of "Heartbreak Hotel," which catapulted Presley's regional popularity into a national hysteria, opened a fissure in the massive mile-thick wall of postwar regimentation, standardization, bureaucratization, and commercialization in American society and let come rushing through the rift a cataract from the immense waters of sheer human pain and frustration that had been building up for ten decades behind it. Elvis was desirable and desiring, the son of a Mississippi sharecropper with no advantages but the

God-given erotic force that put the gleam on his 300-horsepower hair, the Hellenic beauty in his face, the genital nerve-endings in his voice, and on his lips a sneer with more naked repudiating ideological power than the writings of Thomas Paine, Karl Marx, and V. I. Lenin put together.

Now, put aside any thoughts as to whether this myth, this story Cantwell is telling, or retelling, is true or false, a vision of wholeness or self-congratulatory generational nonsense. Whatever it is, as Cantwell sets it out it is a story you can become part of, one that can help define your place in your society, can situate you precisely where history and legends collide, can help you perhaps to define your own place in your society, or outside of it. It's a complex story—a tale of debts coming due, of the return of the repressed, and much more—but first and last it is a myth of liberation, of legacy and starting over all mixed up together.

You could join this myth by listening to or arguing about or buying records, or writing about them, or making them yourself, by aligning yourself for or against this or that pop figure—or by publicly professing allegiance to one such figure while, secretly, maybe in a secret you half-kept even from yourself, you identified most completely with a figure mocked and scorned by everyone you knew. This was a myth you could join by allowing it to judge the choices you made: between friends, between going to college or not going, studying one thing and not another, between clothes you put on and those you set aside—the choice you made, finally, over just what country, as you defined it, you would be part of, if you were to be part of any country at all.

That is the myth—as it was acted out in the sixties, as it was received, transmitted, invented, codified, and then taken as a natural fact, as a legend of history. In the fifties, this legend wasn't present. There were only events. The myth had to wait—and by the time it arrived, history had faded, faded enough for legend to replace it. At bottom, that's how you join a myth: you join in constructing it, in making it up. Making up this particular myth was to one degree or another the sense or nonsense left to the world by the first generation of pop critics. Does that make the myth untrue? Of course not. It makes it a strange and shadowing standard, a standard all pop music that followed upon the first emergence of rock 'n' roll has to be seen to match, or overtake, or overthrow, or render irrelevant. It's a standard every record, every performance, has to somehow affirm or dismiss.

But as Robert Cantwell writes out the myth of pop transformation—he doesn't call it a myth, I don't mean to imply that he does—it isn't hard to see another, poisonous myth inside of it, as if biding its time: a germ in the idea of equality, the idea carried forth so ferociously by Cantwell's "remorseless spitting Americans," a germ that will emerge not to prove that all might exist on the same plane of legitimacy, but to prove that some are true and some are false. This is the myth of authenticity, or purity—the idea that true art, or true culture, exists outside of base motives, outside even of individual desires, particular egos, any form of selfishness, let alone mendacity, let alone greed.

This myth rewrites the past no less than the myth of pop transformation, and more violently. The earliest version of this myth wasn't written out; it wasn't a story. It was acted out. It was the payola investigations of the late fifties and early sixties, all based in the certainty, on the part of certain guardians of public morals, and politicians who knew a good horse to ride when they saw it, that the only reason the airwaves were filled with garbage, the only reason decent children, white children, had turned away from decent culture, was that someone was paying disk jockeys and radio programmers to play what otherwise would have never been heard. Rock 'n' roll, in other words, was payola: a conspiracy. It was a trick, not unlike that other fifties media panic, subliminal advertising. Both the fear of payola and the fear of subliminal advertising were versions of the ruling postwar myth: that, like the seedpods in *Invasion of the Body Snatchers*, communism could creep up on America as it slept. At the time, in the late fifties, this argument—which was itself vaguely subliminal—didn't even feel like a metaphor. Communist messages secreted in Hollywood movies, like fluoride in public water systems, would weaken the will or the brain tissue itself, until Americans were powerless to resist. And on the radio, among teenagers everywhere, it had already happened.

A different version of this argument came out of the folk revival that took shape concurrently with the payola scandals. Pop music, rock 'n' roll, was looked on as trash, the adolescent indulgence society at large said it was, something to grow out of. It was corrupt; it was all about money; it was all about imitation, every emotion a counterfeit, every gesture second-hand. But with folk music—old mountain music, blues, reels, and story songs, ballads that sounded as if they'd been written by the wind—the soul of the singer came forth. Stripped of artifice in its performance, the music produced a naked person, who could not lie. The speech that issued from his or her mouth was pure; the motive, simply to tell the truth, was pure; and the performance made both singer and listener into authentic beings, who could not lie because they could not want to.

The latest version of this version of the antipop myth comes in Fred Goodman's book *The Mansion on the Hill*, which is about the presumed clash between art and commerce in contemporary pop music. Here, because pop music takes shape in a capitalist milieu, it is inevitably deformed and corrupted, until neither performer nor listener can tell truth from lie. Never mind that pop music, rock 'n' roll, might as usefully be seen as a form of capitalism than as a form of any kind of art—Goodman's version of this myth is really quite bizarre.

Before Bob Dylan stepped from folk music into rock 'n' roll in 1965, Goodman argues, rock 'n' roll was a "pop-trivial medium." There was no such thing as expressiveness, no authenticity of any kind, just—stuff. Money and sounds. But rather than rock 'n' roll then wiping folk music off the cultural map—as the story is usually told—Goodman argues that, through Dylan's agency, folk music completely rewrote the rules of pop music. Now, according to Goodman, suddenly the rock 'n' roll sound could carry truth: true messages and true beings. You could be true to yourself; to thine own self you had to be true. But because there was still money to be made off of rock 'n' roll—in fact, far more than ever before—a fatal contradiction loomed.

Despite suggestions in *The Mansion on the Hill* that the man who once wrote, "Money doesn't talk it swears," kind of likes to, you know, swear—Dylan, Goodman said on the radio recently, had stayed pure. "There's

Dylan and there's everybody else," he said. "He's never made a record to make money; he's never made a record to make a hit." Now, any good pop fan should answer that with, "Well, if Bob Dylan never made a record to get a hit, he ought to. It's not too late." But the whole concept, the whole division, is ludicrous—and still this myth of purity, this folk virus, is today as defining a pop myth as any other. In England it defined punk from the beginning, with some fans all but demanding proof of working-class status before a record might be considered, and it defines much of the punk milieu today. That's the world Adam Duritz of Counting Crows came out of in Berkeley—and it was this myth, far more than anything that can be reduced to an attitude, that drove him out of town. He wrote his songs, formed this band and then that one and then another, made his music, followed where it led, and his music hit—and then, in a drama that Kurt Cobain perhaps acted out within himself, arguing with himself, raining abuse upon himself, Duritz found himself a pariah on the streets of his own town, cursed by those onetime friends and fellow scenesters who did not cross the street or turn their backs and walk the other way when they saw him coming. Not only had he betrayed the purity of the Berkeley punk community, he was like a disease: get too close, and you could catch it. It all goes back, so seamlessly, to the folkies who decided that the Kingston Trio, never mind that they'd somehow gotten the word out first, were phonies.

Now, given the weight of pop myths—and there are of course scores of them, intertwined and overlapping stories about what it means to be a performer or part of an audience, about love and death, identity and facelessness, and on and on—it can be a shock to encounter performances that seem utterly free of myth, that seem to come forth completely on their own terms, as if they came out of themselves. That this might be possible is perhaps the most alluring pop myth of all; myth or not, it's what I heard on *The Golden Vanity*, a Bob Dylan bootleg a friend in Germany sent me.

Bob Dylan acted out an odd, to many incomprehensible or irrelevant little cultural drama in the early and mid-nineties. Onstage, he offered often shockingly powerful versions of his old songs, performed with a tight, relentless band, with himself as lead guitarist, to the point that long, snaking instrumental passages, doubling back and descending into near silence and then, like the Isley Brothers' "Shout," erupting into a greater noise, completely overwhelm the parts of a song that are actually sung. From 1990 to 1997, he issued no new songs of his own, instead substituting records of old blues and folk songs—solo recordings made with an acoustic guitar and harmonica, drawing on material that in his repertoire predates the material on his first album, released in 1962, more than thirty-five years ago. It's these sorts of songs that are collected on *The Golden Vanity*—the oldest of the old songs, ballads, and airs that are hundreds and hundreds of years old, collected in the form of audience recordings made at Dylan concerts from 1988 through 1992. Some of the songs are common coin, numbers everyone sang in the days of the folk revival, "Barbara Allen" or "Wild Mountain Thyme." Some are obscure, at least to me: "Eileen Aroon." These are the sort of songs Bob Dylan recorded in St. Paul and Minneapolis in 1960 and 1961, on cheap tape recorders in cheaper student or dropout apartments, because in those days these songs seemed like a key: a key to another country or another self, a strange music carrying, like all strange music, the call of another life.

In the early sixties, Dylan, then twenty, twenty-one, could invest these songs with flesh and blood. As he sang, men and women, lords and ladies, ghosts and demons, all the figures of the old ballads, appeared before you. But now, as Bob Dylan sings these songs in his late forties, in his early fifties, all that these songs once meant, as talismans of the folk revival, as charm pieces of purity and authenticity, as keys to a kingdom, has been forgotten. As knowledge, as rules, what the songs once meant has been passed down in the form of punk, not in the form of "Little Moses" or "The Two Soldiers" or "The Waggoners Lad"—and so these songs appear, on a bootleg CD, not as culture at all, but as some sort of contradiction, anomaly, or disruption, coming out of nowhere; speech without context.

In a dark, aged, bitter, baffled, chastened voice, Dylan sings these old songs as if he knows they contain all the truth of being, from birth to death, and as if that truth would be plain to all if only the songs could be sung as they were meant to be sung, or heard as they were meant to be heard—if only the world were, for an instant, in perfect balance. Passion lifts the songs, a yearning so fierce it's hard to credit, hard to listen to. A retreat, a withdrawal in the face of a world that was always the way it is and that will never be any different, overwhelms the singer, and he seems barely to sing at all. All at once, he can sound like a man singing a given song for the first time, or the last time. But inside the audience, where these recordings were made with hand-held microphones and hidden tape recorders, there is a completely different world, and people live in it.

People are shouting, cackling, growling like dogs, yelping Deadhead yelps and whooping hippie whoops, imitating each other, vocally high-fiving, barking and drunk. It's the weirdest thing. This is no collision of history and legend—the collision, as I've been trying to say, from which myths arise, whether the collision is accident, the myth emerging like a new language no one has to learn, or whether the collision was arranged, the myth set forth as a new language everyone has to learn. Here, in these recordings, as what the singer is doing and what the crowd is doing cancel each other out, there is no history and there is no legend. The centuries of persistence in the ancient songs Dylan is singing, and the ancient singer he appears to be, make the noise of the crowd seem like vandalism; the refusal of the crowd to listen makes the wisdom of the songs, and the passionate body of the singer, seem like vanity. The result is the most compelling music, or the most compelling event, I've heard, or become part of, in a long while: monumentally irritating, utterly confusing, impossible to hear and in moments impossible to pull away from. You hear someone struggling to turn what he believes to be timeless, what he believes to be outside of historical time, back into ordinary time, and the instinctive effort of others to stop him.

There's no myth I can pull out of that or drape around it. It's a new incident, without a story, so far—like the two shouts that open Sleater-Kinney's "Little Mouth," the film-noir theme in DJ Shadow's "Stem/Long Stem," or a thousand other things anyone could name.

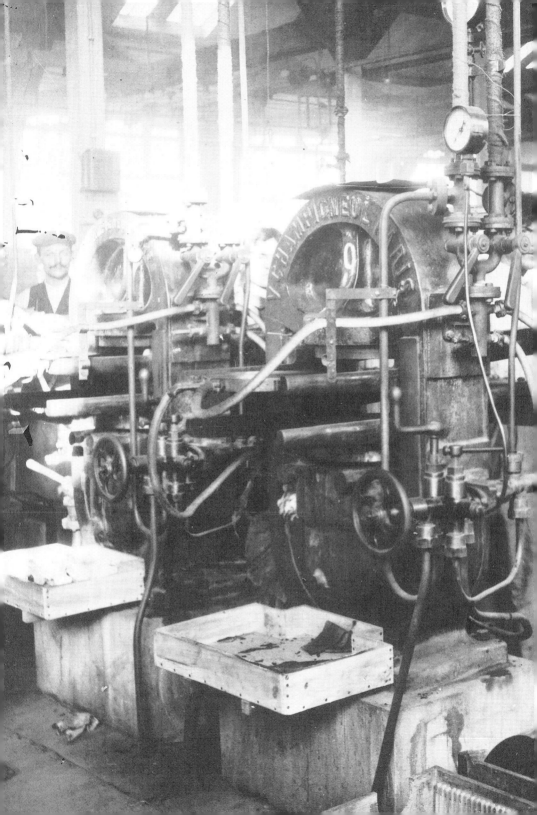

Commerce

Lost in the Supermarket:

Myth and Commerce in the Music Business

It should surprise no one that, in the determinedly one-track mind of the music industry, myth, like everything else, is merely something to be marketed. The hipster point of view would argue that, of course, that's true about Whitney Houston but certainly not about Pavement. But the fact is it's true across all genres and styles, regardless of whether the myth is "DIY" or "classic rock," "the year of the woman," or "keeping it real." It was true back in the hallowed sixties, when record companies would run campaigns with slogans like "The Man Can't Bust Our Music," and it is even more true today, when most consumers do not require or appreciate ad slogans that distance them from "the Man." In fact, the very idea of myth has been drained of its significance. Essentially at this point myth is, at best, inseparable from a celeb-addled notion like "charisma" or a tossaway word like "legend." At worst, it is synonymous with "image"—and synonymous as well with all that term implies about the calculated re-creation of the self for the marketplace.

Myths, of course, have very different meanings depending on the frames in which they are placed, the filters through which they are viewed, and the times in which they emerge. We are far more suspicious today, for example, of myths of the hero than people were two centuries or even two decades ago. The question is: are any of the meanings that myths accrue politically progressive or helpful in any other way?

To the degree that myths, in their purest sense—that is, as religious systems—serve to mystify the material circumstances out of which they arise, the answer to that question would be no. In a more secular sense, myths also reinforce the conservatism of the status quo when they are exploited—as they so often are—by huge corporations that care nothing about the emotional or spiritual role of music in people's lives, except as a potential source of profit. Artists are people, after all, people who grew up and live in specific historical conditions, which the work they create partly reflects and partly helps shape. Myth can be a means of concealing those simple but critically important facts. Prince's relationship to an entire history of African-American culture, or Liz Phair's privileged upbringing, were issues that rarely came up as he was being cast as somehow beyond racial category, and she was portrayed as an indie-girl rebel sexpot beyond class.

The real lost meaning of myth, however, is as a symbolic repository of a people's deepest hopes and fears, an expression of all the complex, contradictory, incomprehensible elements of their lives. Rock 'n' roll has all-too-frequently been described as a kind of religion, and at the point of each young true believer's discovery of it, the music absolutely shimmers with those mythic qualities. For reasons that extend far beyond rock 'n' roll itself, however, it is difficult now for any adult—or even for most sophisticated young people—to retain that deep belief in the possibilities for social change and self-transformation that once seemed inherent in rock 'n' roll.

The ironic sensibility that governs so much alternative rock—a mostly futile response to the culture of marketing that infects both fans and the bands themselves—pretty much renders a serious consideration of myth impossible. In fact, it's probably not too great a simplification to say that the real question is: do the myths surrounding rock 'n' roll at this point have any life at all independent of the economic uses to which they are put? Is myth now exclusively a creation as well as a function of marketing?

From a sociopolitical standpoint, the most suggestive cultural moments are those in which the profit motive clashes with other ideological priorities—as, for example, when Warner Bros. is pressured by law-enforcement groups and stockholders to drop Ice-T or to sell Interscope Records. These are the times when myths collide and explode. Such moments isolate the flash points at which peddling the myth of the invulnerable black gangsta clashes with the myth of "law and order" or with the ingrained racism of American society. Such clashes strain the system, as artists who have proven themselves profitable are unable to continue the role scripted for them in the economic drama, and genuine political battles ensue from sociopolitical situations that had been assumed to be purely economic in nature.

The basic underlying premise of American corporate culture is not so much conservative as apolitical: it assumes that anything that commands the attention of a sizable group of people can be sold, regardless of how potentially inflammatory or disruptive it is. It assumes that all anyone really wants is money; so as long as artists with supposedly progressive messages are cut in on the deal to some manageable extent, there should be no real political consequences to making even seemingly revolutionary music available to vast numbers of people. For the most part, however unlikely it may seem, that viewpoint has proven to be correct.

What's interesting in this regard is that popular music does far more to agitate conservative elements in American society in opposition to it than it does to mobilize progressive elements in support of the allegedly idealistic goals some artists espouse. Law-enforcement groups, family-values organizations, conservative politicians, and corporate shareholders have successfully pressured record companies to withdraw support from rappers, for example, by using the supposed deleterious effects of their music as a wedge to advance a conservative cultural agenda. It's an agenda that contradicts right-wing economic politics, in which the free market ultimately determines the value of all things.

In the case of "Cop Killer" by Ice-T's thrash band, Body Count, the almighty marketplace had already (and rightly—it wasn't very good) doomed the album containing that song to a quick and painless death. The furor over the song caused by irate law-enforcement groups revived it—and jacked up its sales—for the very purpose of ending Ice-T's business relationship with Warner Bros. The song's actual cultural and political significance to that point had been negligible at best. Whatever impact the song had is due entirely to the attacks on it. Strangely, conservative critics apparently have more faith in rock's mythic power than alternative cynics do.

Unquestionably, rock 'n' roll occasionally eludes commercial demands to create deeply satisfying art. And, occasionally, the creation of great songs— as in the case of Motown—actually seems to be aided by the strictures of commerce. Popular art is supposed to be popular, after all, and the communal impulses the music is so good at exciting are premised on its ability to find an audience of some measurable size. But how do the bottom line and the matters of myth that often come into play in such art—spirituality, idealism, community, transcendence—interrelate? Are they pure oppositions or can they survive in creative conflict, or even in some version of harmony?

As we near the end of the twentieth century, it's hard to evoke a vision of that potential harmony. The language of business has overwhelmed all other forms of discourse. Everyone speaks it with surprising ease and regards all other ways of speaking and thinking as foreign. Alternative languages are not merely rejected, they are experienced as meaningless and alienating. As has been the case with the movie industry for some time, a blockbuster mentality has overtaken the music business, and sales have become the only generally shared measure of an album's worth. The weekly *Billboard* charts, far from being the sole province of people in the trade, are now discussed by teenagers, and the twists and turns of the marketplace are monitored with rabbinical zeal. Albums "open" just as movies do, with first-week sales playing a crucial role in how seriously people regard the fate of every new release.

Cynics would suggest that this is simply a more honest state of affairs than in the past, that in the immortal words of one manager, "It's not called show art, it's called show business," and that's just the way it's always been. Certainly nothing about the, shall we say, "colorful" origins of the music industry (founded by a group of men primarily distinguished by an odd combination of traits: monumental self-interest, piratical greed, and extraordinary good taste) would suggest that the motivations of its founders were primarily idealistic. And, as an industry, it's simply followed the general movement of the national economy and the culture as a whole. Moreover, every aspect of popular culture derives part of its charge from the dynamic between art and commerce, between the impulses of the individual creator and the demands of the crowd.

Still, no one but a fool could deny that the market is a far more over-whelming factor in every matter connected to music than it was even twenty years ago. The current market was defined by the single-driven blockbusters of the eighties—Michael Jackson, Bruce Springsteen, Prince, U2, Madonna—and even the seemingly anticommercial gods of grunge who emerged in the early nineties conformed, however unconsciously or unwillingly, to that model. Just as the Reagan years defined an era in which it was possible to utter racist ideas in public without the slightest apology, no one even has to pretend today that money might not be the single most important reason for making music. A development like that, of course, is at least once removed from the structural forces behind how the music industry works, but those forces have themselves changed dramatically over the past twenty years.

Record companies are no longer run by people who, despite their innumerable other flaws, rose up through the ranks and may even have been musicians—or at least fanatical music fans—themselves. They are owned by multinational conglomerates—Sony, Bertelsmann, TimeWarner, and so on—with many other holdings, and they are expected to show the same types of steady returns as other, more traditional, less creative businesses. The vagaries of artistic inspiration—another element in the creation of myth—are ironed out into trusty formulas, and artists who don't play by the rules better justify themselves with millions of sales (thereby generating the next formula), or they're gone.

Myth thrives in environments and times that admit the idea of the unknowable and reward faith. Today people say, "that's a myth," when they really mean to say "that's not true," in order to dismiss a commonly held belief. *Myth* simply means *wrong*. The idea of a truth that might be deeper and richer than fact, or of an artist who might provide a bridge to an unseen world of possibility, doesn't have much currency. People are understandably skeptical, but they don't really believe anything that's worth being skeptical about. They're desperately lost in the supermarket and, far from being unable to shop happily, as the Clash suggested, they now mistake sneaking a couple of extra items through the express lane for an act of rebellion.

The one unquestioned truth, the truth beyond all skepticism, is the market. It is too deep and all-pervasive to be questioned; examining it is like examining the air as we try to breathe. But, while myth is no better able than anything else to resist the market's lure, it cannot survive there. Stars certainly don't stand still in the sky, but they do fall out of it, and no amount of wishes can compensate for the losses of hope and inspiration all those sad descents embody.

Angela McRobbie

Thinking with Music

Who Is That By?

Nowhere is the marriage between art and science more happily secured than in the extraordinary profusion of cheap-to-produce popular musics that over the last fifteen or so years have created a music-society that rivals and even outstrips the image-society in which we now live. This forces a reassessment of the meaning of music in everyday life; but so prolific is the output of so many different genres, which converse with and against one another, that few critics seem capable of creating a credible map, or writing a story, of contemporary pop. Music-making defiantly slips the net of language, setting itself, as Susan Sontag memorably put it back in the sixties, against interpretation. Current music styles leapfrog backward and forward in time, snatching phrases, chords, and strains of sound from unlikely sources, placing one on top of the other and throwing issues of authorship and ownership into disarray. Who is that by? becomes an absurdly naïve question. These musics play teasing, competitive games with the audience for whom, listening on the car radio, or even half-submerged in the local swimming pool, there is always the chance that they will never hear the same track again. (For a moment last summer, I thought of getting out of the water at the Archway Pool in North London to ask the DJ-lifeguard the name of the hip-hop track whose fluid inter-play of spoken word and backing track so evoked the bare-bone aesthetics of rap that it was good enough to drown in.)

Hip-hop and dance musics propose newness, not just by applying bedroom-size computer technology to old, discarded fragments of sounds, but also by forging a different relationship with their audiences. So ener-getically bound up are they with their own musical inventiveness, with what can at present be done with music, that the DJs, musicians, and producers can virtually ignore the audience, in the same arrogant way that early punk did. So dispersed and fragmented, so volatile and widely spread are the various audiences for contemporary music, it seems almost pointless to think, Who will this please? Who will want to buy this record? Music is thus allowed to turn in on itself and enjoy a moment of almost sublime self-confidence. This challenge to the audience is passed on in the challenge to the critic or to the sociologist; we too seem suddenly redundant. What role is there now for criticism or analysis?

Indeed, our critical vocabulary seems sadly lacking. None of the old words, like *collage*, *montage*, or *postmodernism*, seem capable of capturing the velocity and scale of this output. Likewise, the older ways of making sense of music by placing different styles into different categories, or by posing the commercial against the creative or experimental, or by talking about white or black music as though they were quite distinct are equally inappropriate. Now, in the late nineties, we have to start with an assumption of musical hybridity, of global cultural crossover and the profound interpenetrations of style, coupled with the reliance on often quite basic machines to engineer a quality of DIY eclecticism that even the huge and wealthy record companies have trouble knowing what to do with. In short, music has become artificially intelligent.

Faced with the sheer challenge that music production poses, music commentary in the more academic journals has actually pursued a fairly predictable and erroneous course. The claim that current dance-music styles appear to embrace a refusal of meaning, in the same way that they suggest a refusal of authorship and authenticity, is patently banal and unsatisfactory. The conclusion that follows, which sees only political nihilism in sharp contrast to the political verve of punk, is equally fallacious and ahistorical.

For example, Jeremy Gilbert has recently argued, "However nihilistic they may have seemed at the time, not even Joy Division . . . can really be located outside this discourse of protest."[1] The problem with this kind of account is that it posits a style of music, i.e. punk, as being inherently close to politics, as though politics were this quantifiable, identifiable thing at the center of social life. Current dance music, in comparison, pursues a logic of pure pleasure rather than politics, Gilbert says, and thus confirms the essentially apolitical identity of young people in Britain in the late nineties. He explains this abandonment of politics in terms of the rave generation's frustration with mainstream political culture. Rave is nihilistic, but it just, and no more, manages to rescue itself from the slur of having no politics whatsoever by refusing at least to share the nostalgic stage of national pride with Blur, Oasis, and the other white boys of Britpop.

In a similar vein, the search for politics continues in Drew Hemment's suggestion that "the ecstatic dance is not in itself political, but it is a micropolitical event—an intervention in the formation of desire."[2] Finally, Dave Hesmondhalgh warns against a too-easy confirmation of the democratic potential of dance music on the grounds that it is authorless music, imagined and produced largely outside the corporate cultures of the big music companies.[3] This is misleading, he argues, because it overlooks how dance-music producers also get sucked into the star mythology of name DJs and the attraction of a record deal with a major company. Yet Hesmondhalgh still wants to hold the torch for dance. Even though drum and bass has become "yuppie cocktail music," he acknowledges in this music an often thrilling mixture of the dark and the uplifting.

In all three of these essays, and indeed across the field of writing academically about music, where it is recognized that in some complicated way something political is at stake, there is this same tension between mistrusting dance music's hedonism and affirming it as political. It is certainly not satisfactory to discount the political dynamic from the viewpoint that it's just music, after all. Nor are most leftist critics willing to adhere to the argument that the writing and discussion somehow spoil the whole experience, that they rob the music of its whole reason to exist (as one of my own students recently suggested). Perhaps the issue is not to search for a political and theoretical vehicle of such sophistication that it does justice to the significance of the phenonema (which is how Gilles Deleuze and Félix Guattari inevitably appear in the footnotes in both Gilbert and Hemment), but rather to be more realistic about the politics of music and the people who make the music, and to adopt a more pragmatic, sociological approach based on the question, What can academics say or do that might be useful?

The purpose of such an approach would not be to court the political approval of a government attuned to the significance of the culture industries by producing a string of policies, or good ideas, out of a hat. Quite the opposite: it might well be to ask very awkward questions of governmental leaders, like Bill Clinton and Tony Blair, determined to use pop to look modern. But neither would such an approach simply succumb to the temptation to replace politics with theory, as though making sense is achieved exclusively at that point where convincing analogies can be drawn between a musical form and the frequently opaque writing of a number of French philosophers (enjoyable though such an attempt might be).

Livelihoods in Music

The more politically relevant point is surely that music today is a place of employment, livelihoods, and labor markets. This fact is obscured because being creative remains in our collective imaginations a sort of dreamworld or utopia, far apart from the real world of earning a living. The irony is that the philosophers are as spellbound by the idea of art and creativity as the rest of us are. Jean Baudrillard, for example, is reported as having said that the real attraction of retirement is that it means he can become a real writer, an artist no less. The popular-music industry has drawn on this conventional language of genius, talent, and charismatic personality, which in turn is how modern society continues to understand the role of the artist. The artist is the romantic outsider whose exceptional gifts are manifest in how different he (occasionally she) is from the rest of us. But this is now a hopelessly anachronistic way of understanding music (and art) production in Britain in the nineties. For a start, there are a lot more people making music and hoping to earn a living from doing so. This is no longer a completely futile dream. The old jobs, which for many people meant a lifetime of unrewarding labor, are gone forever, and there has been instilled into a younger generation, at some deep level, a determination for work to mean something more than a hard slog, for work to become a labor of love, a source of creative reward, a sort of poetics of living. For working-class boys (less so girls) without qualifications, it's become possible to turn youth culture into a job-creation scheme. Too easily, in the demonic media-typecasting of young, often black, males as lurking on the fringes of criminality, do we forget the small humiliations and indignities of low-paid, low-status labor.

What an escape, then, to move into music. Talent, imagination, and even musical genius have emerged as working-class youths choose careers in culture, in some cases transporting the individual from a career in crime (i.e., the rap artist Coolio) in the space of one record. In Britain, the startlingly diverse and imaginative urban soundscapes of Manchester and Glasgow, Bristol and London index the scale of wastage that mark a class-divided society, where middle-class children have every ounce of talent nurtured like a precious thing as a matter of course, while the rest could quite easily have never known they had it in them.

But even this does not exhaust the issues posed by the changes brought about by the culture-society. How much music and how many musicians can the new culture-society accommodate? What kind of livings are being made? How can we gauge the span of talent and creativity? Who judges what constitutes musical genius? Indeed, this line of inquiry can even be taken to the opposite extreme by suggesting that, at some level, to those now doing the producing, the questions "How good is it?" or "Is it great art?" are somehow less relevant. These are replaced by further exploration into some very particular musical directions in a way that is uninterrupted by other, commercial constraints. We can see this especially in the new musics being produced by figures like Roni Size and his colleagues and, also, Björk. With creative work now accounting for a much greater number of livelihoods, it may well be that some of the old romantic notions have already slipped by the wayside.

Artistic work has become more ordinary, it has been edged off its pedestal and turned into more common currency. It's not just that the art schools are churning out more graduates, but, further down the hierarchy, there are any number of sound-production, studio-engineering, and computer-programming courses. The students who sign on for these have been mixing tracks in their bedrooms since they were twelve, and see quite clearly that electronics and engineering no longer mean working for the electric company or steel mill. The emphasis on skill rather than stardom does not mean that the utopian dynamics of these new apprenticeships for the nighttime economies of dance and club culture are denied—quite the reverse. Here we have, with the growth of cultural capitalism, a similar scenario to the one Marx himself looked forward to: cooking, looking after the children, and doing the ironing in the morning, writing lyrics and composing tracks on the home computer in the afternoon, and playing them for money in the evening! Caspar Melville describes how this happens in the world of drum and bass, where it is not unusual for producers, like Grooverider and 4Hero, to make a piece of music in the daytime and play it out at a club in the evening.[4]

How this kind of activity works in the postwelfare society remains to be seen. How much of the labor market can culture mop up? What kind of livings are there to be made in this cultural society? Are we witnessing the emergence in Britain of a new kind of low-pay, labor-intensive, cultural economy, comprising a vast network of freelance and self-employed creative people? What sort of government issues will be thrown up by the emergence of this work force as a long-term phenomenon? Are these culture workers all dutifully paying their taxes? Have they already attended to their private pension plans? How does self-employment tally with the high cost of parenting?

It's doubly difficult to get a real grip on these economics when they encompass such vast differences of income, from the now incredible wealth of the Prodigy to the modest living of Grandmaster Flash, for example. At the same time, what all of these performers (including the twelve-year-olds in their bedrooms) have in common is the possibility of producing cheap music through access to sophisticated, home-based computer equipment.

The opportunities made available by these machines were spotted early on by figures like Grandmaster Flash, who learned how to refine the art of mixing from an electronics course at technical school and then combined this knowledge with his curiosity for old records, which stemmed from his fascination with his father's record collection, locked away and out of reach of children's hands. As he said to David Toop, "I would tiptoe up to the closet, turn the knob, go inside the closet, and take a record."[5] The ability to make music within the budget of pocket money and a Saturday job has also been a key factor in the prodigious growth in music production, twenty years after the birth of hip hop. Making music at home on a school kid's small budget is how the first Prodigy album was cut, with Liam Howlett literally walking off the street into the record company with a sequence of rave songs recorded in his bedroom. This is now common history, but the celebrity culture that almost immediately gears itself up for marketing musical success obscures the local economic outlook in the long term. As far as I know, no attempt has been made to chart, for example, how current DJs' careers are pursued in Britain, even how many are plying their trade, and how sustainable these careers are.

An Avant-Garde of the Self-Taught?

Obviously all this activity does count, more than just economically. Contemporary music culture embraces the banal and the sublime, but because most popular music still registers in the cultural hierarchies as untutored or untrained and associated with talent, emotion, and sensuality, its cerebral and socioeconomic significance is often overlooked. Critics can make all sorts of claims on behalf of the emotional power of popular music, but rarely, if ever, do they dare to propose a thinking role. As French sociologist Pierre Bourdieu would explain, if it's sensual and immediately gratifying, then it must belong to the lower social classes and thus be perceived as incapable of the depth and complexity found in the high arts as enjoyed by the educated social classes. It has been up to black writers in Britain, such as Paul Gilroy, to demonstrate just how much thinking there is in black music. Such music can hardly contain the investment of artistry, politics, history, and literary voice, so that as an aesthetic it is, by definition, spilling out and overflowing, excessive, a first destination for social commentary, dialogue, and rap that leaves those of us still caught in the prison of language far behind. But no establishment person on the quality press (the *Guardian*, the *Times*) or elsewhere ever calls it a spectacular avant-garde, which is what it is. (Though it is also perhaps true that the popular, black idiom of this kind of musical activity also exposes the underpinnings, limits, and exclusions of the term *avant-garde*.)

It's not just music that is directly connected with black culture that provides a language of analysis and critique for its practitioners. Popular music in Britain provides an accessible, relatively open aesthetics for those who want to play. It can be something to think with—to explore class and history, city and space, sexuality, identity, and tradition. And, because this capacity has been grabbed as a kind of philosophical lifeline by some of the most interesting figures in this particular urban, postwar landscape, much music means more than just pop.

The way in which British pop has become particularly aware of its own capacity for reflecting on all sorts of sexual anxieties, as well as other national obsessions, has been commented on since the early eighties. The Pet Shop Boys and Morrissey are usually held up as prime exemplars of this: masters of surface poise and gentle irony, and explorers of white, polite masculinity. There is a problem, however, when debate gets narrowly focused on the work of performers like these big names. It becomes even more difficult to shift from a mode that considers their work, its meanings, how these develop, and where they come from, to one that is concerned with livelihoods and politics. So enormous is these stars' personal wealth, they hardly have to worry about paying their mortgages or about what will happen if they get sick. The challenge then is to find ways of making connections between these success stories and the question of employment in music and, by extension, in the culture industries. We can begin to do this by returning to questions of social class (as well as gender and ethnicity), history, and biography.

Histories of Music, Politics of Class

Three useful examples of how music can function as a way of thinking, as well as a place of working, came to my attention almost by chance last summer. I felt like reading about music again and was suddenly overtaken by a desire to go to hear music the way I used to in the early eighties in Birmingham, when there was such a rich musical crossover of reggae (Steel Pulse), disco (Sheila B Devotion), punk, two-tone, and various well-intended efforts at neo-Marxist pop. I reread Simon Reynolds's influential *Blissed Out* and found myself absorbed in his interview with Morrissey. It showed Morrissey to be remarkably aware as a child that pop culture provided him with a kind of personalized map, a way of making sense of place, identity, and existence. He told Reynolds that at the age of six he had his own magazine, and how, listening to the Top 30 every Tuesday, he would "run off instantly to the typewriter in order to compile my own personal Top 30, which totally conflicted with how the world really was. . . . It was a Top 30 of contemporary records, but the new entries were very unlikely, and obviously I favored certain musicians, like T. Rex."[6] This doesn't just prove that popular culture has replaced nursery rhymes and fairy tales as a source of image, narrative, and information; it also reveals an incredibly intelligent child looking to the charts as a way of working things out. A more middle-class environment might gently discourage this attitude. But in a single-parent and class-dislocated household, Morrissey was free to consume as much pop as he wanted. You get the impression of him being a rather pompous, old-fashioned child, giving radio his full, unbridled attention.

A week later, the *Guardian* ran a lengthy interview with Terry Hall, who had started off with the Specials, then set up the Fun Boy Three, and has recently released an excellent new album titled *Laugh*.[7] This was a distressing story of a working-class boy making it into the local grammar school, only to be perceived as socially vulnerable by a teacher who then kidnapped and sexually abused him and another thirteen-year-old. Unable to describe to his parents back home what had happened to him, his schoolwork went out the window and his days at grammar school were numbered. His talent was only able to surface inside the safer confines of Coventry's grim and hard-edged, two-tone youth cultures in the early eighties, where he wrote "Ghost Town," a classic single that conjured up the history of black ska music by allowing it to haunt the outskirts of the song, and that envisaged and documented the new intersections of black and white youth in Britain's inner cities.

The same week this interview was published, I slipped into a sweatbox in Islington to hear Jah Wobble's Invaders of the Heart play on one of the hottest nights of the year. It was a great performance with a lineup of reggae musicians and the drummer Jaki Leibezeit from Can. Wobble's bass playing (and his looming, expressionless physical presence) led and connected the whole set, from a pared-down jazz introduction, through a reggae section that combined Celtic instruments and Blakean lyrics, through to a solid dance dub ending. The thudding bass line also told a story of class and history, of manual labor and then later of urban multi-culturalism. In his earlier incarnation with John Lydon, this bass was put to spectacular effect in the first Public Image single. The dark rumble (miles more ominous than anything the Prodigy have come up with), combined with Lydon's psychotic screechings, make it one of the most memorable (and influential) records ever made.

Wobble had done a number of extended interviews following the release of his most recent work.[8] He recalled walking out of a shabby, run-down East London school (this was "no Dead Poets Society") and stumbling into Lydon, with whom he went on to share a squat. Eventually he picked up a bass guitar left lying around by Sid Vicious. Interwoven with this narrative was another one, of Dickensian cityscapes, of fifteen-mile hikes around Lea Valley to Greenwich and back to Cambridge Heath Road, of reading Yeats in Shadwell Public Library, of parents and grandparents who made their livings from the river and its trade, of falling into music after falling out of hopeless jobs. He also went on to recall abandoning music for a spell after Public Image and taking a job in the London Underground, then finding his way back into music and rediscovering ability and talent and a sense that it couldn't be wasted.

Morrissey at Madison Square Garden, 1991

   Apart from the fact that this particular story vividly illustrated the cultural-studies work of at least three of my colleagues produced over the last twenty years, including Phil Cohen's seminal essay on youth cultures and the breakup of the working-class community in East London,[9] Dick Hebdige's still-magnificent structuralist reading of punk,[10] and also Paul Willis's *Learning to Labor*,[11] all three interviews prompted more general questions about how academics engage with the sort of people who have been living and breathing what we scholars then write about or analyze. For example, it seems scandalous, after thirty years of comprehensive education, the so-called decline of class society, and its replacement by consumer culture, that there remains a need to draw attention to the forces that continue to conspire against young people's having access to forms of encouragement and finding ways of making good use of their talent. It is politically demoralizing to have to continue to specify the obstacles that must be overcome by young people and the sheer contingency of achieving against a backdrop of active discouragement.

It must be better, however, to run that risk than to disappear entirely into the more intellectually tantalizing, but politically less useful, project of searching for a theoretical language to measure up to the dizzying brilliance of contemporary music-making. Of course, one should not counteract the other, but the stakes are high when (mostly male) academics set themselves the task of making sense of modern music. They are, it seems, haunted by the image, style, and reputation of the (usually white) music journalist (again, check the references to the halcyon days of the *New Music Express*). In this context, the writing has somehow to be a parallel text to the music. This is a boy's language that avoids at all costs soft subjects like those raised above in favor of a breakneck breakdown of mutating styles, names, gadgets, and equipment. Alternately, the aim is to elevate the music to the realm of the philosophical by introducing poetic fragments from Michel Foucault, Deleuze, or Guattari. This would be more welcome if the authors were willing to take their arguments further and ask what exactly does it mean that the ecstatic, dancing, raving bodies of working-class boys (girls have always danced), in some field off the highway, correspond at some level to the bodies without organs that are so central to Deleuze's concept of the social? Or, indeed, to challenge the new hegemony of the superhuman black body and the power attributed to it in contemporary hip-hop music, as Gilroy has recently and provocatively suggested.[12]

But even the inclusion of these questions should not overshadow other issues, such as those involved in earning a living or learning a skill in the new culture industries. The current flowering of talent and energy across the creative industries will need more than just symbolic public or governmental support; it will require a postindustrial strategy, which, in its most hopeful mode, might mean that among those less supported by their own cultural capital, less is left to chance.

Thanks to Jah Wobble for his useful comments.

Notes

1. Jeremy Gilbert, "Soundtrack for an Uncivil Society: Rave Culture, the Criminal Justice Act, and the Politics of Modernity," *New Formations*, no. 31 (Spring/Summer 1997), pp. 5–23.

2. Drew Hemment, "*e* Is for Ekstasis," *New Formations*, no. 31 (Spring/Summer 1997), pp. 23–39.

3. Dave Hesmondhalgh, "The Cultural Politics of Dance Music," *Soundings*, no. 5 (Spring 1997), pp. 167–79.

4. Caspar Melville, "New Forms and Metal Headz: Jungle, Black Music, and Breakbeat Culture" (master's thesis, Goldsmith's College London, 1997).

5. Grandmaster Flash, quoted in David Toop, *The Rap Attack* (London: Serpent's Tail, 1984), p. 62.

6. Morrissey, quoted in Simon Reynolds, "Morrissey," in *Blissed Out* (London: Serpent's Tail, 1990), p. 26.

7. See *Guardian Weekend Supplement*, 10 July 1997.

8. See Eric Fox, "Songs of Innocence and Experience," *Guardian Weekend Supplement*, 9 July 1996, pp. 26–29; and Suzy Feay, "Here Comes the Stubble," *The Independent*, 6 January 1997, p. 20.

9. See Phil Cohen, *Rethinking the Youth Question: Education, Labor, and Cultural Studies* (Durham, N.C.: Duke University Press, 1998).

10. See Dick Hebdige, *Subculture: The Meaning of Style* (London: Methuen, 1979).

11. See Paul Willis, *Learning To Labor: How Working-Class Kids Get Working-Class Jobs* (New York: Columbia University Press, 1981).

12. See Paul Gilroy, "After the Love Has Gone: Bio-Politics and Etho-Poetics in the Black Public Sphere," in *Back To Reality? Social Experience and Cultural Studies*, ed. Angela McRobbie (Manchester: Manchester University Press, 1997), pp. 83–116.

Concealing the Hunger

I have a tendency to believe that any story that moves you is true.

—Terry Allen (singer and artist from Lubbock, Texas)

The Myth of Rock 'n' Roll

Going through Checkpoint Charlie into East Berlin in the late eighties, I'm pulled over by a border guard for having some Soviet insignia on the arm of my leather jacket.

WHERE DID YOU GET THIS?

I'd bought it in a goth-rock store on Hamburg's Reeperbahn some days earlier and sewn it onto my jacket out of boredom in the van.

THAT IS NOT POSSIBLE . . .

Oh, yes it is, they sell this stuff all over Western Europe, even in Leeds. There's much shaking of heads and pointing before we're finally let through. We soon find out that about the only place you can't buy cool Commie paraphernalia is in the East. Fur coats, perfume, watches, no problem. As long as you've got Western currency to pay for them. But all we've got is a pile of East German marks smuggled in inside someone's knickers . . . and there's nothing here to spend it on. Hey! We're from the West, products of capitalism, raised on rock 'n' roll, born inside the belly. . . . We demand the right to procure choice Stalinist nuggets and the hammer 'n' sickle souvenir bric-a-brac of your crumbling sector in exchange for this toy money.

Come back in a few years, and you can buy a chunk of the wall, slurp Miller, and watch MTV at TGI Friday's in Karl Marx Platz with your previously owned Red Army tank parked outside, stuffed to the brim with contraband plutonium. And the same border guard will say:

Herbert Marcuse said that whatever you throw at capitalism, it'll just sell it straight back to you. The music business is capitalism's muscular right arm with a big fat catcher's mitt on the end.

For a while punk rock was too hot to handle (a brief, formative moment of opportunity and danger), before the major labels donned their oven gloves, held their noses, and swallowed it whole. When the Clash signed to CBS, some odious little PR drone came up with a marketing slogan, "The only band that matters," just to rub corporate salt into communal wounds. It was in the papers and on posters all over the States. We thought we could climb into the dragon's mouth and piss the flames out, but we learned: the only band that matters is the one that makes money. . . . Punk rock is reduced to Malcolm's swindle . . . . It's reassuring for the industry: WE ALL WANT THE SAME THING.

By the mid-eighties, rock 'n' roll had grown up and gotten a job on the board of directors. The myth of a social conscience saw pop stars posturing to conceal a hunger that feeds on the world, thinks globally, and acts locally—to screw everybody.

Wednesday, February 12, 1997: satellites beam U2's press conference all over the pop-saturated planet. It doesn't matter if it's from the lingerie department of Kmart, the laundry room at Trump Tower, or from up a dead bear's arse, the irony is transparent, the meaning plain: ignition engaged, the engine turns over.

I can't hear you, Bono, my ears are full of shit.

The Myth of Expertise

Letter from Bob Wills's attorney, David Randolph Milsten, to Saul H. Bernstein of Irving Berlin Inc. Music Publishers on July 16, 1940, regarding changes the firm had made in both the music and lyrics of Wills's song "San Antonio Rose" in an attempt to popularize it.

Dear Mr. Bernstein,

Mr. Wills did not contemplate such a radical change in the tune as has been made. According to Mr. Wills the original tune has been abandoned and the song has been revised so that now all that is heard when playing the piano score is harmony to the original melody.

You have so changed the words and the tune that the patrons and fans of Mr. Wills will no longer accept the song. Mr. Wills now almost continually has embarrassing moments when his orchestra plays the song as published because his patrons refuse to dance to the tune and call for the original to be played and the original words to be sung.

In November 1969, people all over the world heard "San Antonio Rose" sung in its original form by Apollo 12 astronauts Charles Conrad and Al Bean on their way to the moon.

Advertising copy from Tiffany Music Inc. of Oakland, California:
Medicine men to cure listener's dial fidgets—Tested selling power

On Tulsa's KVOO, during two prewar years, the Texas Playboys sold Playboy Flour in Texas, Arkansas, Oklahoma, and Kansas in quantities that matched those of brands that had been on the market for forty years. (The sponsor was Red Star Division, General Mills.)

While Bob Wills and his Texas Playboys were transcribing their compelling songs and melodies between dance engagements, the selling power of these transcriptions was being tested on California's non-network KLX, Oakland. A few of the selling successes:

Pocket-type adding machines . . . . 10,086 in 10 months
Candid cameras . . . . 5,000 in 4 months
Plastic Easter bunnies . . . . 4,000 in 2 months
Bob Wills picture giveaways . . . . 11,265 in 18 days

Time magazine quotes Bob Wills: "They say that guy made $340,000 last year and don't know what he's doin'. Hell, I know what I'm doin' all right—I'm just playin' the kind of music my kind of folks like to hear."

The Gnome of Zurich

December 1996: the *Wall Street Journal* reports that Dave Bowie is considering floating a fifty-million-dollar bond issue. Future royalties would flow into the fund, and once investors earned back their initial investment, plus interest, Bowie would get the overflow. Karsten Sindt, music buyer at Hamburg retailer WOM, says that Dave Bowie's popularity seems to have waned of late, while Gerd Pannen from the Saturn store in Cologne, Germany, adds that at present, "We don't sell a lot of Dave Bowie CDs."

John Artale, senior buyer for the Carnegie, Pennsylvania–based National Record Mart chain, says, "You never know what he's going to do, now he's taking jungle . . . to the masses."

From *Living in Sin*, the Mekons' novel-in-progress:

Time for a word with the Captain!—Aye aye, breathed Sophie, unscrewing the cap of the body-heated bottle. She felt the rum instantly warm her flesh and muscle as it hit her throat. She sat down on the curb feeling giddy, but listening—

"anyway a lot of their plans consisted of variable indicators and many elements of the plan would be inconsistent with each other, I mean quite often the supply plan frequently failed to match up to the production plan, so output targets had nothing to do with meeting user requirements; the labor or wages or financial plans were out of line with each other and with output plans and so on, right? One of the best examples of this that Khrushchev himself quoted was the giant sofas, sofas far too big for anyone to climb up on or even fit in a normal house, because it was the easiest way of fulfilling plans in rubles. I mean, in fact, it would be a miraculous coincidence if the product mix that accorded with the requirements of the user also happened to add up to the aggregate total required by the plan."

The lad they'd met in the pub paused to light his ciggy stub.

New designs or new methods were avoided because the resultant disruption of established practices would threaten the fulfillment of quantitative output targets.

—Alec Nove, *An Economic History of the USSR*

Sophie was feeling better. She thought of climbing up and over large sofas, and turned and looked at Colin with huge, open eyes. He smiled and said softly, "The record companies produce straight commodities and mainly useless ones at that. If chart position is the only universal criterion of the commodities' worth, then by definition the record industry is structurally compelled to produce waste in vast, unimaginable quantities. The drive of monopolistic enterprise to control, not only the market in which they are directly engaged, but adjacent market areas creates chains of local absurdities. Record companies with formidable resources can produce objects, e.g. microgroove records and CDs with an accuracy measured in microns, utilizing the most advanced technology. But the idea of international industry, organized in such a way that—even on its own terms—the majority of its products are failures, would leave even the most corrupt or inept Khrushchevian or Brezhnevian bureaucrat weak at the knees."

They were silent. They watched neon turn fog into gold.

Deena Weinstein

Art Versus Commerce:

Deconstructing a (Useful) Romantic Illusion

**I really believe deep down that rock 'n' roll is an art, man, and I
really just don't see totally sellin' out everything for a buck.**
 —Chris Robinson, Black Crowes

**A major theme of this album is staying loyal to the art you believe in
and never compromising—you know of the confrontation in the music
world of "art versus commercialism." Well, all musicians try to blaze
their own path with their own art, but a choice has to be made, as in
"A Matador's Poem" [by Charles Bukowski] which says, "Are you
going to love your life or are you going to face death every day in
the bull ring?" In the end, the matador chooses death in the bull ring.
It's a very profound poem.**
 —Marc Bonilla, guitarist

. . . and the Head-On Collision of Rock and Commerce
 —part of subtitle to Fred Goodman's *The Mansion on the Hill*

**The fact is that we write to please ourselves, not the fans. We don't
wage an inner war about being commercial or artistic. The artistry is
what matters to us. . . . We'd rather fail with music we believe in than
succeed commercially with music we don't like.**
 —Ian Astbury, the Cult

The second commandment for rock journalists is to elicit and dutifully
quote musicians' proclamations of their artistic integrity. Rock styles and
tropes forever change, but more constant than the guitars and drums is
the understanding that rock is, or should be, art, and that commerce is

Rob Pilatus of Milli Vanilli, March 1994

inimical to art. From its inception this opposition between art and commerce has been a central, even defining, feature of rock discourse.

The notion that art and commerce are in an immutable opposition is not an eternal principle, as its adherents seem to presuppose. It is one thing to acknowledge both the possibility of authentic art and the banal reality of commerce, and another to say that the two can never coexist or supplement, rather than oppose, each other. The art-commerce binary is one of the major myths of romantic ideology. The Romantic movement was the first countercultural rebellion in the modern West, rehabilitating everything nonrational in a reaction against modern rationalism, including, in Thomas Carlyle's famous phrase, the "cash nexus" of capitalism.

Romantics consistently champion will, feeling, passion, intuition, and imagination against regulation by intellectual and practical disciplines. They privilege, as Georg Simmel argued, individuality, eccentricity, abnormal experiences, and excess over common humanity and common sense, and value personal authenticity, variously defined, over expediency and conformity to social rules and cultural models.[1] One of the standard romantic heroes is the Promethean artist, whose courage to dream and genius to create beyond limits struggle against the forces of petty calculation and oppressive conformism.

The art-commerce binary erupted in youth music in the sixties through the counterculture (the last major romantic movement in the West), which nurtured a quest for authenticity: "Do your own thing." "Let it all hang out."

In the discourse of rock music, "authenticity" had two meanings. In the early sixties, as Nat Hentoff observed, authenticity for young urban and suburban whites was borrowed from "authentic" sources, particularly blacks and rural whites.[2] Bob Dylan did not lose his romantic credibility in his own eyes or others' eyes by covering songs written by such authentics as Woody Guthrie. Among others, the early Rolling Stones, the Animals, and the Beatles also covered artists in genres deemed authentic, particularly blues, rockabilly, and rock 'n' roll.[3]

By the mid-sixties, white youth music, except for blues rock, dispensed with exogenous sources and became self-initiating at the same time that a self-conscious youth movement, in and for itself, emerged. From that point on, when "rock" (as opposed to fifties rock 'n' roll) came into being, authenticity no longer meant sincere appropriation of an authentic source but obedience to one's own muse, to oneself. The Beatles, the Stones, Dylan, and the Doors were not considered by themselves or their fans to be simply performers but auteurs, artists. The Doors' Jim Morrison was self-consciously inspired by the nineteenth-century French poètes maudits, such as Charles Baudelaire and Arthur Rimbaud.

In this fully romantic moment, the political and cultural conflict over the "generation gap" fused with the creative impetus of young artists to challenge established models in order to create an oppositional discourse— "us versus them." On the political front, the moral, passionate, youthful change-agents ("My Generation") pitted themselves against the immoral, unfeeling, and decadent establishment. On the cultural front, within rock music, the oppositional binary pitted romantic artists against the capitalist establishment of the Kinks' "Well Respected Man."

The Doors, who took their name from a poem by William Blake, epitomized the romanticism of the counterculture with their injunction to "break on through to the other side." Morrison, after his death, became the quintessential romantic hero with a cult of authority-annoying devotees who still make pilgrimages to enshrine his tomb at Père La Chaise cemetery, where he is buried among his beloved poets.

At the same moment that rock was constituted as an endogenously generated, self-conscious youth music, programmatically structured by the art-authenticity–commerce binary, rock criticism appeared and founded itself on this same binary. The myth of the irreconcilable opposition between art-authenticity and commerce was established: henceforth musical discourse had a literary discourse to police it, indeed, to normalize it.

After the sixties social movements were forced into strictly institutional opposition and the military draft ended, the youth movement collapsed, the counterculture imploded, and youth music fragmented. The art-authenticity–commerce binary, however, has persisted into the present in the successive musical and critical discourses of all of the inheritors of sixties rock: art rock, arena rock, the singer-songwriters, heavy metal, punk, and, later, indie, rap, and alternative.

The binary has become the guiding myth-structure of rock. As such, it can be approached deconstructively to show its circumstantiality, and sociologically to show its functions and effects within the social (-psychological) transactions of the rock "life world."

Deconstructions

The Fifties: An Alternative Binary for Youth Music

Rock has a prehistory: fifties rock 'n' roll. Rock 'n' roll was innocent of the art-commerce binary. Both musicians and audiences structured their discourses through other binaries, especially youth-adult. The relation of artist and audience to commercial mediators was not an issue. Whatever its provenance, rock 'n' roll was "ours" (youth) music, not "theirs" (adult). There were antecedents of "authenticity" rhetoric. The legendary DJ-promoter Alan Freed distinguished between superior and genuine originals, often by black (r & b) or white (rockabilly) artists on indie labels, and inferior covers, often by white pop musicians on major labels.

As rock 'n' roll was transformed into rock and roll, a marketing category larded with schmaltz and dominated by major labels and (my personal nominee for the heir to Satan's throne) Dick Clark, the early binaries were replaced by a smoothed-out teen-adult binary within popular music that lasted until the eruption of the sixties youth movement.

Punk: Pure Mediation

Punk's initial move damned the romantic artist and spewed venom, gobs of it, on business. For the authenticity of the romantic artist, punk substituted the autonomous amateur. Erasing the elitist divide between performer and audience, punk's retro-rhetoric favored a preindustrial folk culture where all members of the community could perform as well as applaud, and the content of the music was an expression of that community, not some unique professionalized and individualized artist.

Damning business did not eradicate the need for business for record companies and distributors, venues, radio, and magazines. Punk damned big business—the capitalism that eats you up and spits you out—and embraced petit-bourgeois business, dubbed DIY (Do It Yourself). Some of these American DIY (anti)business enterprises are SST, Dischord, Epitaph, Alternative Tentacles, and Fat Wreck Chords.

It is not punk music but punk mediators that deconstruct the art-commerce binary: record labels giving total autonomy to their musicians, enabling them to record with the content and in the style that they choose, not what some suit thinks will sell. The free-form, underground FM stations in the United States in the mid-sixties, and their college-radio offspring, are another example of such pure mediators, playing music that did not follow a format designed to grab a large demographic.[4]

With genre-oriented 'zines, radio shows, clubs, and record labels, what prevails are punk's or any other subcultural community's standards, not the mass tastes of the moment that must be served to provide maximum profits. Genre mediators share the artists' own standards and thus erase the binary opposition between art and commerce.

Banal Authenticity and Authentic Audiences

The art-commerce binary is also deconstructed when the artist's authentic output coincides with the tastes of a mass audience. This circumstance occurs in two rather contrasting ways, which I'll sum up as the Beatles meet Neil Diamond.

I won't argue the merits of the Beatles or Neil Diamond, but let me use them as metonyms, the former standing for good art (as the majority of rock critics would understand it) and the latter for dreck. I'll assume that Neil Diamond and Hootie are expressing their authentic selves on their albums; the quality of their artistic expression is dreck, but it happily coincides with the level of mass taste. This situation erases the opposition between art and commerce as cleanly as its opposite, the high sales of Nirvana in the nineties or the post-1965 Beatles. Here the quality and authenticity of the artists is critically acclaimed and the artists appeal to the (temporary) tastes of a mass audience. The happy coincidence that erases the art-commerce schism in the momentary triumph of art also fulfills the populist rhetoric, promise, of rock. It fills critics with joy, temporary, to be sure, since as surely as night follows day, cooptation and rationalization will follow dissent and charisma, and Silverchair and Bush will emerge and sell way more than P. J. Harvey.

Frith and the British Scene

Of course, it is no news that art and commerce are not in eternal opposition. Simon Frith has long argued for the absence of such an opposition. He has traced the ideology of the Romantic Artist in rock to the British art schools.[5] He states, in a grand essay tracing the economic and technological history of popular music, that "by the mid-seventies there was very little tension between musicians and the business. Rock performers were more likely to complain about companies not exploiting them properly than to object to being 'commercialized.'"[6]

Functions of the Art-Versus-Commerce Myth

Given the abundant evidence that the art-commerce binary only applies in limited circumstances, why does the myth of a constant and irreconcilable opposition between art and commerce persist? Why must every rock interview include the requisite quote, elicited from, if not automatically offered by, the musician, about "staying true" to their art, their battles with the industry, their declarations never to sell out? Critics review albums in terms of authenticity versus imitation, with the implication or explicit understanding that imitative work cannot be "authentic" and is only done for commercial reasons. The printed rock discourse, which constantly reinforces the myth of the constant binary opposition, is mirrored in the fans, whose chatter (and now newsgroup postings) is peppered with terms like "sellout."

Cultural inertia cannot account for the persistence of myths. An individual's neurosis, which comes into being in response to some specific situation, lasts long after the initiating cause is gone, maintained by what psychiatrists call "secondary gains." The myth of the binary opposition between the Authentic Artist and Commerce has continued to be regnant for three decades because it produces secondary gains, because it functions for the various interests that comprise the rock world. That is, the myth is sustained by the benefits it provides to the musicians, fans, the commercial media, and critics.

The Artist

The occupation of a rock musician is arduous, not only because it is "a long way to the top," but because hardly anyone trying to get there ever does so. Less than fifteen percent of the artists signed to major record labels ever break even,[7] and only a minute proportion of would-be rockers even get signed.

How do you recruit and motivate people to try? And if they have managed to create some great music, how do you get them to continue to do so? The myth of the struggling romantic artist and of romantic excess offers some solace and possibly compensation. Musicians can avoid being demoralized by the pesky problems of everyday existence through belief in their music or the promise (or actuality) of a lavish, lascivious, or merely dazed-and-confused-with-drugs-and/or-alcohol lifestyle.

Rock's populist ideology, stronger at some times and in certain genres than others, presents a serious problem for the artist. Populism, the "build a better mousetrap and they'll beat a path to your door" myth, assumes that if the music is good, it will go gold. Reminiscent of Calvinism, which, as Max Weber noted, practically contradicted its belief in God's unknowable predestination of souls to salvation and damnation by obsessing on the outward signs of inward grace, populism argues that massive sales are the sign of a successful artist; poor sales damn you to perdition.[8] The myth of the opposition between art and commerce consoles those whose records stiff in the marketplace—and the vast majority of records are financial failures. (Populism saves the myth for the musicians whose work does go gold, allowing them to avoid being labeled as "sellouts."[9])

The Commercial Media

Business's interests are served by the perpetuation of the opposition between the artist and commerce, insofar as that divide helps to recruit and motivate musicians to create new products to sell in the marketplace. And when artists find it to be outside their role to concern themselves with business, and when such concerns are an otherness that they feel would detract from their artistry, business can more easily take advantage of them. Leonine contracts that leave the musicians without monetary profit from their work are legendary. The case of the Jayhawks was well documented,[10] and punk magazines such as *Maximumrocknroll*[11] and the *Baffler* have published many screeds against, and analyses of, this phenomenon.

Commerce also benefits from the art-commerce binary because the romantic artist that the myth creates sells records. "If record companies

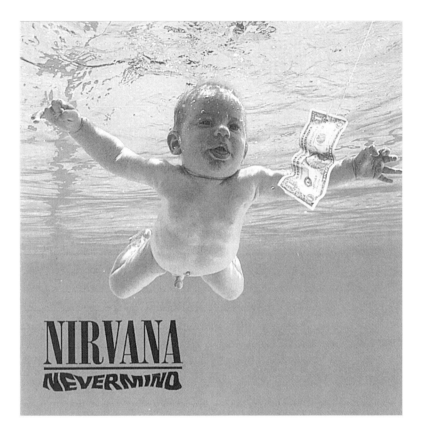

can get listeners to fall in love with the person rather than the song, there's a better chance fans will buy the next album—and concert ticket, T-shirt, video, book, and poster," one rock journalist admits.[12]

Fred Goodman's *The Mansion on the Hill* hails such managers as Dylan's Albert Grossman and Bruce Springsteen's Jon Landau for their ability to mediate the art-commerce binary—they are larger-than-life beings who can worship both Art and Mammon. The rise to power of the record producer[13]—this half-man-half-beast with one ear tuned to art and the other cocked to commerce—also demonstrates the development of specialized roles to mediate the opposition.

The Audience

The mass audience never bought into the art-versus-commerce myth.
One need only look at the top-selling records year after year to realize that
authenticity is not a concern of the general music-consuming public. But
fans who are more serious, more subcultural, more hip, and in other ways
less mass, readily embrace the myth of the opposition of commerce and
artist. It allows them to identify with the musician as the heroic rebel,
fighting, or at least tilting, at the windmills of business. Insofar as rock
musicians also embody nonbourgeois statuses, such as black, working class
(in truth or only in accent), gender-bender or out-of-the-closet, or junkie,
they become romantic artists evincing the other to conventional society.
They provide fans identifying with them with a feeling of rebelliousness.

Further, the mythic opposition between art and commerce allows fans
to believe that their tastes are not a product of the publicity machine but
are valid aesthetic decisions; the myth validates the fans' sense of autonomy.

Rock Writers

The art-commerce binary functions for rock journalists in several ways.
Merely perpetuating the myth makes their writing agreeable to their readers,
the rock fans. And clearly the rock industry approves of their ideology and
supports much of it with advertisements, which often exalt the image of
rebellion, and with free records and concert passes for the critics.[14]

The interviews and reviews that critics write focus on the aspects of
musicians' lives that fans find romantic—sex, drugs, and rock 'n' roll—
generally omitting references to the solitary practicing, the long hours of
rehearsals, and the innumerable taking-care-of-business activities. Conflicts
of artists with their record labels are not omitted, of course. One particularly candid rock journalist, Geoffrey Himes of the *Washington Post*, states
that the content of rock journalism can be explained by "the fact that it's
easier to write about personalities than art."[15]

Ease, however, cannot account for obsession. Take death, for example.
Death is a great career move, in part because rock journalists provide the
dearly departed with more exposure than even the most ample publicity
budget could provide. Critics celebrate romantic rock deaths because they

affirm the myth of the artist. A drug overdose, a shotgun suicide, or a gangland gangsta slaying: these deaths show, rhetorically, that the romantic artist was authentic, not merely assuming a (Christlike) pose. The right kind of death is the most powerful authenticity effect, the indefeasible outward sign of inward grace. "The artist must be sacrificed to their art; like the bees they must put their lives into the sting they give," Ralph Waldo Emerson wrote.

Death isn't the only authenticity effect embraced by rock writers. They also champion heroin-addicted musicians and rockers who are off their rockers, the mentally deranged like Syd Barrett, Roky Erickson, and Wesley Willis. Addicts and the insane are automatically authentic because their grip on rationality is too weak to allow them to "sell out."

Maintaining the myth of the opposition of art and commerce, and seemingly siding with the artist, allows rock journalists to maintain the aura of art critics, rather than appearing to be members of the hype machine. Or it lets us comfort ourselves that we have a foot in both camps.

The Myth Persists

With the triumphal gloat of capitalism in the wake of Communism's collapse, as *ur*-rock songs wind up as ad jingles, with the dominance of music videos (commercials for musicians that are not authored by them), and as iconic indie labels have grown in power, income, and practices so as to closely resemble or merely join major labels, the myth of the opposition between art and commerce is more difficult than ever to maintain. Tom Frank, writing in the critical 'zine the *Baffler*, argues that both the counterculture and contemporary business recycle sixties ideologies, demonizing "the exact same figure: the blue-suit-wearing-conformist 'organization man' of the fifties."[16]

Nonetheless, in the nineties the art-versus-commerce myth persists tenaciously. It can account for much of the popularity of gangsta rap and grunge, genres whose visual and verbal discourse center on claims to authentic expression. The revocation of Milli Vanilli's Grammy award (because they had lip-synched at concerts) is an excellent example of what Jean Baudrillard calls a deterrence machine: taking back the award made it seem that Grammies only go to authentic artists. Pearl Jam's quixotic fight with Ticketmaster and Dischord's Ian MacKaye's refusal to raise prices for CDs, tickets, and T-shirts are other authenticity effects referenced by rock writers to promote the art-versus-commerce myth.

Less believable than it ever was, the art-versus-commerce myth is promoted and probably believed in as much if not more than it ever has been. The myth persists because too many people gain too many different things—money, identity, prestige, or a common critical standard—from it to give it up. As long as this continues to be true, the participants in rock discourse will continue to take cover under romantic illusion.[17]

Notes

1. See, for example, Georg Simmel, "The Metropolis and Mental Life," in *The Sociology of Georg Simmel*, ed. Kurt H. Wolff (New York: Free Press, 1950), pp. 409–24.

2. See Nat Hentoff, cited in Steve Jones, "Reviewing Rock Writing: Recurring Themes in Popular-Music Criticism," *American Journalism* (March 1992), p. 148.

3. By doing such covers, the artists were trying to grab a piece of authenticity for themselves. See Deena Weinstein, "The History of Rock's Past through Rock Covers," in *Mapping the Beat: Popular Music and Contemporary Theory*, ed. Thomas Swiss, et al. (Malden, Mass.: Blackwell, 1998), pp. 137–51.

4. MTV basically argues that some ad or movie directors' quirky attention-grabbing visuals are more significant than the sound of the music.

5. See Simon Frith and Howard Horne, *Art into Pop* (London: Methuen, 1988).

6. Simon Frith, "The Industrialization of Popular Music," in *Popular Music and Communication*, ed. James Lull (Newbury Park, Calif.: Sage, 1987), pp. 53–77.

7. L. Silverman, "Finding Fame Without Fortune," *Rolling Stone*, no. 561 (21 September 1989), p. 33.

8. Max Weber, "Judaism, Christianity, and the Socioeconomic Order," in *The Sociology of Religion* (Boston: Beacon Press, 1964), pp. 246–61.

9. When Nirvana's Kurt Cobain posed for the cover of *Rolling Stone*, he wore a T-shirt stating: "Corporate Magazines Still Suck."

10. Fred Goodman, "Between a Rock and a Hard Place: For the Jayhawks, the Price for Dancing on the Threshold of Rock 'n' Roll Fame Is Compromise and Debt to the Tune of $1 Million," *Worth* (March 1995), pp. 102–06.

11. See columns by Steve Albini and Ben Weasel in *Maximumrocknroll*, no. 112 (June 1994).

12. Geoffrey Himes, "Why It Doesn't Matter if Kurt Cobain, Snoop Doggy Dogg, and Axl Rose Are Jerks in Their Personal Lives (And Why It Does if They're Jerks in Their Songs)," *Request* (May 1994), pp. 38–41.

13. Obtaining not only fees, but royalties for their work, producers make musicians meet their schedule and their locale preferences.

14. Those in the rock-crit business know about what befalls writers who dare to see and write beyond the myths.

15. Himes, "Why It Doesn't Matter," pp. 38–41.

16. Tom Frank, "Alternative to What?" *Baffler*, no. 5 (1994), n.p.

17. Here is an alternative postmodern conclusion: The art-versus-commerce myth is less believable today than it ever was, yet it is promoted and probably believed in as much if not more than it ever has been, witness *The Mansion on the Hill* and all the publicity and media attention it got. We have here an imaginary that is at odds with its circumstances, yet affects those circumstances by shaping people's actions. The imaginary is not an epiphenomenon; it co-constitutes its circumstances, but not as the major player. The constant and polysemous liaison between art and commerce in rock music while each partner proclaims its opposition, each for its own purposes, has a theater-of-the-absurd, carnivalesque quality. The romantic myth has been inscribed on the bodies of rock musicians—a good death is the best career move. The myth persists because rock is (also) a salable form of religiosity.

Performance
and Image

Evelyn McDonnell

Re: Creation

When you look in the mirror

Do you see yourself

Do you see yourself

In the magazine

When you see yourself

Does it make you scream

   —X-Ray Spex, "Identity"

When Karen Kelly and I were putting together the conference on which this book is based, I thought of "Performance and Image" as our panel devoted to artistic process. I also thought that we used both words, *performance* and *image*, because we assumed they were not the same thing, that there was in fact a tension between them: *performance* is what the artist does, *image* what the audience receives. Bringing together a performer (Kathleen Hanna) and an image-maker (video- and filmmaker Katherine Dieckmann) would provide perspectives on both ends of the *performance* → *image* communication equation. The critic (James Hannaham) and the scholar (Lawrence Grossberg) would provide insight on what happens inside and around the arrow. That we chose this title instead of, say, "Creation and Voice" may have been an at-the-time unanalyzed indication of our own media-saturated cynicism—or perhaps it was just a result of our respective positions in curatorial and critical institutions, where Karen and I are privy to but still outside the act of creation.

   Creation is a bad word these days. Conservatives have wrecked it, first by setting it in opposition to scientific, rational thought and the teaching of evolution ("creationism"), then by making it the antithesis of choice, freedom, reproductive rights, and feminism ("procreation"). A term that should indicate the birth of life and its attendant possibilities has instead

Lou Reed in London

become lead-thick with religious meaning and dense with funereal absolutism. It is a dead, dead concept, so that even people in this book who would nominally be considered the "creators" of music don't have much faith in it. Paul D. Miller, a.k.a. DJ Spooky That Subliminal Kid, quotes Emerson, "The originals are not original," while Hanna, in conversations outside of and surrounding her essay, has spoken of her disbelief in artistic genius or even distinction, and her acceptance of the postmodern truism that the concept of "the real me" is passé—that we're all just a series of performances/images. Throughout this book and in music criticism in general, authenticity is mocked as the biggest pose of all; the "self" is roundly dismissed as a marketing concept.

In theory circles, if something isn't "constructed" it's "performative." Both terms are used—interchangeably, or with a differentiation that could perhaps itself be dubbed *performative*—to describe/define the artificiality of experiences and creations that we perceive as whole or genuine. Judith Butler, in her seminal book *Gender Trouble*, has written about how sexual identity itself is performative; it's something we try out and put on, like changing fashions.

Suits Me, Diane Wood Middlebrook's biography of Billy Tipton, is a case study in gender trouble. Tipton was the jazz musician née Dorothy who spent fifty-six years of her life passing as a man, fooling even five wives and three adopted sons. One of the fascinating aspects of the book is the glimpse it provides of a twentieth-century working musician's life in western America—the touring circuits where vaudeville, country, and jazz converged. Because she already lived in the alternative world of an entertainer, virtually no one questioned Tipton's strangeness; many of the musicians Middlebrook interviews find the author's curiosity impertinent. As the author says, being a man was part of Tipton's performance. But that's not giving Tipton enough credit: music was her life, not her act; sexual preference and persona were her life, not her lifestyle.

Those musicians, in being creative types, know what critics think they've discovered: that art is short for artifice. Traditional rock critics— i.e., those steeped in the "performance" of rock criticism that was birthed in a hot-tub purple haze in the sixties—seem romantically fixated on searching for some authentic Platonic ideal, some Edenic state of creationist grace, that all subsequent music either moves away from or connects back to—e.g., the devil-driven blues singer Robert Johnson or the dustbowl chronicler Woody Guthrie. But Johnson's story is a model of inauthenticity—yeah, right, he met the devil at the crossroads and traded his soul for his voice. Talk about myth! And Guthrie was a story-teller who, when he came to New York, went to the Rainbow Room—that penthouse of idle rich idolatry—because he knew that he was in show, not truth, biz.

Today's critics, on the other hand, those who started their craft in the last two decades and probably studied semiotic theory in college, seem intent on demystifying artistry. Acts—and I do mean acts—like Swirl 360 or Natalie Imbruglia are held up as paragons of pop because they've been so perfectly assembled by A&R men and other bottom-line feeders. They are constructed performances, proof positive that simulation has triumphed over stimulation, and that the music biz, like Hollywood, has become a place of group collaboration, with the performer least likely to be nominated for the auteur role.

It seems a distressingly short leap from the relativism espoused by pro-gressives like Hanna to the cynics' embrace of Imbruglia. Like most good radicals, these cultural margin-walkers may have thrown out the baby with the bathwater (another creation metaphor). If "the talent" doesn't believe in talent, then that doesn't give her much bargaining power against "the corporation," does it? If the artist doesn't believe in him "self," then what is he worried about selling out? (Of course, the Artist—formerly known as Prince—does believe in himself, even when no one else does, and he's certain he *was* sold out like a slave.) The death of the author is a convenient notion for people who don't have a creative bone in their body and can only pick apart others—actually, *j'accuse* critics of assassinating the author and assuming her throne. Deconstruction has replaced creation as the primary activity for an active mind. We live in a culture of analysis, not imagination.

Most performers, at some point in their lives—with the possible exception of Joe Cocker—have practiced in front of mirrors. They do this to see how what they feel their faces and bodies doing looks. Is that grimace really scary? That kick high enough? That hair better slicked back or teased up? They want the image in the mirror to reflect back the image they're trying to project. The mirror may even reveal to them new gestures, faces, poses.

When I write, I am constantly aware of the plasticity and insufficiency of words. My thoughts come out in established syntaxes: a professional voice, a confessional voice, my Greil Marcus imitation, my Ellen Willis impersonation. For example, because while editing this book, I've read more academic essays in one year than I have since I got my B.A. twelve years ago, I can tell I've taken on a professorial tone in this essay that I didn't use when I was writing for my fanzine, *Resister*. And yet I fight against mere mimicry or replication, not simply in pointless reaction, but because I'm struggling toward something. Calling that something a voice of my own sounds hopelessly sentimental, even reactionary, but that's because the words, "a voice of my own," are a cliché, they've again failed. And yet I assemble and reassemble the words, the performances, endlessly. I hope someone could read "Re: Creation" and "Resist Stance," my editorial for the first issue of *Resister*, and see a similarity, even say to themselves, "That sounds like Evelyn."

Sometimes, when I read a bunch of my articles, or a lot of criticism in general, it all seems pointless, like so much peacock pontificating, mental masturbation, "brainworked to death," as my lumberjack boyfriend would say. This is the problem with text when it is separated from context, when it's a goal in itself instead of a vessel for communication. Then I'm stuck in the hall of mirrors, my words endlessly reflected back at me in 2D images.

A performer knows that you don't play before a hall of mirrors, that you need an audience. That is when art becomes art—or doesn't—when it risks danger and triumph. An artist also knows the importance of lighting, that it's something that can—and should—be manipulated, that that manipulation is part of the "truth" of art.

Oscar Wilde said that truth is told only with the most exquisite of lies. It's as if journalists and scholars, whose lives after all are dedicated to discovering the "truth," found out they've been lied to—that performers practice in front of mirrors, that they adjust the lighting to make themselves look better and the reverb to make themselves sound better—and they feel so disillusioned they don't see the exquisiteness. Sometimes, the more artificial something seems, the more real it is. Hanna changed her stage name to Julie Ruin and found her voice again. Glam, the most mannered rock 'n' roll style, is also the hardest rocking.

"Art-i-ficial." Poly Styrene sang the word in syllables on the X-Ray Spex's brilliant *Day-Glo World* album. About twenty years ahead of her time, Styrene sang about poseurs, plastic rats, warriors at Woolworth's, and other identity crises in a consumerist society. She wore a pith helmet and braces in a Day-Glo world; hers was a brilliant triumph of style over style, at least for one album (until she said she saw a UFO, disbanded X-Ray Spex, then became a Hare Krishna—a conversion, not a pose). Whatever her influences, Emerson be damned—Poly Styrene was a true original. There was no one like her before and no one has been since.

When I'm around children, I don't feel like I'm giving in to mystifications when I reward their creativity. It's what's going to keep them from becoming drones, or vidiots. My seven-year-old friend imitates Missy Elliott and, through her consumption of that image, finds a style of her own. The performance becomes a creation; a star is born.

James Hannaham

Bela Lugosi's Dead

and I Don't Feel So Good Either: Goth and the

Glorification of Suffering in Rock Music

If rock 'n' roll is the blues with an emphasis on adolescent sex, then goth rock is rock 'n' roll with complete dysfunction—where death, sex, and madness combine into a heady potion. Gothic imagery and influence have skulked at the margins of rock music for decades, and even the blues have plenty of subject matter—mortality, eroticism, insanity, and loss—in common with what came to be known, in the late seventies and early eighties, simply as "goth."

The blues, however, were meant to be part testimony and part catharsis. Black blues singers wailed in order to explain and share their hardship, and by extension build a sympathetic society. One of the tributaries of the blues, the Negro spiritual, attempted to accomplish this feat in a more literal way: the spiritual was often used as a code to signal slave escapes, and its lyrics usually drew parallels between making a break for the promised land in heaven and stealing away to the promised land up north.

Once rock 'n' roll became the engine of American youth culture, however, the social meaning of the blues was altered. When people who were fans, rather than originators, began to play the blues, the subject matter became an end in itself. The pain described could be not only felt by the singer but fetishized and focused inward as well. Pain could be treated, not just as something to express, but something to strive for. As Shel Silverstein once sang, "What do you do if you're young and white and Jewish . . . and you've never spent the night in a cold and empty boxcar . . . and the only levee you know is the Levy who lives down the block?" The answer, as Bob Dylan proved, is that you sing the blues anyway.

Siouxsie Sioux in 1986

It's easy to forget that most white Americans first heard the blues and rock 'n' roll created in their backyards only once it had been filtered through the ears of the British Invasion. It arrived, not sanitized exactly, but translated, idealized, and somewhat abstracted. Not that England's bluesmen couldn't feel authentically disenfranchised or sad, but their sadness was the result of an entirely different environment than, say, your average Mississippi bluesman. By the time it reached England, the form of the blues had been established. It then became possible for the most salient component of the blues—misery—to switch from impassioned declaration to a kind of rapture, the ultimate state of being for a blues singer. Chances are, when a black American sang the blues, she just had them. When an Englishman did, he also wanted them.

The simple glorification of suffering, of course, was not enough to give rise to the excesses that became gothic rock. For that, a certain degree of showmanship and capitalism was necessary. Gothic rock may have begun with Screamin' Jay Hawkins's 1957 hit "I Put a Spell on You," which radio stations banned for his "cannibalistic" howling—supposedly the result of Hawkins's intoxication during the recording session. Legendary DJ Alan Freed encouraged the natural showman Hawkins to milk the controversy for all it was worth, advising him to make his stage entrances from out of coffins (an act for which Hawkins was later paid five thousand dollars per performance) and dressed in high-vampire style, with a black cape and a walking staff adorned with a skull. Hawkins eventually sold two million copies of the record and later quipped, "I wish they'd ban all of my records."

As the late fifties progressed into the sixties, rock 'n' roll became the theater of the world. Pop stars got more ambitious and successful, following the Beatles' example and turning their bands into entertainment industries—making films and stage shows and producing the work of other artists. Their positions of wealth and power became ironic: they chose to play rock music as idealistic young rebels, determined to dismantle the system, only then to be swallowed by it. Their creative output and personae were used by advertisers to sell products, rather than to change society. The hypocrisy of packaging grandiosity and teenage rebellion for mass consumption led to another gothic monster: Alice Cooper.

Cooper, a minister's son who named himself and his band after a girl at his Sunday school, was discovered by rock's mad genius, Frank Zappa. Unlike its mentor, however, Alice Cooper the band was not known for musicianship but for bizarre theatricality. Audiences at Alice Cooper shows were regularly treated to mock chicken-slaughterings, simulated autoerotic erections, and fake blood. In a particularly notable dramatization of his epic song "Dead Babies," Cooper, made up in the runny black mascara that became his trademark, brought out hundreds of plastic dolls and dismembered them, to the delight of his audience.

Though Cooper's antics shocked people, his Grand Guignol rock-theater seemed rooted deeply enough in the realm of fantasy to let his audience retain a sense of order. Cooper himself, born Vincent Furnier, was usually quick to make a distinction between his onstage and offstage images. "My posture changes when I become Alice, even my voice," he told *Kerrang!* in 1987. "It's like a possession—well, I wouldn't call it possession, but it is like being overcome with this character." Offstage, Cooper is an avid golfer. His character, Alice Cooper, the iconoclastic, gender-bending social misfit, not only exorcised Furnier's personal demons but channeled that suffering into a larger-than-life cartoon of pain. Furnier created in himself a grotesque rock star who symbolized music-industry excess, self-absorption, cult of personality—in short, he took counterculture to its illogical extreme. Cooper's influence remains one of rock's biggest triumphs of style over substance.

That same style-over-substance equation turned into the albatross around the neck of the branch of subculture that emerged from punk in 1978 and later become known as "goth." In fact, it's difficult to distinguish between "goth" and "post-punk," for the simple reason that goth is more of a fashion statement than a coherent musical style. In the period from 1978 to about 1984, hundreds of bands dyed their hair black and wore black lipstick, white pancake makeup, black lace, and chains. Despite stylistic similarities, heavy-metal music remained separate from this phenomenon; in fact, the two genres might be said to have been divided along gender lines. Heavy metal was aggressive, sexist, and therefore "masculine," while goth had a softer, more accepting, "feminine" cast.

You can hear that passivity in "goth-chick" Claudia Hazzard's description of how to appreciate a goth classic: "You can totally immerse yourself in the music, the consuming power of this song. This conjures up images of horror films, dark skies, castles, and forbidden vaults. The lyrics are of a vampire nature and intoxicate you."[1] Goth inspired a euphoric if cheesy utopianism rather than heavy metal's warlike feudalism.

At the same time, punk flicked its emotional switch from anger to depression, and became more ethereal in the process. But not all atmospheric post-punk bands sported goth fashion, and not every death-rocker played wind-swept post-punk. The careers of the most successful atmospheric post-punk bands—the Cure, Siouxsie and the Banshees, New Order, Cocteau Twins, Dead Can Dance—tended to be long and uneven, and their music ranged stylistically from New Order's "death disco" to Dead Can Dance's Middle Eastern and medieval-influenced ragas. The Cure switched gears a number of times, from snappy power pop to ponderous dirges to happy ditties about being in love on weekends.

Punk and goth were indistinguishable at first. In 1976, at age seventeen, Siouxsie Sioux, the *ur*-goth, was part of a clique of Sex Pistols fans known as the Bromley Contingent, famed for their outrageous modes of dress. At the time, Sid Vicious of the Pistols was drumming for an early incarnation of Siouxsie and the Banshees, which had played a date at London's 100 Club that was either disastrous or cathartic, depending on your point of view.

A wall of noise illuminated the fact that no one could play. Siouxsie said the Lord's Prayer. The mélange lasted twenty minutes. They walked off, bored. "She is nothing if not magnificent," Caroline Coon wrote at the time. "Her short hair, which she sweeps in great waves over her head, is streaked with redlike flames. She'll wear black plastic nonexistent bras, one mesh and one rubber stocking, and suspender belts all covered by a polka-dotted transparent plastic mac." Another observer said that the set was "unbearable."[2] Already, those enraptured by the visual rather than musical aspects of punk began to idolize Siouxsie. After the Bromley Contingent made their way into the studio audience when the Pistols played England's *Today* show, the rules changed. "From that day on,"

Sex Pistol Steve Jones recalled, "It was different. Before then it was just music—the next day it was the media."[3]

Once she had helped give punk a name, Siouxsie wanted no part of it. Avidly antiestablishment, the Banshees took two years to land a record deal despite their high profile, partially because their lead singer had made it a habit to insult record-company executives in the audience. Fans were writing "Sign Siouxsie Now!" on the sides of record company buildings. By 1981 the Banshees had converged upon London's legendary Batcave, the Soho establishment run by members of the band Specimen. "It was a light bulb for all the freaks and people like myself who were from the sticks and wanted a bit more from life. Freaks, weirdos, sexual deviants . . . that's very much the spirit of what the Batcave was," former Specimen keyboardist Jonny Melton remarked.[4]

Siouxsie and the Banshees' material took a turn from punk's habit of rooting out poser hypocrites—"Too many critics/Too few writing," she summed up in "Love in a Void"—to obsessions with madness and exotica. In the center of a scene that idealized and emulated old horror films and witches, the powerful vibrato howl that won Siouxsie "best female singer" polls in the British music press for years running became a siren song. Her heavy black makeup, tangled pile of black hair, and smear of red lipstick, pioneered during gigs when Cure leader Robert Smith became the Banshees' temporary guitarist, became a trademark of eighties "New Wave" fashion.

Rock 'n' roll's gothic undercurrents, however, have rarely merged their dramatic elements—think vampires—with their purely existential ones. Everyone feels a certain amount of alienation, mental stress, and fear of death. However, not everyone puts on white pancake makeup and black lipstick, teases their hair, and then gets onstage and sings about it. The requisite adornment that goes hand in hand with a "gothic" aesthetic, as rock 'n' roll defines it, calls the sincerity of the wearer into question. Goths have dealt with their feelings of alienation from society by reinventing themselves as "monsters"—or, as Morrissey puts it, wearing "black on the outside/'Cause black is how I feel on the inside." But does this artifice reinforce the message of the music or cancel out the sincerity of the wearer by further obscuring his identity?

The pop-culture legend that finds his way into the Hall of Fame is an eloquent, unpretentious, and genuinely tortured soul who can represent the pain of his listeners in the mass media—a secular Christ figure. It's an extraordinary person from humble beginnings—the poorer the better—who lives his pain and often dies young and/or tragically, à la John Lennon or Kurt Cobain. Except for his race, the archetypal rock icon remains essentially unchanged since the heyday of the blues. The more rock stars live up to their images, the more "real" they appear. Rap stars are held so closely to their outlaw standard that Snoop Doggy Dogg's murder trial only raised his credibility, and Tupac Shakur was killed in a drive-by shooting.

Goths, by turning death, madness, and violence into archetypes, depersonalize their connection to horrific events. They position themselves as reporters or tour guides of the macabre, rarely as its victims. Even when Siouxsie puts her own memory of an encounter with a child molester into song, she casts herself, not as nine-year-old Susan Ballion, but as the sex offender, "Candyman" himself, who intones, "Oh trust in me my pretty one/Come walk with me my helpless one."

When Peter Murphy of the seminal goth band Bauhaus informs us in a scary voice that (as we already suspected) "Bela Lugosi's Dead," or Siouxsie, decked out in Theda Bara exotica, serenades the victims of Mount Vesuvius, they emphasize the distance between their own pain and that which they describe. Their icy remove doesn't leave us with the impression that it matters to them if Lugosi has passed away, or if the volcano petrified hundreds of Pompeii's citizens under molten lava, but merely with the feeling that death is forbidden, mysterious, and therefore glamorous.

Goth rock continues to be blamed for suicides among fans, but it remains an open question whether the music can actually cause mayhem or simply supports existing instability. Of course, any long-lived movement for which fetishizing death is a primary directive must be taking this stance in the service of art—or it wouldn't be long-lived. Those artists who truly had the courage of their convictions would simply kill themselves, or so the logic seems to go.

If this is the case, Joy Division was the only atmospheric post-punk band that managed to combine the ideals of blues-style confessional, of which legends are made, with the bleak vision of goth. As Jon Savage explains in his foreword to *Touching at a Distance*, a biography of Joy Division lead singer Ian Curtis written by his widow, Deborah:

[Joy Division's] first album, Unknown Pleasures, released in June 1979, defined not only a city [the depressed, post-industrial Manchester, England] but a moment of social change: according to writer Chris Bohn, they "recorded the corrosive effect on the individual of a time squeezed between the collapse into impotence of traditional Labor humanism and the impending cynical victory of conservatism." Thus, death rock became a moot point on May 18, 1980, when Ian Curtis's wife Deborah discovered that Ian had hung himself to death in their kitchen, their phonograph's stylus still stuck in the dry groove of a copy of Iggy Pop's The Idiot *in the next room. He was twenty-three. At the time, Joy Division was well on the way to becoming famous for a gloomy, impressionistic sound and lyrics that didn't just describe feelings of doom and hopelessness, but embodied them. Curtis's suicide, coming on the heels of an attempt a month before, and at least one other when he was fifteen years old, put the stamp of authenticity on Joy Division's dour oeuvre.[5]*

At the time of Curtis's suicide, the band's discography consisted of a few EPs and only one full-length LP, the stark and lonely *Unknown Pleasures*. They'd completed their second, *Closer*, in March of that year, but had not yet released it. Amid much British music-press fanfare, the band had made plans to embark on their first tour of the United States.

Joy Division defined what goth could have become. When they began in 1977, under the name Warsaw (later changed when they got word of a London band called Warsaw Pakt), their angular guitar hackery and fuzz-bass echoed the Sex Pistols and the Buzzcocks. But by the time they recorded 1979's *Unknown Pleasures*, the angst-y minimalism of songs like "Digital" had given way to a slow, dreamy brooding that was heretofore unheard of in punk rock. Joy Division started the movement from the energy and anger of 1976's punk revolution to the self-pity that would characterize the new wave of the eighties.

Plenty of bands had used echoing reverb before, but with the assistance of producer Martin Hannett, Joy Division pioneered its use as a metaphor for emptiness. Many Joy Division songs sound as if they were recorded in deserted school buildings, abandoned factories, or under the lonely bridges of Manchester. These bleak soundscapes reinforced Curtis's lyrics, which nakedly display his obsession with isolation. Curtis wasn't simply describing the alienation of the individual from others and society but the way in which numbness and surrender divides the self. On "New Dawn Fades," he sang, "Oh, I've walked on water/Run through fire/Can't seem to feel it anymore/It was me, waiting for me/Hoping for something more/Me, seeing me this time, hoping for something else."

Despite his youth, Curtis's voice sounded old. He was off-key a great deal of the time, but his intonation had a haunting power and creaky authority. It lurched unevenly from vulnerability to anger, from deadpan to melodrama. It was the perfect instrument to deliver his vision: shaky and unsure of itself, at times nearly conversational in tone, it said nothing if not that Ian Curtis was an ordinary man in extraordinary pain.

Though Curtis's pen touched on subjects such as Nazi death camps (Joy Division was named for the term the Nazis used to describe women prisoners used as prostitutes) and, on "Atrocity Exhibition," an insane-asylum-turned-roadside attraction, his view of death leaned toward existentialism. "Existence, well what does it matter?/I exist on the best terms I can/The past is now part of my future/The present is well out of hand," he sang on *Closer*'s "Heart and Soul."

In their image, too, Joy Division lacked the theatrical pretensions of other bands that grew up alongside them and in their wake. Instead, they used funereal black-and-white photographs of religious statues on their record sleeves. They presented themselves onstage without referring to glam-rock image-makers, such as T. Rex or David Bowie, who influenced their peers, preferring to appear simply as regular, if dull and remarkably disaffected, working-class Mancunians. They were blokes who happened to be suicidal, a stance that contrasted heavily with the usual methods of incorporating gothic influence into rock music. Despite their punk roots, they didn't accessorize with makeup, safety pins, or outrageous hair. Nothing was posed. Curtis had developed a reputation as an energetic live act, due in no small part to his epilepsy. His bandmates were not even fully aware of the degree to which he owed his stage presence to his seizures. As guitarist Bernard Sumner reminisced, "[Ian] had a fit and we went on, he was really ill and we did a gig. That was really stupid."[6] Curtis's wife also observed:

The fact that most of Ian's heroes were dead, close to death, or obsessed with death was not unusual and is a common teenage fad. Ian seemed to take growing up more seriously than the others, as if kicking against it would prolong his youth. He bought a red jacket to match the one James Dean wore in Rebel Without a Cause. *He wanted to be that rebel, but, like his hero, he didn't have a cause either. Mostly his rebellion took the form of verbal objection to anyone else's way of life.*[7]

The restraint with which Curtis and Joy Division approached their misery was one reason for the pervasiveness of their influence, which stretched far beyond the black-lace set and showed up in the approach of fellow Mancunians like the Fall and the Smiths. Perhaps not all of the goths who flocked to Joy Division's posthumous releases, who dressed as creatures of the night to prove their love of death, really wanted to die. They just needed a way to express their disenfranchisement. Lacking a blues of their own, they created a community of the living dead, a society that aligned itself with death because life was substandard. They needed a folk hero like Ian Curtis to die for them, so they wouldn't have to discover for themselves that death had no sting.

Notes

1. Claudia Hazzard, quoted in Mick Mercer, *Gothic Rock* (Los Angeles: Cleopatra, 1993), p. 37.
2. Jessica Berens, "Portrait: The Masque," *Guardian Weekend Supplement*, 14 January 1995.
3. Steve Jones, quoted in Jon Savage, *England's Dreaming: Anarchy, Sex Pistols, Punk Rock, and Beyond* (Boston: Faber, 1991), p. 260.
4. Jonny Melton, quoted in Mercer, *Gothic Rock*, p. 102.
5. Jon Savage, foreword to Deborah Curtis, *Touching From A Distance: Ian Curtis and Joy Division* (London: Faber and Faber, 1995), p. xii.
6. Bernard Sumner, quoted in ibid., p. 113.
7. Ibid., p. 5.

Hide the camera, YOU.
It's against the law to shoo[t]
a rock video here.

Katherine Dieckmann

MTV Killed the Music Video Star

Not so very long ago, back in the eighties, or "The Big '80s" as one short-lived video-revival show liked to call them, MTV provided fruitful ground for the pop-minded scholar. The music video was, in fact, often considered the ideal mass-cultural artifact. In an essay titled "Fatal Distractions: MTV Meets Postmodern Theory," contained in *Sound and Vision: The Music Video Reader*, Andrew Goodwin notes several of MTV's key traits—"its fusion of high art and popular cultural discourses (or perhaps more accurately, its refusal to acknowledge such cultural boundaries)," its play with and against narrative, its predilection for borrowing and intertextuality—although Goodwin ultimately argues against a singular analytical take on the field.

My interest in MTV is less theoretical and more pragmatic, partly because music video is an industry I've worked in (never all that happily, I might add), partly because a highly intellectualized approach to the medium feels just about as dated now as Madonna's conical bustier. It's hard to talk about a history of MTV, even though, of course, there is one, because the channel has produced constant streams of imagery, ads, promos, and shows for sixteen years now, which start to seem like one long, unindividuated, jangling blur in retrospect.

But there are a couple definitive moments to be plucked from the flow. When MTV debuted in 1981 (although it didn't air in New York or Los Angeles until two years later), the first clip played was the Buggles' minor hit "Video Killed the Radio Star." That sentiment now feels quaint, if not downright fossilized, but it recalls early arguments against MTV: that it forced schlumpy-but-talented musicians to be visually arresting, and that it cramped listeners' imaginations by proscribing pictures that might not fit their visions of a song.

Difficult as that line of thinking may be to conjure up now, it's even more unfathomable to realize that, up until 1984, MTV promoted a lily-white, "rock"-only playlist, until it began rotating the landmark videos from Michael Jackson's *Thriller* album. Shamed by that record's multi-platinum success, the cable channel could only respond in the way in which it was trained: to plump up and reflect what the market demanded, color be damned, a tendency realized even more dramatically when rap and hip hop proved bankable in the late eighties.

There have been other epoch-defining moments in the ensuing years: the ambitious, diverse, and overanalyzed Madonna videos; the one-hit-wonder clips that connote a particular stylistic moment by foregrounding a hairstyle or outfit; the videos that have virtually on their own helped create niche markets (like Nirvana's "Smells Like Teen Spirit," which defined grunge); even videos that have broken down formal barriers and occasionally proven more stimulating than the experimental films and art photographs from which many of them so blatantly crib (and that "borrowing" has only become more shameless and virtuosic in recent years).

By the early nineties, MTV seemed smoothly and effortlessly entrenched as an industry, not only in its cozily productive relationship to the record business, but also in its tacit legitimacy as a form that often had something to say about the passions and preferences of youth culture. No one really bothered to question what had now become MTV's world dominance, with successful channels scattered all over Europe and Asia. Thinking pop-culture fans everywhere seemed content to accept MTV's ubiquity, even to celebrate the moments when a music video managed to be provocative or—God forbid—fun.

This acquiescence overlooked signs of a coming crisis in music video, one that is now so pandemic that it's actually difficult to watch music videos on MTV even if you want to, so overwhelmed are they by a jamboree of dating-related and reality-based shows. There are still music videos, of course, and acts that are aided immeasurably in their ascent because of them—Alanis Morrisette, Jewel, Garbage, No Doubt, Prodigy, and the Wallflowers are just a few recent examples. Yet people aren't really talking about these videos very often, because formally (with the exception of Garbage's "Stupid Girl" clip, which managed to make worn techniques like faux-scratching, silhouetting, and stutter-cutting seem lively and fresh), they're largely a snooze. Their shopworn devices and marketing intentions are so obvious as to make any interest in content seem totally beside the point.

No longer does the MTV world premiere of a new video demand to be regarded as an "event"—and I'm judging this not only by my own possibly cranky thirty-five-year-old standards, but by the level of perceptible excitement generated by the network itself. Reliable old auteurs like Madonna and Michael Jackson are too involved with breeding to worry about reinventing their image—or they have achieved such reinvention through it. The respective births of their children prompted day-into-night MTV programming takeovers featuring old videos, archival footage, and interviews (Jackson's bearing the logo, "It's a Jacko!"), which only made their accomplishments as signal MTV artists feel more remote. Even rap video, which for a spell thrived as a separate genre with its own codes and rules, appears to have arrived at something like a dead end with the Roots' sardonic "What They Do," directed by Chuck Stone III, which sports mocking intertitles that point up tired tricks like the digitizing out of T-shirt and baseball-cap logos, the foregrounding of gyrating B-girls ("Money Shot," reads the intertitle), and stale effects ("Wow, lightning," reads another).

Three years ago, there arrived a definite clue that we were on our way to the current state of crisis. It came in the form of a humble little clip called "Loser," starring Beck, and directed and shot by Steve Hanft. If you watched MTV even occasionally in 1994, you couldn't escape this crude, shambling minimasterpiece, a deadpan pastiche of seemingly random vignettes: a plain pine coffin mysteriously shuffles along on its own volition across fields and suburban parking lots; the grim reaper does a squeegee job on a windshield, using blood instead of wiper fluid; grinning, barely pubescent girls perform slomo cheerleading moves in a graveyard; and, of course, the slight, pasty Beck himself, who sporadically and lazily lip-synchs while alternately sporting a *Smokey and the Bandit* T-shirt, an Indian headdress, bad flares, and even worse breakdancing moves.

"Loser" insisted upon a kind of genial, morbid disregard for the stature of the music video (it hardly seemed like anyone needed to make another one in its wake), as well as the ascent of a kind of stubborn geekiness that doubtless reflected a big chunk of MTV's demographics: young, male, white, and vaguely loserish, if only in their own tortured teenage minds. The video established Beck's indelible persona as a smart, aw-shucks mix-and-matcher of idioms both musical and visual, a persona that became further legitimized when he won numerous Artist of the Year awards in 1996, and turned out another brilliantly parodic video, "Where It's At."

But "Loser" also exposed MTV cool for a sham, giving credence to a kind of offhand clumsiness that somehow seemed even hipper than cool. Your average, meticulously styled video star, doling out coy, studied poses, suddenly seemed even more inane in Beck's wake (not to mention post–*Beavis and Butthead*, who ascended around the same time as Beck and did an even more thorough and hilarious job of substituting MTV chic with their own dorky snottiness, taking on the channel's most ludicrous products and slyly cutting them to shreds).

Music videos began to look more bloated, self-indulgent, and generally pointless, with the exception of work by other shambling ironists, most notably director Spike Jonze, whose clips for the Beastie Boys' "Sabotage" (a kinetic riff on seventies cop shows and grade-B movies); Weezer's "Buddy Holly" (in which the band appears to perform in the soda shop from TV's "Happy Days"); Björk's "It's Oh So Quiet" (a neo-Godardian minimusical set in an auto-repair shop); and Wax's "Southern California" (in which a man engulfed in flames runs in comical, excruciating slow motion down a Los Angeles street, only to catch a bus around the corner)—these and a few other videos pushed pop-culture rifling and high-concept execution to their stylistic limits. Yet while these videos injected MTV with some fresh air—or, perhaps, supplied an imaginative crescendo before the inevitable fall—the music-video medium itself was faltering on a grand scale.

A year after the debut of "Loser," TimeWarner Cable pulled the plug on The Box, music video's version of an all-hours Viewer's Choice channel. Operating something like the jukebox from which it derived its name,

The Box scrolled a lengthy list of possible selections on the screen along with the video currently in play. Fans could call in and, for a nominal fee, order up their most-wanted videos. The Box favored rap and hip-hop clips far edgier and inventive than those selected for MTV's *Prime Time* and *Yo MTV Raps!* shows, and often picked up on offbeat indie work that tended to screen once on MTV's *120 Minutes*, only to be forgotten. (That show, devoted to more underground videos, still airs every Sunday in a deadly midnight-to-two-A.M. slot.) Consumer response to the cancellation of The Box was indignant but short-lived. (Maybe it's just symptomatic of the overall forgetfulness that attends music television as a form.)

As The Box disappeared, and VH1 shifted even more firmly into its retrospective, boomer-friendly programming, MTV playlists began to shrink, as well as become unbelievably monotonous. A key cause of the numbing sameness was the growing entrenchment of a small roster of male directors, what I like to call the all-boy show-off school, a privileged group that in some ways recalls the group of established male movie directors hired to dabble in what was a nascent medium during MTV's early days. (These included Brian DePalma, Martin Scorsese, Tobe Hooper, Jonathan Demme, Paul Schrader, John Sayles, Bob Rafelson, and John Landis.) Now, the boy directors, many of whom far younger and products of film schools, were using music video as a springboard to feature-film careers. (Needless to say, women directors remain a rarity on MTV, and the ones that do get over have to be willing to adopt the manmade rules of the genre, including embracing the boy school's bag of tricks and sexing-up all female talent.)

The boy camp, led by video stars like Matt Mahurin and Samuel Bayer, began to dominate the playlists with their top-this visual pyrotechnics and their seemingly unshakable control over a large number of videos in production. The effects they pioneered remain a stale staple of music videos today: heavy use of strobes, gels, smoke, blurred focus, blink cutting, and pretentious "symbolic" imagery (including, inexplicably, animal masks). Their style enshrouds musicians in obfuscating devices; it's the pure antithesis of something like the now-moribund "MTV Unplugged," where bands were shot naturalistically and without effects performing stripped-back or orchestrally expanded versions of their best-known numbers. Rarely is something so simple trusted to carry a video now.

The general rule of thumb these days, growing directly out of the boy school's fixation with freighted, epic visuals, is that a musician or band's worth is measured by how much cash was obviously ladled out to create the most ambitious clip possible—take U2's recent embarrassment, "Discothèque," featuring a conspicuously middle-aged Bono crotch-thrusting inside a gigantic mirrored ball, or Bush's video "The Fly," which is closer to a blockbuster action flick than the mere amplification of a pop song.

While more and more money is doled out for top bands, or to dramatically introduce an act with potential widespread appeal, budgets for music videos for less-sure bets have shrunk or vanished. This reflects in part the overall stagnation besetting the record industry, which has suffered sharply diminishing sales over the past two years. The decline can be attributed to a drop in the marketability of genres that caused profits to soar in the early nineties: alternative, hip hop, and country. And recently, there have been surprisingly lackluster chartings from previous guaranteed top-sellers like Pearl Jam and R.E.M. With no new superbands surfacing to replace the previous successes, the record business is in something of a holding pattern. Belt-tightening has hit every department, including video.

MTV was originally created to help revive a stagnant music industry in the early eighties, and for a while it did just that, creating new personalities and pushing the comeback of a Top 40, singles-based market after the dominance of album-oriented rock in the seventies. But at this moment, MTV seems incapable of recharging a flattened field, except in very occasional cases. Whether the network sensed this coming cataclysm or in fact helped to create it, MTV has opted to radically back off of music video programming, and what remains sends out a decidedly schizophrenic message.

Take *MTV Primetime*, the one regular show in MTV's weeknight lineup between seven P.M. and midnight still devoted to screening music videos. One week, veejay Simon Rex was broadcasting from a U.S. Army base in Fort Benning, Georgia, where soldiers showed off high-tech video equipment, and visits into the barracks produced such conversational gems as "I love metal, sir!" Before a break, Rex remarked, "These guys are risking their butts for us. Please stick around for a Buzz Clip from the Cardigans."

Why the sudden interest in the armed services as a viable lifestyle option for impressionable young MTV viewers? Because the U.S. Army was sponsoring *MTV Primetime* for the week, producing the weird effect of "alternative" music videos being juxtaposed with the Army's gonzo ads, which only make the military seem like one of the more challenging twentysomething road-trip specials or sports adventure shows MTV likes to program these days. This is a far cry from the MTV that has always championed progressive, even liberal, causes, whether in its *Week in Rock* bulletins, its public-service announcements, or the successful Rock the Vote campaign. Activism seems to have been placed on the back burner at the revamped MTV, replaced by a need to grab sponsors from wherever they might come—sure, the major labels are lagging, but the U.S. Army has a few good dollars to throw around.

MTV's mandate has always been about survival via change. Keep the videos moving, the programming shifting, the promos bubbling, the flow continuous and subtly different, all to maintain consistently fresh entertainment for an ever-rotating stratum of youth culture: thus the spate of new shows currently clogging MTV's schedule, none of which has much, if anything, to do with records. All carry the emphasis on youthful libido previously displayed solely in videos into reality-based programming, where cute-yet-ordinary folks act out MTV's narratives of romantic yearning and desperate with-it-ness.

Most notorious is MTV's *Singled Out*, a histrionic update on the *Dating Game*, where a group of horny young'uns answer a series of inane questions and perform embarrassing stunts before narrowing the field to arrive at a final "dream date." (The show was neatly lampooned for its strident heterosexism and general idiocy by James Hannaham in *Spin*.) Then there's *Loveline*, a call-in advice show where no problem is too personal, no libidinal dilemma too explicit, to preclude some weirdly voyeuristic scrutiny from the hosts, guest advisors, and, one presumes, a television audience. MTV also continues to run its ongoing vérité soap, the *Real World* (occasionally in back-to-back marathon screenings), and *Road Rules*, where recently, a gang of multiculti Euroteens pouted and argued their way across Italy. All these shows take the fantasy elements of music videos—fine dudes, hot babes, tortured romance, general angst—and displace them into so-called true narratives and situations. These are new dream sites, not necessarily that different from music videos in terms of the needs serviced, but remarkable for the fact that they've wholly excised the "music" element, except as background soundtrack.

Meanwhile, the energy and visual savvy of the better music videos are being dispersed into other outlets—which may not, in the end, be such a bad thing. Commercial advertising, always informed by and informing MTV, has picked up where the channel has left off: one could easily argue that the frequently broadcast Nissan spot, which cast Barbie, Ken, and G.I. Joe in a love triangle, bolstered by some *Toy Story*–esque animation and Van Halen's stomping remake of "You Really Got Me," was the best music video of last year. Ditto Spike Jonze's ad for Levi's Wide Leg Jeans (although the product has nothing to do with the commercial), where the tuneful beep of an emergency-room monitor prompts a patient to recall Soft Cell's eighties classic "Tainted Love," turning the ER chamber into a raucous dance party.

While commercials get more savvy, and music-image sites multiply online, the MTV market is splintering. The continuing rise of electronica may cause MTV's ambient *AMP* show, currently broadcast in the wee hours of the weekend morning, to cross over and create some new music-video genres, ones based more on repetitive abstract imagery and laser theatrics than the cult of personality. And straight-up music video is getting a revival of sorts on MTV's mostly veejay-less branch network, M2, which exhibits a slightly anarchical, irreverent approach to the medium, somewhere between The Box's video-first emphasis and a smart grad student's thesis. M2 operates around mini "themes," such as "teenagers," where Cracker's "Teen Angst (What the World Needs Now)" bumps up against Alice Cooper's live performance of "Teenage Frankenstein." It also likes to program three or four videos in a row by the same director, acknowledging that individual vision can actually inform the genre.

MTV is increasingly making its programming less about stars and top tunes and more about a kind of all-encompassing lifestyle that embraces fashion, relationships, and even, in the case of the Army-sponsored *MTV Primetime*, dubious career choices. Less and less does one find a clear, singular object to scrutinize. Instead, MTV is, now more than ever, about a pattern of aggressively teen-and-twentysomething-driven behaviors, looks, and norms, which remain largely unanalyzed—possibly because it's a struggle for almost anyone over the age of twenty-five to sit through MTV's current programming.

The school of MTV-generated academic criticism, which coupled music videos with postmodern theory in the eighties, has long receded into the past. One wonders what, if anything, might take its place as a way of thinking about the network. My title, "MTV Killed the Music Video Star," is only half-serious, but we are in fact witnessing a moment where MTV is concerned less with its traditional practice of creating telegenic chart-makers than with promoting a lifestyle channel for what seems like an increasingly narrow demographic. Could we even imagine the existence of a youth-oriented popular music unencumbered by MTV's playlists and mandates, by the demands of calculated style, by the tyranny of the Buzz Clip? It's a sign of how very tightly MTV has held the hit-makers and their audience in its embrace that that's virtually impossible to do.

Lawrence Grossberg

Same As It Ever Was? Rock Culture.

Same As It Ever Was! Rock Theory.

I have been going to conferences to talk about rock and popular music for almost twenty years now. At the more academic conferences, I have usually assumed that I was invited to play the role of the *rock 'n' roll* professor, to talk about the ways rock culture challenged the adequacy and utility of traditional modes of academic work. At less academic conferences, I have usually assumed that I was supposed to play the role of the rock 'n' roll *professor*, defending the need for and value of both theoretical and empirical (which is not to say "objective") work. Usually, it was easy to tell which role I was supposed to play and which role was necessary on a particular occasion, and I was more than happy to play either. But I must admit that something has changed, for I can no longer separate the roles or the audiences. Increasingly, the same arguments have to be made to both (academic and nonacademic) audiences—and to tell the truth, I am tired of making them.

The Place of Theory in Rock Discourse

What has changed? Two things: first, I do not think that writing about popular music has significantly changed—to say nothing of "progressed"— in forty years. I realize that progress is a suspect concept in the contemporary world, and I do not want you to read more into it than is intended. Simply, I do not think that we have gained a significantly better understanding of how popular music works, nor have we developed a vocabulary in which to argue about the differences between musics, or between critical interpretations and analyses. In fact, we would be hard-pressed to describe the major paradigms of either journalistic or academic writing on pop music.[1] Second, I am no longer confident that the academic study of popular

A Kabuki-style musician plays rock 'n' roll before a crowd in Tokyo, on the tenth anniversary of Elvis Presley's death, 1987.

music is a particularly useful place from which to begin the sort of project—the project of cultural studies—that has always driven my work.

My commitment has been to theorizing and analyzing the relations among popular culture, popular politics, and the systemic structures and forces of political inequality and domination. Consequently, I have argued for more than twenty years (and I have certainly not been alone in this) that rock music cannot be studied in isolation, either from other forms and practices of popular culture or from the structures and practices of everyday life. Studying rock for me was never about further carving up the field of popular culture into media and genres, or the field of cultural studies into increasingly narrow and less relevant disciplines. But recently, I have become convinced that the academic disciplinization of popular-music studies (through organizations, journals, and so forth)—by which I mean the identification of popular music as an object of study and specialization equivalent to film, television, and other media—has taken on such a force of its own that it has now become a serious stumbling block to the kind of work I want to do. Furthermore, I believed that popular music offered a particularly powerful place to enter into the fields of culture and power because, however naïvely, I thought that it had at least the potential to serve as an organizing site, if not force, of resistance and alternatives. It no longer strikes me as having any such privilege in the field of popular cultures. And there is growing evidence that people make the sorts of investments that were reserved for postwar popular music in a wide range of media products and practices.

Much of the academic writing on popular music, like journalistic work, operates *within* the discourses and relations of popular-music culture and fandom, and often from within specific taste cultures, even though it presents itself as offering something else—namely, an analysis of such discourses, relations, and cultures. Sometimes, this occurs because the biography or taste of the author (or some surrogate) is taken to exemplify, if not the story of rock 'n' roll, then at least a normative version of that story. Some circumscribed experience of the music and its social context are taken to signify its proper meaning or social effects. The aesthetic and political stakes overwhelm everything else. In such work, the line between the academic and the nonacademic disappears. At other times, it occurs because popular music has become little more than an excuse for the scholar to reenact his or her own theoretical (and aesthetic and political) agenda. In such work, it almost doesn't matter that one is talking about popular music, and the line between the academic and the nonacademic becomes overwhelming. (I suppose I must admit that my own work shows a strong tendency toward this sort of practice.)

Before elaborating any further on this situation and its conditions of possibility, I should add a more personal vector into the scenario; if I am describing what has changed in my relationship to writing about popular music, I should also acknowledge what has changed in my relationship to popular music itself. In fact, a lot has changed. My wife likes to remind me that I used to say I would stop teaching rock when I turned forty. Now I am approaching fifty and still teaching it—partly because I can't seem to find that new generation of scholars to take over the classes (I suspect that this is more a matter of institutional hiring and teaching demands than of the interests of younger scholars). Yet at the same time, I find that I am no longer able or willing to invest the quantity of time and money I used to into keeping up with the music. I listen to what I like of current music and constantly defer listening to what is happening; although I think there is still lots of great music being made today, I no longer expect to listen to all of it. Perhaps the nature or quality of my investment in the music has also changed, or perhaps it is that the nature of the investment demanded by the music in the present context is itself different. I do not think that the music matters less to me (in fact, there are still lots of times when the music keeps me alive, and even more when it gets me through the day). Yet I cannot help but think that, for whatever reasons, the ways it matters are also changing.

The result is that my ability to use myself (and my own role as a fan) productively, which has in the past given me a certain access not only to the music but to other fans as well, has become increasingly problematic. And simultaneously, I find it increasingly difficult to relate to younger rock fans, or to convince them to relate to me and trust me—which is absolutely vital to the kind of empirical work I have always used as the basis for my writing. Having said this, however, I want to pull back from the idea that this is all a matter of age, of getting older, and at least suggest that it is as much or more a matter of generational differences and relations.

These changes, however, have not diminished my commitment to the need for specific, academically defined intellectual work around popular music. Such work would not attempt to offer or to defend a particular set of judgments about musical texts and tastes; and it especially would not begin with such judgments.[2] The question is not whether or how one defends popular music (or some part of it) but what popular-music practices are doing and what is being done with them and to them, and such questions cannot be entirely answered in terms of individuals, whether texts or audiences. Nor are they questions about intentions, experiences, and uses, although these might be relevant dimensions of the empirical puzzle. Obviously, important questions are at stake here about one's relationship to everyday popular culture, and about the value of different voices or positions from which to speak: e.g., the immersed participant; the ethnographer (externalized visitor); the fascinated describer.[3] But perhaps, at least for the moment, we can circumvent the question by accepting that "our attention must be turned away from that mythical popular subject immediate to observation, and focused instead on the relation between two different kinds of practice: a first-order practice of everyday culture and the second-order practice of analysis conducted by a reader [*sic*] endowed with significant cultural capital."[4] It is this reference to "significant cultural capital" that I want to elaborate, although I have my doubts that the market in such capital is booming these days.

The academic study of popular music—considered as an everyday cultural practice within specific and multiple contexts, in definite relations with other practices and relations—is then defined by two distinguishable but related projects: first, to gain empirical knowledge, at a variety of levels of everyday and social life, about the music, its institutions, audiences, producers, and so on; and second, to give us a better understanding of how popular music works, of what it is doing in the world and how it is changing in relation to a changing world. (One version of this second project is what I call cultural studies.)

In arguing for these two projects, I do not intend to dismiss the writing that has been done both inside and outside of the academy. I don't want to deny that this work is often full of insights or that it is often valuable and fun. Different kinds and sites of writing and criticism about popular music can and should serve lots of different functions. It would be interesting to know something about these differences, differences concerning the questions they attempt to answer and their relationships to or places within the cultures of popular music. Consequently, I am not demanding that all writing about popular music be defined by a single definition or project, least of all by my own. But I do think that there are specific—empirically, theoretically, and politically inflected—academic projects that have yet to be significantly addressed in anything like a sustained or collective way. This is not a matter of one's theoretical paradigm or one's empirical research practice; it is a matter not only of knowing more but of understanding better. Most fundamental is the question of how popular music works—as popular and as music (i.e., as sonorial); and it is the fact that we have not advanced significantly toward answering this question that, I believe, provides the most damning judgment of the field of popular-music studies. Again, it is not that interesting and important contributions have not been made but that we seem collectively unable to discuss these proposals and to move beyond our own individual agendas and positions.

Empirically, we are certainly, if slowly, increasing our knowledge about some of the various dimensions and aspects of the existence of popular music. There has been a proliferation of studies of the music and musicians, of audiences and taste (cultures). And yet, only slowly are scholars beginning to realize that the musics and audiences that constitute popular music are much more diverse and multiple than we have been willing to admit (including, even in the U.S., Indian film music, Vietnamese pop music, Vegas pop, and Broadway musicals). Moreover, such work is only now beginning to confront the limitations of using communicative models to study such mass phenomena. Such models isolate texts from audiences and contexts and then struggle to reconstitute the relationship through notions of expression, signification, and representation. But popular music is so deeply and complexly interwoven into the everyday lives of its fans and listeners that its study, even more than that of other cultural forms, has to recognize that the music is inseparable from the entire range of activities that fill up our lives, activities that are defined by and respond to the contrary, sometimes terrifying, and often boring demands of work (paid and unpaid, domestic and nondomestic), education, politics, taxes, illness, romance, and leisure (whether sought out or enforced). As a result, the meaning and effect of specific music always depend upon its place within both the broad context of everyday life and the potentially multiple, more specific contexts or "apparatuses" of other texts, cultural practices (including fashion, dance, films), social relationships, and emotional investments that define the material reality of so-called taste cultures. I define an apparatus as, first, a set of practices and relations; and, second, a set of logics—modes of operating, working, communicating, producing effects—which is simultaneously similar to and distinct from other popular musical and even broader popular cultural apparatuses. Consequently, the study of popular music poses what seem to be almost insurmountable methodological problems: How does one limit the number of texts or trends to be studied? How does one locate significant exemplars or trends? How can one isolate a particular text (or what aspects are responsible for its success) from other texts, media, and activities? How does one know what the relevant relations between texts or between texts and other practices are? Similar questions can be raised about the attempt to identify and isolate particular audience factions, taste cultures, or communities. In the end, it is unclear what one can conclude from such research.

At the same time, even as we learn more about some aspects of popular music, we seem to know less and less about other absolutely crucial dimensions of its existence: namely, its institutional and economic conditions. Moreover, scholars have ignored the relations among these various dimensions and aspects, to say nothing about how they are contingently linked together within specific contexts and apparatuses. Finally, such empirical research is further exacerbated by the fact that there are, as it were, three (and a half) different projects, almost conspiracies, attempting to occupy and construct the world of popular music in their own image. First, there is what I have called the industrial logic of production and commercialization, which attempts both to construct and to market music by segmenting it according to isolable generic distinctions supposedly grounded in "objective" features. Second, the (fans') multiple logics of consumption, through which the music is appropriated into and constructed within the terms of the specific context and apparatus of some set of fans. (The half-conspiracy is that of critics, who operate somewhere between the industrial logic and the logics of consumption.) Finally, there is the academics' logic of effects, which purports to describe the place and operation of popular music in the context of people's lived realities and the structures of power of the social formation.

Moreover, whether such empirical work presents itself as a description of the world (the writer's position being merely a matter of access) or as an interpretation (the writer's position enabling a privileged set of aesthetic and political judgments), it is often strangely content to rediscover what we already knew; in fact, it often seems to "discover" what it has already presupposed (e.g., either that music is increasingly hybrid or that it has always been built on appropriation; that musicians make compromises or that they are caught in a rigid choice between artistic and economic pressures; that pleasure is an alibi for ideological domination or that audiences are actively involved in feeling and doing things; that record companies don't feel anything and seldom do anything). Rarely am I surprised; instead, my most common experience is that I have heard it before: been there, done that.

But an understanding and analysis of popular music demands more than either empirical description and/or interpretation; at the very least, it requires theoretical work, and a vocabulary in which one can begin to describe what is the same and what is different (between popular-musical and other cultural apparatuses, and among popular-musical apparatuses themselves), what is changing and what is not. That is, as an academic at least, I am committed to what Marx called "the detour through theory," to the need to develop concepts (and a logic by which they can be related) that will enable one to redescribe and transform the empirically available world into something else, what Marx called "the concrete." Such theoretical concepts are, inevitably, abstractions, operating without all of the specific determinations that provide the density of everyday life.

Here I think the critical and academic study of popular music in general, and of rock culture in particular, has failed (and this may be true of my own efforts as well). In the first place, we simply have failed to offer theories of the specificity of popular-music apparatuses. Insofar as such apparatuses are part of larger spaces of popular culture, one would assume that any account of them could, to an extent yet to be determined, make use of (and overlap with) the theoretical resources developed elsewhere. But in fact, whatever theoretical resources are generally deployed in the study of popular music—whatever theoretically based work there is—are almost entirely drawn from theories developed to analyze other (broader or equally specific) cultural domains. It seems to make little or no difference, in such cases, that we are talking about music, despite constant reminders in the writing that we are dealing with music and vague claims about its specificity. Such reminders are usually made through the use of a set of signifiers—the body, fun, affect, feeling, energy, pleasure, sentiment, emotion—without any attempt to adequately theorize them.[5] Moreover, while scholarly work on other popular media is often dominated by the attempt to read the (ideological) message of a particular text (perhaps in relation to a particular audience or issue, and sometimes in relation to a more general textual genre), popular-music studies are rarely concerned with the specific meaning or effects of a single text. Rather, popular-music studies are usually triangulated by a concern with texts, trends, and larger organizing concepts (such as rock, hip hop, or country and western).

A better understanding of the place and effects of popular music, then, demands that we develop theories that have some specificity to them. I would like to compare the absence of any conversation aimed toward such theoretical advance with the emergence of so-called film theory[6] as my model here, especially as it developed out of *Cahiers du Cinéma* and *Screen*. It seems to me that the discipline of film studies became productive (and progressive—at least in the sense that there was a common position to argue with, over, and against, and a common vocabulary to argue in) when it moved beyond common-sense-based discussions of texts, oeuvres, and genres (although it can and has come back to them after the moment of "screen theory" but in new and I think more productive ways). So-called screen theory embodied an attempt to develop a theory capable of describing the specificity of cinematic communication both in general (e.g., by arguing that the cinema was a language deeply implicated in psychoanalytic processes) and a particular (classic Hollywood) cinematic apparatus. This is not to deny that there are problems with both the actual theory and the ways it is enacted and practiced. Too often, film analysts privilege, if not universalize, a particular apparatus, thus ignoring the radical contextualism of the theory, or the radical implications of such a contextualism (e.g., viewing videotapes at home cannot be explained in the terms used to analyze the classic Hollywood cinema). They seem to forget that concepts (of the gaze, of subjectivity) are specific to and gener-alized from specific apparatuses. Too often, the discourse of film theory seems to assume it can provide answers to all of the significant questions one might want to ask about film (or that the only significant questions are the ones it can answer).

But it is not the particularities of screen theory that are at issue here; it is the model of cultural theorizing based on the complex relationship between general and specific concepts, where the latter are adequate only in response to particular contexts and apparatuses. Even more interesting is its success at enabling an ongoing theoretical conversation.[7] I could offer another and perhaps less controversial example: Raymond Williams's concept of flow as a description of the televisual text has provided at least a common starting point for many, if not most, discussions—theoretical and empirical—of the televisual text.[8]

My claim then is simple: the study of popular music has either never found an appropriate starting point (from which the argument can begin) or, more likely, it has never undertaken such a project in a serious and col-lective way; in fact, for whatever reasons, it seems unwilling and apparently unable to take on this project.[9] It is interesting to speculate on why this is the case, and I want to offer a few suggestions. First, the struggle to legitimate popular music did not have available to it an accepted model, whereas both film and television studies had the model of the literary text with its associated celebration of the author. Thus, the latter initially appealed (and often limited their studies) to the study of film and television as art. The struggle to legitimate popular-music studies (outside of the models of art and folk culture) has been a much more difficult one. Partly as a consequence, the field of popular-music studies is made up of a smaller and more intimately connected body of scholars and students (often with little or no power). The social relations that have contributed to its successes have perhaps also made it more difficult for individuals to seriously engage with and criticize each other's work. Moreover, the fact that popular-music scholars come from a very wide range of disciplines has not made the task any easier. Finally, and perhaps most importantly, I believe the nature of the investment that those studying popular music have in the music is often qualitatively different from that in other areas of research. Perhaps we are too invested, but most certainly, the music matters in ways that often transform the intellectual project into a defense of particular tastes.[10]

An example might help: at another panel in this conference, a friend asked the keynote speaker about the role of backup singers (often black and female) in rock performance. The speaker, a leading figure in rock criticism, responded in rather vague terms that such singers served to legitimate the (white male) performance, a kind of performative pat on the back. It is not just that this is totally inadequate; rather, my point is that an adequate answer begins to make theoretical and contextually specific demands on us. For example, a better answer might begin by suggesting that postwar popular music is, in part, about identifications, both real and imaginary, of all different kinds (e.g., fantasy, alliance, affiliation), between different factions of the population (e.g., black and white, male and female, gay and straight). Such identifications usually involve complex economies of perception, imagination, and desire around issues of subordination and alienation, on the one hand, and response and transcendence, on the other. To go further we would need to begin to develop a better theory of identifications and their relations to musical practices; and then we would need to develop a better vocabulary for making useful distinctions between apparatuses and economies of identification. But, to return to the question, I would also reject the universal form in which it was asked, as well as the assumption, implicit in the answer at the time, that the differences could be described in purely generic terms, as if identifications were necessarily correlated to genres.

In fact, perhaps the most commonly debated question in any discussion of pop music—"What is new?"—is unanswerable without this kind of theoretical work. How can you talk about what's new or different and what is the same (or what is "the changing same") unless you have a vocabulary in which both sorts of relations can be described? How can you begin to offer new insights into the concrete workings of particular musical and cultural practices if you have not yet figured out a vocabulary within which to ask and answer questions about the effectivity of such practices?

The Performance/Image Couplet

I would make the same argument for any question worth asking. But let me take the issue of the relations between performance and image and let me proceed by using Karen Kelly and Evelyn McDonnell's elaboration of this question in the call/program for the Dia conference as my starting point.[11] To begin with, we have to recognize that this phrase, "performance and image," condenses a number of different questions at different levels of abstraction. First, as the introduction to this panel suggests, it demands that we "explore the relationship between the creation of music, the translation of that creation into a public space, and the reception of that translation by an audience." It also requires us to reconsider the meaning and role of live performance in rock culture, not as something separable from or opposed to image, but as one term in a complex set of relations among the various forms of the objectification-commodification-exploitation of the performance-image couplet.[12] This question does assume that the live event produces certain experiences unavailable through other means. Consequently, it would seem that the experience cannot be understood simply in terms of the constitution of a community or of the feelings that go along with being with other people and having a common object of investment, since such experiences need not depend on live performance; they could be produced through the collective viewing of videos, or simply listening to records together. However, I think this argument—searching for some unique experience produced by the live experience—is mistaken, for it takes the productivity of the performance as a necessary and universal effect. My own sense is that, at the most abstract level, the social investment in rock culture does not depend on the specificity of the live moment but upon the possibility of producing "the coming community."[13] Moreover, at this level, it isn't only that performance and image are inseparable from one another but that they are and always have been inseparable from rock culture itself.

Second, has the relationship between performance and visual image changed? Is there a new ratio, as it were, between an emphasis on the music and on the visual image, or has the quality of the visual image changed, presumably making it easier to overwhelm the music? And, following from that, are there now two kinds and meanings of performance? Can one see an opposition between live performance and "a whole visual package," or has rock performance always deployed a whole visual package, whether spectacular or minimalist? Beyond the fact that image and style have always been a crucial part of rock (which is not to say that the ratio has always been the same), it is worth recalling that, at least since the sixties (if not earlier), a part of rock culture (especially in Britain, where it is often identified as pop) has championed the artificiality and ironic possibilities of style. While often presenting itself as different from (even opposing) mainstream commitment to authenticity, such pop apparatuses, I would argue, are equally implicated in such logics of authenticity, but I will return to this point shortly.

Third, assuming that something has changed, what are the politics of this new "performance in the guise of style and impudent imagery"? What is its relation to late capitalism? To conventional iconographies? And on the other side, what are the politics of live performance in the face of this new visual economy? Of course, it is important to point out that nothing is new about the form of this question. In fact, it is part of the logic of rock[14] (and of being a rock fan), for it simply records the fact that rock culture always involves a distribution (actually, a number of competing distributions) of texts, audiences, and practices along at least one of the following dimensions: economics (majors versus independents); success (mainstream versus marginal); audience (mainstream versus subcultural); sound (commercial versus underground or alternative); and sometimes even a political/ideological difference (mere entertainment versus resistance). Such distributions or differentiations are precisely how rock culture works. Often, the different dimensions of this distribution are all conflated, as if they were guaranteed to be equivalent, as if one could read from one "fact" to another. This condensation is linked to notions of authenticity and cooptation, and is usually tied up with claims for rock's power (as transcendence or resistance, etc.). I mean neither to dismiss this logic nor to buy into it entirely, although in a sense I do want to argue that, from a theoretical point of view, the question (asked at the beginning of this paragraph) is that of a fan or critic. I simply want to point out that such questions were a necessary and constitutive part of an emergent popular formation in the fifties and sixties, a formation that, by the eighties, had become dominant, at least in terms of youth culture and popular music, if not more broadly in terms of the national popular culture of the U.S. The result is that the question of authenticity has been reproduced over and over again, albeit in slightly different terms of reference, wherever fans and critics speak.

If we are to answer any of these questions concerning the (changing) nature and place of the performance-image couplet, we need to put them in the context of what has happened—is happening—to rock culture. At the very least, we need to ask ourselves: are we assuming (and if so, why) that such questions—the meaning or value of live performance, the politics of style—have only one referent, only one answer, which is adequate to the entirety of popular-music culture? Instead, I would argue that in order to begin to answer these questions, we need to locate the questions (as well as the performance and style) in a specific context, understood both as an apparatus and as the conditions of possibility of that apparatus (a doubling that, unfortunately, film theory too often ignores).

Mapping Rock in the Nineties

Let me begin by offering the barest outline of my own research on and theories of rock culture.[15] First, I have argued that the emergence of rock has to be understood in relation to a number of conditions of possibility operating in economics, politics, everyday life, youth (as a population and signifier), culture—including technologies, industries, "media economies" (comparative investments in different media), and, I would certainly add, music[16]—and the available images of alienation and rebellion.[17] Second, I have argued that what emerged (in the most general and abstract terms) was a cultural logic or mode of productivity that can be described in the following terms: affective (rather than ideological); differentiating (us versus them); a celebration of fun (where "fun" takes on different meanings depending on what it is opposing); politicized, primarily within the realm of everyday life; and operating as a mode (or practice) of survival in the face of the very conditions that called it into existence.

So the question of what is happening to what we might broadly call rock culture in the nineties, in my opinion, has to begin by addressing these two issues: how have its conditions of possibility changed, and how has its mode of productivity changed? For the sake of time and space, I will assume that the former discussion is unnecessary since the contours of the changes that have taken place between the fifties and the nineties are, I hope, fairly transparent.[18] Instead, I will offer something like a map of rock culture in the nineties by distinguishing four broadly defined apparatuses of popular music.[19] First, the formation that I have described throughout the body of my work emerged in the fifties to become the dominant U.S. cultural formation of "American" youth (if not of the United States) from the sixties until the mid-eighties. But by the end of the eighties, I believe this apparatus is, to borrow Raymond Williams's term, "becoming residual." Williams defines the "residual" as follows:

The residual has been effectively formed in the past, but it is still active in the cultural process, not only and often not at all as an element of the past, but as an effective element of the present. Thus certain experiences, meanings, and values that cannot be expressed or substantially verified in terms of the dominant culture are nevertheless lived and practiced on the basis of the residue . . . of some previous social and cultural institution or formation. It is crucial to distinguish this aspect of the residual, which may have an alternative or even oppositional relation to the dominant culture, from that active manifestation of the residual . . . which has been wholly or largely incorporated into the dominant culture.[20]

This apparatus, usually organized around generic commitments and differences, although still active and important, is slowly moving toward the edges along paths that are often erratic and sometimes even reversed. It is no longer dominant where dominance is a matter not of commercial success but of what might be called cultural or discursive power.[21] I do not think this apparatus can speak any longer for or as the most widely distributed or most powerful "version" of rock, although there is no doubt that it is still struggling to speak normatively as the "proper" form of rock; and in so doing, it sometimes has the effect of marginalizing other apparatuses, and other forms of cultural practice and social relationship. At the same time, we have to acknowledge that, given the changes in the conditions of possibility of rock, it is harder to anchor this residual formation in actual social and cultural relations than it was, say, twenty years ago.

Within this apparatus, live performance is both the imagined originary event and the site for authenticating the claim of authenticity. As a result, the presence of the fan is not only the measure of his or her own commitment but also the occasion for him or her to measure the performer's commitment. Furthermore, while the logic of this apparatus can allow for the recognition of image as part of performance, this recognition is usually actualized in an experienced contradiction between the image and the performance, or at least as a fear that the image can and is overwhelming the performance, which is the essential moment of rock culture itself.

However rapidly this apparatus is becoming residual, it continues to dominate most of the writing and thinking about rock among academics and journalists; this is one of the few things these two groups have in common. But I think this is largely a function of the generational identity of the writers, and of the lack of an adequate theoretical vocabulary that would allow one at least to talk about the incongruity of the claim of continued dominance. This claim of dominance for a residual apparatus is helped along by the fact that both rap and alternative musics share its explicit ideology of authenticity, even if authenticity may mean different things to these different fans.[22] But there is another issue at stake here: how is this change—from dominant to residual—itself being accomplished? I believe that the residual status of this classic-rock apparatus is being constructed by the growing power of three other apparatuses: a new dominant neoeclectic apparatus, and two relatively recent, closely related, emergent apparatuses. I am not denying that these apparatuses may have histories of their own, but as their places and relative power to speak for rock culture have changed, their relations to each other have also been significantly restructured.

The new, increasingly dominant apparatus defines a new mainstream that actually looks a lot like and is committed to much of the logic of the Top 40, itself another often ignored apparatus of popular music. The Top 40 was always hybrid, bringing together in a statistical sample the disparate tastes of various taste cultures. The result was a collection of music the totality of which no one actually liked, but that, given the alternatives, many people listened to. Yet I believe that today, the apparatus, which is "becoming dominant," embraces a similar kind of eclecticism. Rather than claiming some sort of rock purism, it celebrates rock hybridity at its most extreme. This mainstream operates without the mediations of a logic of authenticity. On one level at least, it gives up rock's differentiating function insofar as it refuses to draw and empower generic distinctions as meaningful. It does not set classic rock, rap, country, etc., in opposition but embraces at least selected examples of each. In fact, this apparatus— and the individuals within it—embrace an extraordinarily wide and (at least by my musical sensibilities) jarring range of music. The fans within

this formation may like some classic rock, some country, some punk, some disco, some rap, and so on.[23] And spending an evening with them can be a strange experience for someone who still lives within the becoming-residual formation, because they happily switch among these genres from song to song. And yet this neoeclectic mainstream does not give up the differentiating function all together, since it is selective about what songs it includes in its own space of acceptability. It refuses to allow popularity or radio-play to define inclusion (as in Top 40), but instead relies upon the judgments of specific members with investments in particular genres and sounds, but such investments can never be so strong as to result in the exclusion of other genres and sounds. In other words, rather than either success or authenticity, this apparatus operates with a logic of sampling, in both senses of the term (i.e., as a production technique and a habit of listening). This apparatus willingly embraces, simultaneously, the global megastar and the local rebel, the rock star who requires an appearance of authenticity and the dance-music star who couldn't care less about it.

Moreover, if these new listeners are tolerant and eclectic about their own musical tastes, they are also tolerant about musical tastes more generally. That is, they do not seem to use musical taste and judgment as the basis for a differentiating logic, and they do not judge other people's tastes at all. They have given up the differentiating function of rock even as they attempt to hold onto its "territorializing function" in relation to a politics of fun and everyday life. They are tolerant beyond anything that "rock culture" could understand. Taste may be the last site for individuality, nothing more and nothing less. Finally, at least for the moment, I would argue that this apparatus cannot be so clearly described, at least in the first instance, as a musical formation, insofar as its center is defined as much by visual practices and commitments (and media, including film, television, video games, and computers) as by musical ones. Often they like music because of the other activities (e.g., collective movement through line dancing) that it enables them to carry out. It is not that the music is not there all the time, but that the quality (rather than the quantity) of the investment in it has changed. Music's power is increasingly defined by its relation to other activities and functions. And, consequently, music's ability to organize other investments, to define what matters, has diminished considerably. I suppose one could argue that this is a nonutopian yet integrative apparatus (unlike the older apparatus, which tended to be utopian and disintegrative). Yet it is also cynical: if those within this apparatus embrace commodification without illusions, it is because they cannot imagine a way out of commodification. If they continue to seek a way to challenge everyday life, they can only imagine such a challenge within an economy of entertainment as an isolable fraction of their lives. They are no longer "dancing all over their blues" but for their right to party, for some claim to feel and care, usually about each other rather than about the music, and to reassert some sense of their own agency, even if it is within an extraordinarily constricted space of their lives. Of course, this vocabulary sounds more critical than I intend, for the logic of this apparatus can be understood and judged only in relation to the context from which it emerges and to which it responds, the context within which youth is constructed and must survive today.[24]

To be honest, I have yet to figure out the politics of style and the relationship between image and performance in this apparatus. It is perhaps too early to know the answer, but the question of the meaning of live performance is a different matter. In fact, I can find little or no evidence that any significance is attached to it; there is little or no commitment to the value or necessity of live performances in defining some sort of unmediated relation to the performer and the music. The performative side of rock seems to be secondary. It is not that those interpolated by this logic do not appreciate the occasions of live music; such occasions are important opportunities for a variety of social activities that have little or nothing to do with the music, or else they are occasions for making identity-claims that everyone knows to be somewhat artificial and temporary.

Finally, contemporary rock culture also involves at least two intertwined emergent apparatuses, both built on a spatial reorganization of the fan's investment in the music. One is already redefining the notion of authenticity, and even affecting the operation of the concept in the residual rock formation. This apparatus is based on a network of dispersed and differentiated scenes, where scenes are geographically identifiable and define a system of differentiation, which is not binary but territorializing.[25] Authenticity here is spatial rather than temporal: it is a measure of commitment to and investment in a particular place, although place itself is being redefined within the logic of this apparatus.[26] Certainly part of what is interesting about this apparatus is that a scene, despite the attempts of the industry to give it musical content, is usually defined less by a sound than by a social style and/or a set of social relationships and allegiances. Thus scenes can bring together dance, rap, and alternative musical communities. (The image of Minneapolis, in which Prince is a major figure, is an interesting example here.) Scenes have no generic identity, and hence they are not equivalent with the commercialized notion of scenes, which are actually residual and/or mainstream formations. These spatial scenes are often utopian, precisely because they are based on an integration of the audience, even while they compulsively differentiate themselves from (and form alliances with) other scenes. I am convinced that this logic operates at the center and border (simultaneously) of everyday life by imagining an identification between the various populations (so that increasingly youth equals black) integrated into the self-representations of the scene. Here the function of live performance is obvious—it involves the constitution and affirmation of the local scene through a sense of a local space of performance. On the other hand, the relation between performance and image is more difficult to analyze, precisely because the scene can be diverse. I would guess that the relation is polyvalent and situational; rather than defining a single standard or proper relationship, such scenes are bound to celebrate the possibility of diversity here as well.

The fourth apparatus is very similar to the apparatus of scenes (and much of what is said about that is true of this one as well), although I am less certain about how to describe it or what its limits and parameters are. The spatiality of the investments in and of this apparatus is defined by the place of music itself, or more accurately, the place of that activity— dancing—which becomes the affective alibi of the music itself. This dance apparatus has explicit ties with (and may include) hip-hop culture, but it hybridizes hip hop, disco, techno, and "world-beat," into a vibrant, largely urban "house" culture. Here live performance is increasingly irrelevant; mediation—by the DJ and/or the technology—is everything. While it began as a variant of a logic of scenes (with the distinctions between dance cultures across space being as important as what happened in the local scenes), I think that hybridization across scenes has overpowered the scenes themselves, creating a rapidly changing global apparatus. The odd thing about this apparatus is that, like certain instances of a scene, it returns to a logic of authenticity, which is, in many ways, identical to that of the becoming-residual apparatus (often thought of as "classic-rock culture"[27]). It celebrates its marginality, not in spatial terms as an invest-ment in the local (as opposed to the globality of capitalism), but in terms of its marginality and (explicit claim to) resistance.

I am cautiously optimistic about these two emergent formations, and even the new mainstream: I wonder if they each have an affective politics that is significantly different from that of the becoming-residual rock formation, maybe even a polemological (explicitly antagonistic) politics, operating on the borders of everyday life by imagining an identification between country's poor white trash, black youth, and white middle-class youth; between male and female; between gay and straight. Punk tried to get to such a politics, but in the end, it failed (perhaps because it also failed, even though it tried, to escape the classic-rock apparatus). Somewhere among these new apparatuses, I would like to begin to imagine new possibilities for a popular politics. But I have to return to my cynicism as well. I do not know how we can begin even to argue about such possibilities unless we develop the theory and vocabulary necessary to such efforts. My sense is that there is little commitment, within a discourse of popular-music studies, to engage with such a project.

Notes

1. I think the truth of this can be seen in three recently published texts that purport to survey our "knowledge about rock"; one even explicitly claims to do so in terms of "theory." What is remarkable is how identical these are in both structure and content, and how little theory there is in any of them: see Keith Negus, *Popular Music in Theory* (Cambridge: Polity, 1996); Roy Shuker, *Understanding Popular Music* (London: Routledge, 1994); and Brian Longhurst, *Popular Music and Society* (Cambridge: Polity, 1995).

2. Although obviously the very fact of my decision, twenty years ago, to teach and to write about popular music already embodies a whole set of judgments. But I don't want to talk about issues of what is good or bad music. I don't want to talk about my taste, if only because I believe that taste is always determined elsewhere, through a complex set of relations. The question of quality, of which music is good or bad according to whatever cri-

terion one might use, is only interesting and important, at least within the project I am trying to describe, in the last instance.

3. See Meaghan Morris, *Upward Mobility: Popular Genres and Cultural Change* (Bloomington: University of Indiana Press, 1998).

4. John Frow, *Cultural Studies and Cultural Value* (Oxford: Oxford University Press, 1995), p. 87.

5. Without such theoretical work, these terms are little more than mystifications.

6. I recognize that film is a medium as well as a broad cultural form, while popular music is not in any usual sense a medium.

7. This is not to say that everyone writing about film has joined the conversation, but it seems to me that even someone who rejects the semiotic-psychoanalytic-Marxist discourse of this theory has to define himself or herself against this theory. I also want to avoid celebrating the historical moment of screen theory or the practices by which it was, however briefly, made hegemonic. There were lots of

negative aspects and results of the historical moment. I only mean to appropriate its model of general and specific concepts.

8. Similarly, Lynn Spigel's book *Make Room for TV* (Chicago: University of Chicago Press, 1992) transformed the field of television history.

9. To some extent, I must admit, the problem is not endemic to popular-culture studies: thus, Dominic Strinati's recent survey of theories of popular culture is organized by paradigms of cultural theory (structuralism, poststructuralism, etc.) that have no obvious or direct relation to competing notions of the popular. (See Dominic Strinati, *An Introduction to Theories of Popular Culture* [New York: Routledge, 1995].) At the same time, I want to acknowledge that there are some serious attempts at least to begin to develop, usually in only the broadest of terms, a theory of popular music. Here one would have to mention the work of authors like Michel Chion and Jacques Attali. Additionally, there are now bodies of work that I find rather unconvincing although sometimes insightful, drawing on either phenomenology or semiotics. On the other hand, I want to acknowledge that there have been many valuable and significant contributions to this project: e.g., Charles Keil and Steven Feld, *Music Grooves* (Chicago: University of Chicago Press, 1994); Will Straw, "Systems of Articulation, Logics of Change," *Cultural Studies* 5 (1991), pp. 368–88; and Charles J. Stivale, "Of *hecceitis* and *ritournelles*: Movement and Affect in the Cajun Dance Arena," in *Articulating the Global and the Local*, ed. Ann Cvetkovich and Douglas Kellner (Boulder: Westview, 1997), pp. 129–48.

10. Interestingly, such relations of taste and fandom may be becoming more common as a generation raised on television and other forms of popular culture comes to power in the academy.

11. Unless otherwise noted, quotations in this section are taken from the call/program for the Dia conference.

12. These issues were raised in the web discussion preceding the Dia conference.

13. See Giorgio Agamben, *The Coming Community*, trans. Michael Hardt (Minneapolis: University of Minnesota Press, 1993).

14. Of course, such a binary question is also constitutive of certain forms of critical theory, although it is opposed by cultural studies: see Stuart Hall, "Notes on Deconstructing the Popular," in *People's History and Socialist Theory*, ed. Ralph Samuels (Boston: Routledge and Kegan Paul, 1981).

15. See Lawrence Grossberg, *We Gotta Get Out of This Place: Popular Conservatism and Postmodern Culture* (New York: Routledge, 1992); and Lawrence Grossberg, *Dancing in Spite of Myself: Essays on Popular Culture* (Durham: Duke University Press, 1997).

16. David Laing is correct to point out that I have often not stressed this last point enough. I suppose I assumed it was obvious when I should not have. (David Laing, "Rock Anxieties and New Music Networks," in *Back to Reality? Social Experience and Cultural Studies*, ed. Angela McRobbie (Manchester: University of Manchester Press, 1997), pp. 116–32.

17. I think the fact that rock culture is willing to acknowledge its debt to black culture and music but always seems to underestimate its relation to country-and-western culture and music can be explained, in part, in these terms.

18. See Grossberg, *Dancing in Spite of Myself*.

19. These apparatuses do not correlate in any simple way with radio formats, partly because, as has been commonly observed, the logic of economics of radio is significantly different from that of the music industry.

20. Williams continues, "at certain points the dominant culture cannot allow too much residual experience and practice outside itself, at least without risk. It is in the incorporation of the actively residual —by reinterpretation, dilution, projection, discrimination, inclusion, and exclusion—that the work of the selective tradition is especially evident." Raymond Williams, *Marxism and Literature* (Oxford: Oxford University Press, 1977), p. 123.

21. After all, in commercial terms, the dominant forms of popular music would be pop, Top 40, etc. Both of these overlapping apparatuses exist outside of any logic of distinction, the former often characteristic of preadolescent tastes. The Top 40 has become more interesting since the mid-eighties, since the emergence of what can be called, following Tony Kirschner, a "hip mainstream." But these must still be recognized as changing apparatuses. For example, it would be interesting to talk about the changing temporality of pop: in the nineties, one hears statements like, "Oh, that's so 1994," and even, "Oh, that's so five minutes ago."

22. While the logic of rap production might be built upon sampling, it still operates with an ideology and logic of authenticity.

23. This description is based on ethnographic research I conducted with a group of high-school students during the summer of 1995 in Illinois. In fact, there were limits to the generic possibilities for the kids in the group—they were unwilling to listen to techno, for example, but even that may change as they are now in college. Also, interestingly, these kids were not, despite common assumptions, into computer culture as much as video games. I hope to publish this work in *Do You Know Who Your Kids Are Tonight?*

24. See Grossberg, *Dancing in Spite of Myself*. At the very least, we must acknowledge the collapse of liberalism as state policy and ideology, the collapse of an ameliorist economy built on a corporate compromise, and the devaluation of youth (carried out to such an extent as to put youth at material risk).

25. See Mark J. V. Olson, "'Everybody Loves Our Town': Scenes, Spatiality, Migrancy," in *Mapping the Beat*, ed. Thomas Swiss, John Sloop, and Andrew Herman (Oxford: Blackwells, 1998).

26. For a discussion of the meaning of place, see Doreen Massey, *Space, Place and Gender* (Cambridge: Polity, 1994).

27. Which is not the same as classic rock as a radio format.

On Not Playing Dead

The creation of a singular, static image has never been a priority for me. In fact, it runs contrary to much of my value system. This doesn't mean that when I get onstage I don't think that I'm being perceived by people, or even right now being perceived by all of you. Being a performer, I realize that there's a certain amount of objectification that's going to happen. It's just that I'd rather play around with the idea of images and roles than fit into a specific one.

Performance isn't just about what happens when a performer is on the stage; it's also about context. The context includes what happens before, during, and after the performance, as well as the general climate the performance takes place in.

Part of my personal context has to do with being a white female who grew up in the suburbs of Maryland. From the time I was little till I went out on my own when I was seventeen, I was submerged in a really boring middle-class lifestyle, one that rewarded me for keeping quiet and not asking too many questions, questions about what my race and class had to do with the access my family had to jobs and housing, questions about what my gender had to do with the fact that I experienced a lot of sexual, verbal, and psychological abuse in my childhood (and beyond).

The abuse I experienced as a girl reinforced the denial I was already submerged in as a member of a suburban family. A lot of times the only defense I had against oppression was to go completely numb: if I wasn't "present" or "in my body" when bad things happened to me, it wouldn't hurt. As an adult, I have begun to question numbness's validity as a strategy. I have also become interested in its relationship to the capitalist structure in general.

It seems to me capitalism thrives on denial and numbness. People who are dead to the world make really good bosses, and in some cases, really good workers. When you're numb, you don't question things when people tell you to do them, even if they're going to hurt you or hurt other people, potentially people you don't even know. (For example, who is being exploited by the companies we work for, or in some cases create/own?)

Since I have a commitment in my life to not being a boring, bullshit square and to actually fully living, I have to hate capitalism. As a performer, part of what I'm interested in is how live performance feeds, or doesn't feed, into capitalism. This is where the idea of "image" comes in. If I, as a performer, accept the idea of "image," basically what I'm doing is accepting objectification of myself and allowing my work to become an easily digestible commodity . . . a commodity to be consumed and shat out, just like any other capitalist product. It seems far more disruptive to incite people—whether through how much they hate my work, how much they like it, or how ambivalent they are toward it—to find their own voices instead of just consuming mine.

Disrupting capitalistic-type viewing situations can be really tricky. Kids who watch a lot of MTV tend to expect a certain seamlessness even when it comes to live performance. A lot of times "fans" come into live settings expecting to hear the songs they want with no glitches or mistakes, no talking in between, etc. They want a flat image that they can consume. In order to disrupt that, one thing I do as a performer is try to stay physically present onstage, and that means being in the *now*. (Oh my god, I sound like such a hippie.) I try not to think about creating a perfect, flawless performance; instead, I try to pay attention to what is going on in my body and what is happening in the actual room, because in a lot of cases, what the crowd is doing on the floor is just as interesting and important as what's happening on the stage.

Take moshing, for example. It used to be this thing that was fun, and at times it seemed really radical. It was one of the only public activities I know of where it was okay to get physical with people you didn't know. I'm not sure what happened, what video it was that had moshing in it, but at some point all these boneheads started coming to shows and moshing in a really gross, macho, anticommunity way. Since I'm a performer who, as I said, thinks it's important to acknowledge the dynamics of the whole room when I perform, I tend to notice if moshing is forcing people who want to see the show into the back. I mean, it's totally cool if guys wanna get all sweaty and touch each other and stuff, but they're not watching what's going on onstage, so why can't they do it in the back? I thought one of the things about punk rock was that it demystified playing instruments. Well, if most of the crowd literally can't see, then it's just not working. Also, how fucked is it that women have to watch a feminist band from the back of the room because they are too scared (or too grossed out) to be in the front? When women are moshing or it's a mixed group and everyone's having fun, that's cool, but if it's messing up a lot of people's ability to have a good time, that's when I've asked the moshers to step to the back. This is just one way paying attention to what the audience is doing affects how I act when I'm onstage.

Another thing that indirectly affects my performance style has to do with how I do (or in some cases don't do) business. I think it's helpful as a performer to be involved in booking shows, doing artwork, and making tour and studio arrangements, because it keeps you in control of what you're putting out into the world and how it's getting out there. I also like putting work out through independent labels, because getting involved with a major corporation can not only widen the gap that already exists between "musicians" and "fans" but further alienate performers from their own work. Being on a major label might also mean letting people who are functioning on a really gross and boring level have control over how I am represented and have access to my money. Which doesn't mean everyone who decides to be on a major label is an asshole (people do have to eat). I just think it can be really alienating and bad for both performers and audience members.

Having glossy pictures of themselves everywhere can also alienate performers from their audiences—and from themselves. Don't get me wrong: I think it's important, especially if you're on a small indie label with little-to-no advertising budget, occasionally to use the mainstream press. But, as a capitalist-hating artist (who still has to work within a capitalist system), I also try to support underground writers and people who do fanzines, because these are the people who are challenging the control corporations have over what gets written (and what doesn't). Also, doing interviews with people who do 'zines puts me in closer contact with people who actually listen to and support underground music and culture.

Another way I've tried to keep open the communication between myself and my audience is by reading all the mail I get and, whenever possible, answering it. It seems kind of like using Morse code sometimes, but I think it's important. I don't always say: "Thank you so very much for your support," and send them an eight-by-ten glossy or something. Sometimes I tell people who write me that I think they're full of shit, have outrageous, out-of-control expectations of me, etc. Sometimes I send them a Xerox explaining that I don't have time to write back right now (which seems a fuck of a lot more honest than writing a fake, bullshitty reply). I just think it's crucial, if performers really want to disrupt capitalism, that we don't treat the people who support our work and contribute to our livelihoods like fools. Communicating with "fans" through letters and stage banter and by the kinds of business decisions I participate in is a way to show that I respect them and, I think, to ask for that respect in return.

Unfortunately, this doesn't always happen. A lot of men at shows I've performed at seem to feel "empowered" to speak their minds in really hateful, retrogressive ways. Guys come to our shows and yell stuff like, "Show us your tits" and "Take it off," or call me a cunt, a bitch, a femi-nazi. . . . Because a lot of times I am "present" while I'm onstage, these things can really hit me very hard. The thing is, even though it sucks when guys yell stuff at me or my bandmates, I have to appreciate it to a certain extent, because at least they're expressing themselves. I mean, a lot of times, there is sexist shit happening in a room but I can't respond to it because it's totally undercover. And while it is fucked up and sickening, I still appreciate the opportunity to confront sexism publicly, without all the fear, silence, and isolation I usually feel when stuff happens to me behind closed doors or when I'm alone on the street.

Experiencing the harsh reality of sexism isn't the only drawback of the performance style I've chosen. Some people get upset with me because I'm not acting how they think a performer should. I think people have been trained by television and capitalism to have shallow, necrophilic relations

Edy Ferguson, *We Can All Agree That This World Has Taught Me Nothing* (detail), 1997

with each other. When confronted with an actual human being, we are startled, sometimes to the point where we lash out in confusion. So many of us function at the level of machines; when something sexy and amazing and real happens, it just doesn't compute.

One common thing is for people to yell at me to "shut up" when I'm talking between songs, as if what I'm saying is not a valid part of the show. It's as if, because music is involved in what I do, speech must necessarily be excluded. This purist notion is particularly frightening to me because, like sexism, it tends to incite some pretty big hostilities in people, i.e., I have been physically threatened, and in some cases attacked, by men who were pissed off because I wouldn't "just play the song"—just as often as I have by men who called me a "man-hater" or a "slut."

Because of negative shit like this, my bandmates and I had to come up with strategies to deal with violence and harassment at our shows. One strategy is to ask the audience what they want to do about certain situations, like to ask people in front if the moshing that's going on is cool with them. Also, I try to let it be known that if people are having a problem they can get us a message so we can either do something about it (like refuse to keep playing until security throws out a sexual harasser) or, again, ask the crowd what they wanna do . . . which sometimes means groups of girls escorting harassers out themselves. If an individual is having a problem, like they are being fucked with, I try to give them the mike so they can speak for themselves (and, again, everyone in the room can decide what they think appropriate action is, how believable the person is, etc.). This has been good because just pointing out "troublemakers" in the crowd can get weird and put me in too much of a teacher-authority position (which is part of what I am trying to disrupt, even though I am not always successful at it). We've also tried to have more women security people, because in certain cases security men have abused their power against our female fans. Another thing that we've done in terms of dealing with harassment, particularly sexist harassment, at our shows is to have flyers or posters up that say it's not cool to yell "slut" or "cunt" at us. It's not cool if you take your dick out and rub it on the woman in front of you, or punch her, or whatever. Like no duh. And if you do it, you'll get thrown out.

I've also asked women to be up front at shows because I feel physically and psychologically safer that way. This makes sense to me because men tend to yell grosser, more fucked-up things at us than women do, also because men are the ones who've tried to pull me offstage on those occasions when shit has gotten violent. There've also been times when guys have said physically threatening things that lead me to believe they might attack me or my bandmates when we're trying to leave the club or venue. In these cases, having women up front made it easy for me to ask for their help. Sometimes having a group of girls surround you while you're walking out to the van can be incredibly important.

What is interesting is that all these things I am talking about, strategies to disrupt capitalism and strategies to avoid violence, these things have now essentially become my "image," even though they were meant to be context oriented and in constant flux. Like sometimes moshing sucks, and sometimes it can be really cool, so sometimes it makes sense to ask people to knock it off, and sometimes it makes sense to just let it be. The problem is, people have been taught to expect some kind of consistency, even though contexts and dynamics change and are incredibly inconsistent. So when I wouldn't say, "Hey, you all stop moshing, it sucks," "Move to the back," or whatever, people would get bummed because they weren't getting what they got last time. Having girls up front became my calling card, and then if I didn't try to make that happen every time, it was like, "Where's the feisty feminist that is supposed to always say, 'Women up front'?" But saying it every night, even when it's not applicable (because there are already tons of women in front or whatever), that can become just as much an "image" as anything. And, to me, it's more important that I don't insult the women who're already standing there than it is to say the thing everyone expects me to say.

To a certain extent, I feel like I've been punished for not having an image and sticking with it, for not being professional in terms of performance, and for opening the communication between myself and the audience. Even though interesting things do happen, it seems like people get mad at me a lot. Sometimes audience members get mad because I don't meet the traditional expectations they have in terms of performance, or sometimes they get mad because I don't buy into the idea that "opening the communication" means they get to be abusive or disrespectful toward *me*. It can get really dualistic: either you are totally disconnected from audiences when you perform or else you are the perfect martyr, willing to cater to their every need.

What I am trying to say is that performers cannot disrupt boring, product/consumer, male/female schemas all on our own; we need audience members who are equally committed to resistance. We need audience members who are willing to open themselves up to the possible instead of just re-enforcing bullshit rules about consistency and image (whether the image is one of an aloof rock star or a completely giving, martyrlike entity, it is still 2D and fully boring). I mean, if we are really going to successfully challenge capitalism's intrusion on live performance, we not only need performers who are unwilling to commodify themselves, we also need audiences who will actively participate instead of just consuming.

I don't want to leave you with the impression that all the strategies I've used as a performer to try to disrupt capitalism have been totally unsuccessful or have always led to harassment and violence. In some cases, I think, they've worked. I've gotten letters from all over telling me that girls feel confident sticking up for themselves and each other at our shows. Also, because I'm present onstage a lot, I get to feel really, really amazing when thirteen-year-old girls are in the front row, singing lyrics that I wrote, as if they're their own. Or when I get to go back to a town that we were at before and see girls who two years ago were talking about starting a band but thought they couldn't do it (sometimes because their brothers had told them that if they plugged in amps without knowing how, they would get electrocuted and die)—when I get to play a show with the band these girls started and I get to be influenced by what they're doing, then it's not just a thing that's coming from here down to there, it's a thing that's circulating.

I have also met kids from all over who're creating their own scenes based on what is going on (or not going on) around them. Kids who are making fanzines, starting bands, setting up shows, and doing all kinds of political work. I've met people who are trying to create writing/musical styles based on nonhierarchical models, and many audience members who truly engage with what I, and other performers, are trying to do.

What I am trying to say is that in opening the communication between myself and "the audience," I have seen really amazing things happen, and really shitty things. It's sort of like how escaping denial in my own life has allowed me, not only to experience great joy, but also to experience great sadness and great pain as well. And even though some shows suck and some shows don't, it doesn't mean I'm not entirely grateful for the experience.

I still think that live performance can be really, really, really important. It's one of the only places where we give and receive pleasure publicly (which seems radical for a myriad of reasons, especially because it challenges the idea that sexuality/pleasure is only for people in straight, monogamous relationships and not something we as a community can have together through music). I also think that having live performance that isn't based on strict consumptive models is important because it creates community, and when we create community, we create the self-esteem we need to fight oppression, not only our own oppression, but the oppression we see our neighbors and friends going through as well.

The Crowd

Cinderella at the Headbanger's Ball

In the hugely popular 1983 movie *Flashdance*, an eighteen-year-old Catholic girl from Pittsburgh welds steel together all day, then goes out to go-go dance at night. Michael Sembello's number-one single from the soundtrack says she's a "maniac," dancing her crazy ballet into the danger zone of her mind. The steel-town girl from *Flashdance* is an archetypal character in pop songs. In "She's Only Happy When She's Dancing" by Bryan Adams, she works nine to five to make ends meet, then on Friday night she heads down to the Ball and Chain and loses herself in her fantasies, going insane until Monday, when her carriage returns to pumpkinhood like some updated version of the Cinderella myth. In "Dancing Queen" by Abba, the girl hunts for a place to dance on Friday nights, then has the time of her life to the beat of a tambourine. And in "Working for the Weekend" by Loverboy, white-trash hard rock from the early eighties, her whole junior class toils at the minimum wage all week, forever impatient to go off the deep end and be in the show.

In a way, these kids are not just working for the weekend—they're working *on* the weekend. In his 1991 *Atlantic Monthly* cover story "Waiting for the Weekend," Witold Rybczynski discusses how the weekend has progressed as an institution from its mid-nineteenth-century, London, Saturday-night music-hall, and Sunday-go-to-meeting roots to the point where people now take their leisure time even more seriously than "real" work. So "playing tennis" becomes "working on your backhand," and the Protestant work ethic puts on a new disguise. "The freedom to do anything has become the obligation to do something," Rybczynski theorizes. "The need to do something well, whether it is sailing a boat or building a boat, reflects a need that was previously met in the workplace." According to Susan Orlean in her essay collection *Saturday Night*, people in the late twentieth century are driven by something called the "fun imperative."

Jennifer Beals, in a film still from *Flashdance*, directed by Adrian Lyne, 1983

Not living it up on Saturday night is often thought to be indicative of a "major failure and possible character flaw."

In 1991, I published a book called *Stairway to Hell: The 500 Best Heavy Metal Albums in the Universe*. On its very first page, I wrote something stupid about how heavy metal has "no redeeming social value." That's utter bullshit, though I suppose what I meant is that metal didn't (at the time) work too hard to be "nutritious" in the sense of public television or protest songs. Really, though, heavy metal has redeeming social value simply by providing a habitat in which social situations *take place*—some cynic even scoffed in a fanzine I contribute to that rock criticism hardly makes any sense at all because "let's face it, the main reason people go see rock music is to *get dates*."

Most people I know find out about new Prodigy and Toni Braxton and Garth Brooks songs the same way people have always found out about new songs: from the radio, from TV, from hearing the songs in bars or malls. So, the fundamental things apply as time goes by: the real world is no more "post" rock than it was in 1990 or 1966. I'm not convinced anything has changed except the technology.

When Angela McRobbie distinguishes between the Spice Girls' "commercial audience" and the "active audience" of what she calls "dance subcultures," I really don't understand what she's talking about. For one thing, Spice Girls fans are *themselves* a dance subculture. If you go to a show by that group, you're certainly not gonna see a huge crowd of thirteen-year-old girls *standing still*. They'll be on their feet, singing at the top of their lungs and bouncing all over the place. Angela's cryptic dichotomy reminds me of the old fifties Situationist myth about capitalism making people passive consumers, as if all those bobbysoxers were shrieking and wetting their pants over Elvis "passively." The Spice Girls and Alanis Morrisette, and Claire Danes, for that matter, are now heroines and role models to preteen girls just like Cyndi Lauper and Madonna and Molly Ringwald used to be. To me, their fans seem *more* actively involved and critically discerning than, say, most techno or mosh-pit crowds, who seem to settle for *any* music sonically screwed-up enough to serve as a backdrop to their selected antisocial activities. In Donna Gaines's 1991 book about youth suicides in New Jersey, *Teenage Wasteland: Suburbia's Dead-End Kids*, the boys all go slam to Slayer while the girls stay home picking up occult tips from Stevie Nicks songs. I don't think that means the girls are more passive—it just means they have better taste.

One Saturday night in the spring of 1998, I DJed my son Linus's first school dance (sixth, seventh, and eighth graders), and it was really educational for me. The girls all dressed up and seemed three years older than the boys, who were all drably dressed wallflowers, and the girls were really aggressive in trying to get the boys to dance. The genders had widely different musical tastes, so it was quite a challenge trying to strike a decent balance. The girls mainly wanted to hear Spice Girls, Hanson, Savage Garden, OMC, Aqua, and Miami bass-booty music, and the boys mainly wanted to hear noisy guitar rock. I didn't play the Metallica and Alice in Chains songs the boys asked for because I don't own them, and they'd be too slow and ugly to dance to anyway, but I did play their Everclear and Sublime requests. The only music both the girls and the boys seemed to love equally was "Tubthumping" by Chumbawumba, "Brimful of Asha" by Cornershop, and No Doubt.

A couple of summers before, I covered the first show of the Lollapalooza tour in Kansas City. I was watching the trendy indie band Girls Against Boys on the third stage, and most of the girls in the audience were shimmying to the band's sexiness, and most of the boys were thrashing to the band's noise. So this guy about my age who looks like an ex-Deadhead asks me what the band's name is, and when I tell him Girls Against Boys, he says, "That's *great!* Girls are *always* trying to do shit better than boys! *Fuck* that!" But what I thought was even more wonderful, after years of being annoyed at indie rock's chronic fear of sex—no obvious effort put into making bodies look pretty in the videos, and no body in the rhythm or voices either, like it was all proud to be celibate, which to me just made it prudish and monklike—was that here were finally these handsome boy rockers wearing snazzy suits again, helping ladies lubricate their loins.

In the fanzine *Maximumrocknroll*, Charles Lamer theorized once that most sixties garage-rock angst resulted from frustration over stringent high-school dress codes, and from boys in Beatle shags being beaten up by greaser gangs. Lamer figured that garage-band musicians dressed to please female fans, who liked their boys wearing lacy, bright-colored shirts and pointy-toed, high-heel boots. Their girl fans supposedly returned the favor by wearing miniskirts and mod corduroy hats and ironing their long hair. Which in turn led envious teenage boys to wish the girls were paying attention to them instead!

If rock criticism is going to start analyzing "The Crowd," these are the sorts of issues I'd want it to deal with. But it has to stop being scared of its *own* audience, and even has to be willing to risk *insulting* that audience sometimes. I want more crowd analysis that people will be able to read in fifty years and still get a mental picture from, but that can only happen if writers sound involved in the action, not detached from it. The best example by far I've read lately came from Sara Sherr, who reviews records and shows for the *Philadelphia Inquirer* and *Philadelphia Weekly*, both of which force her to restrain her personality in print way more than she ought to. She wrote me this review of the ugly mosh-rock band Korn as part of an e-mail, and though I hope I'm wrong, I can't think of a paying outlet nowadays that would let her get away with it:

I got to the Korn show pretty early, and found a good place to stand upstairs. I was initially afraid of the crowd. They were trashier, a little older, and less suburban than the Marilyn Manson crowd two days before. While I'm taking notes, I am approached by this b-boy, let's call him B-Boy Kevin. (He was white by the way, everyone was.) "What are you writin'?" he asks. So I told him. And he asked who I was and I told him, expecting him to hate me immediately. And he said, "Dude, I read your stuff all the time." He wanted to know how I got my job and do I make a lot of money. He also did that Boy List thing: "What are your best bands of all time?" I discovered that he was twenty-three, he worked for a year as a night manager of a supermarket, and now has a more respectable job that involves him having his own car. And he said, "Dude, can I get your number?" I thought that he was cute with short dark hair and a nice face and his clumsy pick-up routine was charming, even if he asked me if I bought my biker jacket specifically for the show. Anyway, by the time the rap group Pharcyde came on, half the crowd was waving their arms like they just don't care and the other half was giving them the finger. This must have been happening all tour, because one of them was saying something like, "If you're a music connoisseur and you like all different kinds of music, say heeeey!" This is ironic because Korn and their fans dress black, talk black, and steal stuff from rap. Later Korn did a song called "Faget" which is just something incendiary and offensive and adolescent repeated over and over again: "Faget, all my life what am I." But the ironic thing is that it's supposed to be about the singer's tormented high-school years. And I wondered if the audience felt like the tormented or the tormentor when they were shouting that—or maybe they just wanted to say a bad word.

Back when I was in high school, in suburban Detroit in the mid-seventies, loud guitar rock was an unavoidable part of my environment. Jocks smoked dope to Ted Nugent and Foghat, who together put on a big show at the new Pontiac Silverdome that all the cool people went to, which did not include me. I was scared of the bad kids in the smoking area, so I didn't start identifying with the search-and-destroy of loud rock until after I graduated. On the other hand, here's what my friend Laura told me about *her* high-school career, as an honor student on Long Island in the eighties: "I wore argyle sweaters and Long Island Jap/preppy wear to school but bought fishnets and bustiers at the cheap mall stores for concerts. I'd leave the house wearing parentally approved outfits to see Mötley Crüe at Nassau Coliseum, and change into slutwear in the car. Still, the burnout kids never knew I was on their side. Although my preppy friends suspected I wasn't entirely on their team either."

She was an unusual case. Most high-schoolers tend to base the kinds of music they like on the kind of clique they want to belong to instead of the other way around, which makes perfect sense—shared leisure tastes are something friends have in common. And once they've joined a clique that considers their color or sexual preference or hair or awkwardness or bad attitude an asset instead of something to make fun of, defending their clique against outsiders is the next natural step. I personally have been told by punk, hip-hop, metal, and disco people that I have no right analyzing their music because I'm not part of the in-group that uses its music in the supposedly "right" way. My friend Rita, who knows way more about your Orbs and Orbitals than I do, says techno music can't be analyzed since there's nothing analytical about fourteen-year-olds tripping out of their skulls and soaking chests in VapoRub. But I never heard heavy metal the way luded-out headbangers did either, and that never stopped me from writing a book making fun of it for two-hundred pages.

My friend Amanda worked in a record store in a suburban Boston mall in the late eighties. "The mall was populated by the polyester-slack brigade, and at night they would give way to the stoners, headbangers, and metalheads," she tells me.

The store's staff was mainly comprised of about five or six metalhead teens, most of them white, though we had an East Indian girl and an African-American lad who were headbangers as well. Heavy metal apparently cut across racial and ethnic barriers in Framingham. It struck me as the ultimate irony that I, who had always leaned more toward the music played on college radio (before the words alternative *and* indie rock *entered the mainstream), was living in Boston, home of a thriving alternative rock scene in the eighties, but spent my days surrounded by people who listened to nothing but hard rock, heavy metal, and the occasional Madonna song. The few times I tried to tune in to the "modern-rock" radio station WFNX in the store, I was shouted down.*

This sort of thing happens all the time in the real world. But then again, everybody wants to feel special, so why *shouldn't* cliques guard their walls against outside threats? This is what the Beach Boys called "being true to your school." Nonconformists join a genre, name their genre "alternative" or "rave" or "Generation X" or "speed metal" or "rock criticism" or "literary theory," then become conformists. The new boss winds up the same as the old boss, and if you're not down with the program, they call you a "glam fag" or "too artsy" or a "boomer" or a "breeder chick" or "politically incorrect" or say you're "using outmoded discursive techniques." That's what life is all about.

When a member betrays the clique, the clique accuses the member of "selling out." Basically, "selling out" means changing your music, usually by opening it up to previously unpermitted sounds, to reach a new, larger audience and perhaps to challenge the cult that used to love you. You do it knowing full well that your new fans might not be as devoted as your old ones, but it has no necessary connection to your music's *quality*. Rock's most scandalous sellout in history happened in 1965, when Bob Dylan wore a motorcycle jacket and fancy boots at the Newport Folk Festival and played electric-guitar songs so loud that his acoustic, purist audience booed him offstage. One of the facets of indie rock I've never bought is *its* whole sellout-whining shtick—"this music belongs to our exclusive little club, and when the bigger audience gets ahold of it, it's no fun anymore"—like that. Once upon a time, I was immersed in indie. I wrote about bands like Soundgarden and White Zombie and the Butthole Surfers years before they became famous. But I never felt indie music or clubs gave me much in the way of a community I'd gain anything from belonging to. Most of my more dogmatic indie-slacker pals nowadays dismiss Scott Weiland of Stone Temple Pilots as a "frat boy," which to me just sounds like a social-class insult or a turf war. I've always had more in common with geeks or freaks than with Greeks myself. But frankly, I've still always considered the drunken dance-party aesthetic embraced by collegiate Animal Houses *lively*, and therefore smart. Though, then again, I've also never been date-raped, and I don't feel frat boys, even the kind who watch the TV show *Friends*, threaten my turf in any way. They're just another extracurricular club, with a different uniform.

Three summers ago, I got allergy shots every few weeks from a pretty twenty-year-old physician's assistant who looked somewhat like Sandra Bullock and somewhat like Gloria Estefan, so before long I started getting them every week instead. Her name was Colleen, and "Smells Like Teen Spirit" was a hit when she was seventeen, and she told me she'd always considered the ten or so girls who "dressed punk" at her Catholic northeast Philadelphia high school scary and strange, but since then she'd got her belly button pierced. Two years later, the best concert I saw was Stone Temple Pilots and the newer MTV Buzz Bin bubblegrunge band Local H at Philly's Spectrum. In the last song in Local H's set—"High-Fiving Motherfucker," it was called—the singer got revenge on all the jocks who used to pick on him back in Illinois by telling them their hair and clothes hadn't changed since 1983, which was funny, because every girl in the stadium had big, ratty, eighties, Jersey–northeast Philly hair, and every boy had a rectangular torso and hockey jersey. And they all seemed completely oblivious to the wrath being directed at them.

"I can often use 88.5 as a test to see if I will like someone I just met," somebody calling himself JayD25 wrote on an internet billboard in 1996.

While it doesn't mean I won't like the person if they don't listen to 88.5, it's almost a sure thing that I will like them if they do listen to the station. It sounds pretentious, but 88.5 just seems to draw a high class of people. Having grown up in a neighborhood filled with Mötley Crue fans, I thought maybe it was just me who had bad taste (liking bands like the Smiths and singers like Kate Bush and Peter Gabriel). When I got to college and found out about 88.5, things changed. I really believe that taste in music and intelligence goes [sic] hand in hand. 88.5, in my opinion, attracts a more intelligent listener than the average station. (And I'm not just saying that because I listen to it. Well, maybe just a little.) In the last few years, I've noticed a lot more people have become listeners. I'm sure some of it has to do with the rise of so-called alternative music, but I also hope it means people are starting to demand a little more than Mariah Carey can offer.

This guy spells his prejudices right out—public-radio fans come from a higher "class" than metal fans, which makes them smarter and easier to get along with! But increasingly, and there's no way poor JayD25 could've anticipated this, "alternative" and "lower-class" people tend to be *the same people.* So more and more, what we're seeing in the antagonism against alternative rock's new mass audience is a newer twist on such snobbish class animosity. Suddenly all these people who get their nails done and call their girlfriends "dude" and major in marketing and go bowling and have big hair are Cinderellas crashing the prince's alternative ball. ("Who's to care if I grow my hair to the sky," glam-metal, working-class heroes

Cinderella sang ten years ago!) Just like progressive rock in the late sixties and early seventies, grunge in its initial Seattle years was a movement created by and catering to college students, whereas so-called greasers or white trash still preferred sixties garage bands over prog rock, and eighties haircut-metal over grunge. Kurt Cobain's mulatto, albino, mosquito, and libido were clearly *misfits*, bringing their friends with them to hunt for entertainment at night because it's fun to lose and to pretend, and when the light's out it's less dangerous. But eventually, as both prog and grunge became more popular, and in most cases catchier and less obtuse over the years—in prog's case, with bands like Styx and Boston and Journey; then in grunge's case, with bands like Matchbox 20 and Local H and Sponge—the earlier, more devoted, more bohemian fans of both genres cried "sellout!" and moved on to music they felt was more honest or esoteric. In both cases, fans of newer, so-called sellout bands were less liberal-arts-oriented and more working-class, trade-school-oriented than fans of the earlier, so-called real bands. The typical newer fan was also younger, and frequently less likely to be male.

So one thing I've been wondering lately is whether, if you left your small-town high school believing Third Eye Blind was the coolest band on earth and then went to college and unwisely sat at a cafeteria table full of Sebadoh fans who told you their music was way more daring, and they gave each other disgusted looks when you naïvely bragged about your quaint fake-alternative tastes, which might be a totally traumatic experience, would it be possible for you to look down on *them*? Did eighties Bon Jovi girls ever intimidate the Morrissey girls they met in college instead of the other way around? Or is that a moot point, since there's a good chance that becoming a Sebadoh or Morrissey fan is partially a defense mechanism against being intimidated by Bon Jovi bullies in the first place? It's sort of like mods against rockers all over again, isn't it?

The Sound of the Crowd

In preparing for this, I did what I usually do when I'm presented with a subject. I went to my records and looked for every single song I could find that had either *crowd* in the title or *crowd* in the lyric. And eventually, I hit pay dirt. I went through a bunch of sixties soul-stompers, like Betty Everett's "Getting Mighty Crowded," Dobie Grey's "The In-Crowd," some mod songs, like the Who's very, very sweet "The Kids Are Alright," where the whole point of the song is that he trusts the crowd so much that he can leave his girlfriend with them and doesn't mind whether she goes off with one of the crowd. On the other hand, there's a punk song like "Shot by Both Sides" by Magazine, where Howard DeVoto says, "I wormed my way into the heart of the crowd, I was shocked by what was allowed."

In those, you already see the variety of responses that any sane person feels when confronted by a crowd: How many people constitute a crowd? Which crowd are you in? You think if you're part of a crowd that you're the in-crowd—well, how do you assess that? Are you really part of a crowd anyway? And do you want to be part of a crowd? What happens if you don't want to be part of a crowd? These choices present real dilemmas during the teenage years, and our choices during these periods stick with us for the rest of our lives, in our relationships to organizations and institutions.

I'm going to focus on one song that places the subject of this session center-stage: the Human League's "Sound of the Crowd," which, released in April 1981, became their first U.K. Top 10 hit. To promote it, they appeared for the first time on the U.K. TV show *Top of the Pops*, which is always a good arena in which to set your stall. As befitted a synth-pop group, they gave a highly stylized lip-synch performance—with even the backing musicians delivering robotic moves. The lead singer, Philip

Disco dancers at the opening of Studio 54, New York, April 25, 1977

Oakey, generated much attention through his lipsticked androgyny, but the eye and camera returned to the sight of two young women—dressed in ra-ra skirts and hair extensions of that period—dancing and singing with the gleefulness of the suddenly empowered.

"Sound of the Crowd" was the second record by a revamped Human League. Before then, they'd been a four-man synthesizer group, with a couple of minor (Top 75) hits. What happened was that the two principal musicians left to form a group called Heaven 17; the others were a bit desperate. One day, Oakey went to a disco in Sheffield, which is where they're from—it's a northern industrial city in the U.K. They went into a disco called the Crazy Daisy and saw there those two women that are dancing in the video. And they were dancing together. Their names are Suzanne Sulley and Joanne Catherall. He did something extraordinary for synthesizer groups at that period: he brought these two women into the group. Before then they were basically like a rock band, a four-man gang.

As if by magic, the group immediately started having hits. Why? Because they were better. And they were better because the Human League had brought the crowd into the group. I want to quote from a rather wonderful interview with the girls in the *Best of Smash Hits*, the seminal volume, six years of interviews, which starts with the Sex Pistols and ends with Frankie Goes to Hollywood. Mark Ellen went to interview Suzanne Sulley and Joanne Catherall in 1982:

Inseparable friends from the very start, and both "completely potty," they jointly set forth upon an early teenage mission to be "really outrageous and do stupid things." They grew out of David Essex the moment that Devo appeared—this being the band's "plant-pot stage"—and donned oil-caked mechanic's overalls, daubed themselves in makeup, back-combed their hair, sprayed it silver, and trekked off to see Devo at every possible opportunity.

Almost as suddenly, Devo were out. Gary Numan had been sighted singing "Are 'Friends' Electric?" on Top of the Pops. *They reckoned him "gorgeous," and on the strength of it, saw him twice, bought most of his records, and memorized the words of every song.*

And something was stirring within their wardrobe.

"We wore black trousers," recalled Joanne, "a black shirt buttoned up to the top with a high collar, black gloves, black boots, exactly like Gary's Chelsea boots with a heel with slants inwards—black hats pulled right down, dark purple lipstick, lines down the side of the face in purple blusher. Punks used to stop us on't street and say: 'ooodya think you are, luv? Going to a fun'ral?'"

In a flash, Gary was forced into the second row. Japan had arrived.

By the age of fifteen, the pair were embarking on hell-raising holidays together, staying at hotels in places like Torquay [which, for Americans, is a really tragic British seaside resort] *and remaining completely drunk for two weeks at a time on such delightful cocktails as Cointreau stirred with vodka. They didn't smoke and they didn't have boyfriends, both were "uncool." In fact, their current boyfriends are their first. "All our friends were boys," Joanne explained, "and they put us off having boyfriends as they'd always say, 'I went to bed with her last night, and she wasn't very good.' I just didn't want to give anybody that advantage over me. And that's why we were always so free and happy-go-lucky."*

Then they say something very interesting, which to me is why the record is so successful. "When we first heard 'Sound of the Crowd,' it was in its early stages—it was just thump, crash, thump, crash—and straightaway, we said 'definite hit.'" The reason? "You could dance to it."

"Sound of the Crowd" was released in the U.K. in October 1981; along with contemporary records like Soft Cell's "Tainted Love" and "Bedsitter," "Planet Rock" by Afrika Bambaataa and the Soulsonic Force, New Order's "Everything's Gone Green," Suicide's "Dream Baby Dream," and the Associates' "Message Oblique Speech," it heralded an intensively creative period in both black and white music.

During the late seventies, there had been a division between white rock and black American dance music (although Jamaican forms like dub did have some considerable influence in the U.K.). It was the time of the punk dictum "Disco Sucks." What happened was that many punks began to realize all around the same time—the late summer U.K. release of Donna Summer's peerless "I Feel Love"—that disco did not suck, that indeed it could be as synthetic/alienated/fantastic as the most extreme rock electronica. Even in dystopian terms, disco was *Brave New World* to punk's *1984*.

The late seventies productions of Giorgio Moroder, Patrick Cowley, and Nile Rodgers made pleasure an issue: by 1978 to 1979, disco bass lines, hi-hat patterns, and lush sythesizer textures began to make an appearance in punk crossover hits like Blondie's "Heart of Glass" and in avant experiments like Public Image's "Memories" and "Radio 4." The impulse was the same: a move away from individual alienation and/or overt political engagement—confirmed by the demise of punk as a U.K. style and the suicide of Joy Division's Ian Curtis in 1980—toward the private spheres of sexuality, gender, appearance, and personal politics.

Modern dance culture started in 1981 and 1982. Many records from the period delight in new synthesizer technology and the still-fresh cutting and scratching DJ techniques developed in the Bronx; the twelve-inch "The Adventures of Grandmaster Flash on the Wheels of Steel"—the first nonnovelty sampling cut—turned the William S. Burroughs cut-up into a brand-new stylistic climate, with its influence on hip hop, electro, and rap. With this increased concentration on sound as pleasure and perceptual politics, you also had an almost psychedelic insistence on the sound journey, whether in the slow, circular build of "Bedsitter" or the New York street effects that you can hear on Grandmaster Flash's "The Message."

The whole point of dance culture is that it is communal, that it is insistent on, at minimum, pleasure, at full operation, pure sex—that it can transcend individual alienation in a very direct and accessible way. The group becomes an important mode of address in many songs from the period, as in the Human League's "Sound of the Crowd":

> **Get in line now**
> **Get in line now.**
> **Stay in time with the rhythm and rhyme.**
> **Get around town**
> **Get around town,**
> **Where the people look good,**
> **Where the music is loud.**

Get around town, no need to stand proud.

—You don't need to be an individual, you know, don't hang yourself up about this—

Add your voice to the sound of the crowd.

—And, what these crowds do, at that point, is said in these real gobbledy-gook verses—

Shades from a pencil peer, pass around
A fold in an eyelid brushed with fear,
The lines on a compact guide, pass around
A hat with alignment worn inside

Now, presumably, that's all about makeup and worrying about street violence, and wearing extravagant clothes, which is a great thing to do if you're involved with pop music. So, "Sound of the Crowd" is a great song. "Planet Rock," "Wheels of Steel": fantastic crowd party sounds—you actually hear the party in the record at various times. Soft Cell, "Bed-sitter": the flip side of the crowd—this is what happens when the party's over. He goes out into the night life—as Marc Almond sings, "Dancing, laughing, drinking, loving"—and he goes back to his bedsitter, where he's all alone, he's waiting for something, he's only passing time, but he DOESN'T CARE. "Torch," again, you don't have to stay in and get pissed off, you can go out to a nightclub and hear a song that cuts you in half. And, that is where you start to feel better, because you actually realize that somebody out there feels the same as you do. I cannot overemphasize the importance of that.

The crowd is what you call yourself if you're in it or wish to be a part of it: the flip side of the crowd is the gang. The word itself was the title of a classic of twentieth-century sociology, Frederic Thrasher's 1927 study of 1,313 gangs in Chicago (and what devilment is contained in that doubled numerical curse!), which, like many sociological works, speaks for the

gangs, whose members rarely get a voice in the book that bears their name. When does the crowd become a gang? When you're not part of it; when you're in the wrong territory, of the wrong gender, sexuality, color, race; when it becomes hostile or is seen as hostile. This has much to do with the mass community of pop being grafted over more traditional forms of social organization: class, race, neighborhood.

But pop does not speak from outside, but from within, and it explores the ambivalences that the individual has when faced with the crowd, the gang, peer pressure. In Grandmaster Flash's "The Message," a brilliantly impassioned rant—rap as sound poetry—segues into a street scene, where the hopelessness of the individual is augmented by the treatment of his crowd: as Merle Mel yaks with the Furious Five, a police car screeches up and our protagonist is arrested. So that's the flip side of the crowd: being feared and picked on because you're an outsider and you've gotten together with other outsiders.

But this is also what pop can do: to bring the isolate out of solitude and bring him or her together with like minds in the classic model of empowerment. Sexuality and gender are extremely important in this, as indicated by the high level of androgyny and nonmainstream sexuality represented in some of these records from 1981 to 1982: the outright mincing of Marc Almond, the lipstick and Veronica Lake bangs sported by the Human League's Phil Oakey, the sheer gleeful assertion of Suzanne Sulley and Joanne Catherall on *Top of the Pops*. The androgyny of the period—in the U.K. at least—is an index of its possibility, its sense of machismo in pop music; it might as well be sport, which it patently is not.

In recognition of this possibility, I'd like to offer two quotes from other pop times. The first relates to punk rock and was told to me by Jayne Casey, who fronted the first Liverpool punk-rock band, Big in Japan, and who is now prominent in that city's life: "We'd all come from these repressive backgrounds, and we'd all discovered the Velvet Underground and

Andy Warhol and William Burroughs and the Situationist anthology called *Leaving the Twentieth Century*. It was an instant bonding, and very deep, because we'd all arrived at the same place individually."

The second relates to the greatest pop story of all time and was told to me by a man called Simon Napier-Bell, who managed the Yardbirds and Wham!, among others, and who wrote the so-far definitive account of pop management from within, *You Don't Have to Say You Loved Me*. It relates to the man who discovered, directed, and made the Beatles: "What Brian Epstein liked was being one of the Beatles. That's what he wanted from the beginning. A lot of stress has been laid on the fact that he was gay or fancied John Lennon, but I think it was much more the fact that he was a loner and suddenly found he was part of a group and that was what interested him much more. What he wanted to feel was that he was one of them."

This impulse, even potential, toward belonging holds much of pop's motivation: that you can, like Dobie Grey, blithely announce, "I'm in with the in-crowd." Pop is a mass form of communication, sometimes a mass art form—which makes it a peculiarly twentieth-century phenomenon. It can offer a promise denied or ignored by other parts of society: that if you are an outsider—whether through race, gender, or temperament—you can transcend your isolation by one small act.

It's that moment that so many people talk about, when you're feeling really upset or alone, completely bereft, and you walk into a club, see a group, or hear a record, and you go bang. That's it. It goes right through you, it makes you want to belong. Within an atomized, ritual-free society, that is no small achievement. That's one of the wonderful things about pop music: that—even if you are an outsider—you can get involved, that you don't have to be alone anymore.

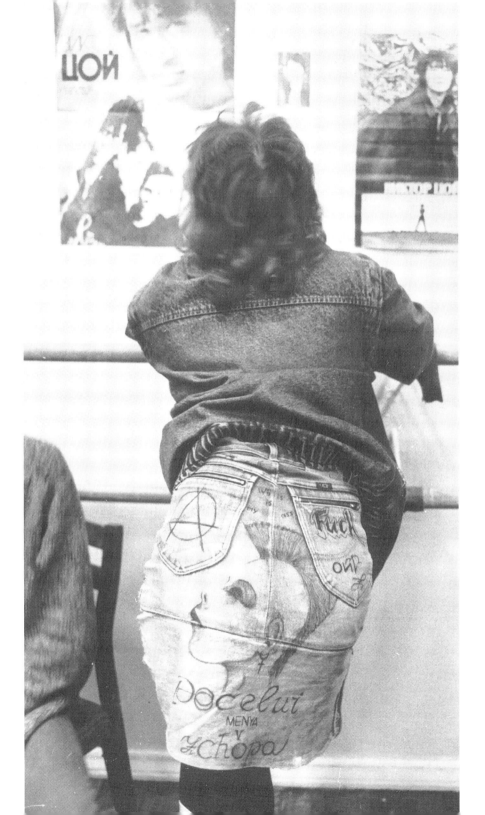

Ellen Willis

Crowds and Freedom

In the course of gathering my thoughts about this panel, I reread parts of Elias Canetti's *Crowds and Power*. It occurred to me that a book about the relationship of rock 'n' roll to its audience would have to be called *Crowds and Freedom*—which is to say that the power of rock 'n' roll as a musical and social force has always been intimately connected with the paradoxical possibilities of mass freedom or collective individuality.

For its detractors, the emergence of rock 'n' roll signaled the convergence of two nightmares—the totalitarian leveling mob, destroying all hierarchy, distinctions, and standards, and the unleashed libidinal, uncowed, and unsublimated self. Both nightmares were connected with a literal darkness, with fear of black people breaching the boundaries of the dominant white culture.

For the American marketplace—if I can metaphorically indulge in the idea of The Market as an entity with a will of its own—the profitability of rock 'n' roll as a commodity translated into an unprecedented mass-mediated dissemination of the sounds and images of freedom. At the same time that the disseminators made continued efforts to package freedom so as to make it as uniform and predictable as any other mass-produced item—efforts that I would argue were partly, but only partly, successful. For instance, the effort to limit the exposure of white suburban kids to rock 'n' roll by giving them watered-down covers of r & b hits ultimately failed. There was too much demand for franker, grittier, more rebellious music—and too much money to be made from meeting that demand.

For performers and fans, the playing out of the paradox of mass freedom has been complex and various. The pop-music crowd has embraced it at some moments and denied it at others—though in my view they never truly escape it. In the context of the whole history of rock 'n' roll, there have really been only brief moments when the possibility of mass freedom seemed fulfilled. Those are the moments from which rock has drawn its utopian reputation, and a good deal of its moral and cultural capital. Yet, for the past twenty years at least, pop music has been in rebellion against its utopian legacy and therefore in rebellion against essential aspects of its own self-definition. I'm going to focus on the formation and devolution of the rock 'n' roll crowd before that point, from the fifties to the late seventies.

When we think of "the crowd" in connection with pop music, we tend to think first of live performance, yet I would argue that historically the primary crowd, the crowd that's central to understanding the relation of music and audience, has been the mass-mediated crowd that was in the first place brought together and held together by radio, records, and the public images of pop performers introduced mainly through TV. This, and not live performance, was the day-to-day pervasive experience that reconstituted the cultural life of youth in the image of rock 'n' roll and built a community that was also in some sense a movement. I'm putting this in the past tense because it seems to me that, while fans still obviously listen to the radio and buy CDs and watch MTV and are influenced by the personae of pop stars, these experiences no longer constitute a crowd in the same way, but, rather, have generated many smaller and less powerful crowds, albeit still deeply influenced by the legacy of this primary crowd I'm talking about.

I guess it's a tribute to the power and ubiquity of cyberspace jargon that I started at one point to think of this phenomenon as the "virtual crowd"; but, when I thought about it further, I realized the term was misleading, since the mass-mediated crowd was in no sense a simulation, but was, on the contrary, the primary, underlying reality that gave live performance its context and meaning. The mass-mediated crowd embodied the paradox of mass freedom in that each of us integrated the music into our lives or our lives into the music in our own way, listened and discussed it with our friends, responded to it according to our own particular filters, and, at the same time, shared it across an enormously heterogeneous spectrum of the population. Rock was the lingua franca of a crowd that could connect without demanding the subordination of the self to the group, and the strangeness and serendipity of that connection was part of the deep, primal pleasure of the music. This was true even at the very beginning, as we all watched Elvis Presley on the Ed Sullivan show—me, my parents, my cousins in Washington, D.C., the working-class kids in my high school, all kinds of people I wouldn't meet until years later. I don't mean that I was self-conscious about any of this at the time, yet the echo of that experience was part of my enjoyment of Elvis, and my inchoate sense of his importance.

I once read a piece about the reception of *Sgt. Pepper's Lonely Hearts Club Band*. I can't remember who wrote the piece, but it expressed very well how I felt about that album and about much of what was going on in rock 'n' roll at that point. The piece described how everywhere the writer went, someone was playing *Sgt. Pepper's*. The music came at you from everywhere. It was a communal event, and yet private at the same time. This didn't mean everyone loved the album. There were already arguments about whether all this fancy studio stuff the Beatles and every other group were getting into was going too far. Richard Goldstein notoriously panned the album in the *New York Times* and got a ton of vociferous mail. The point is, at that moment there was this electric sense of collective engagement—and in response to an album that not only wasn't being performed, but because of its technology couldn't be performed. There was the sense that everyone was connected to each other through the Beatles—from twelve-year-old girls who were turned on by Paul McCartney to musicologists who were analyzing their chord structures. I was much more of a Rolling Stones fan, but without the Beatles the Stones couldn't have been what they were or meant what they did.

If this connection is emblematic of the utopian moment of the rock 'n' roll crowd, there were also always contradictory tendencies toward fragmentation. To begin with, there was race. Despite the significance of blackness for the formation of the rock 'n' roll crowd, that crowd was never really interracial. For the most part, blacks and whites didn't listen to the same music, and, even when they did, there was never any music that was equally at the center of black and white consciousness at any given time. (And, of course, the irony is that there's more of an interracial crowd now in this era of multiple minicrowds.)

The other contradiction was that the intensity and cohesion of the crowd depended on its identity as a rebellious and insurgent crowd, and as that crowd took in more and more people and became more and more ecumenical and more and more acceptable, it also began to lose its force, its center, its reason for being, and its loyalty to itself. So that *Sgt. Pepper's* was really the beginning of the end, or maybe even the middle of the end. Actually, the beginning of the end was probably the arrival of FM rock radio, which divided the radio audience according to class, which became the vehicle for the upward mobility of rock and its integration into middle-class, middlebrow culture, and reintroduced the categories of that culture, such as "serious" and "trashy," into the discussion of pop music.

It's only in the context of this primary crowd formation and disintegration that the significance of live performance during the same period can be understood. The live crowd, and especially the arena or festival crowd, functioned largely as a confirmation of the existence of the community, and a kind of convention of the community's representatives who were empowered to act out its myths and fantasies; these events and the symbols they produced then got recycled by the media back into the collective consciousness of the crowd as a whole. It's possible to trace this function of the live crowd from the kids standing on their seats at the Paramount in the fifties all the way to Woodstock.

In other words, for the most part, live crowds did not themselves create community. There were exceptions to this. One was the Newport Folk Festival where Bob Dylan was booed for playing electric guitar, which divided the folk community and brought a whole new constituency into the pop-music crowd. Probably the early British rock groups were another, though not from the viewpoint of Americans. Definitely another was the San Francisco scene in the mid-sixties, culminating in the Monterey Pop festival. The San Francisco groups and their audience invented a version of collective individuality that was explicitly utopian and insisted on intense physical and sensory contact as the basis of community, and for once transformed the mass-mediated crowd—much more than the other way around.

A girl watches the dawn break at Woodstock, August 1969

Woodstock was the result of the impact of Monterey and all that it entailed on the mass-mediated crowd, which among other things raised the prospect of being able to sell this brand of utopianism, of getting the market in on the act. The festival was at one time both a very real enactment of a moment of mass freedom and a symptom of its fragility. It came about through a marketing scheme that got out of control and succeeded through the sheer will of the crowd to ignore the crisis it had created in the surrounding community, and this was a pretty good metaphor for the situation of utopianism in the outside world. The mass-mediated rock 'n' roll crowd had already begun to fragment in ways that would continue to accelerate; the counterculture was under heavy attack from outside and also vulnerable to its own upper-middle-class illusions. Altamont, when it happened, was the return of the repressed, the countermyth that could no longer be denied. In the seventies, the music and audience that came out of what was left of the counterculture increasingly seemed to be the province of rich dropouts and whiny singer-songwriters, with freedom dissolving into solipsism and any idea of collectivity disappearing altogether.

This, of course, set the stage for the antiutopian period of pop history, in its many forms. There was the divide between "populism" and "avant-gardism" that was foreshadowed by the Velvet Underground and codified in punk. In an era in which populism could not be disentangled from Reaganism, the idea of mass freedom went from being a paradox to being a simple oxymoron. This was the period when Bruce Springsteen became an icon of cultural conservatism, contrary to his own conscious intentions, while the punk definition of both freedom and solidarity was refusal and negation. Punk did form its own collectivity, as did rap and heavy metal, but all these crowds had as their basis the rejection of any sense of possibility, even as their continuing use of a musical language that had possibility at its core belied that rejection. And when "alternative" broke into the mainstream, it was ultimately so trapped in the antiutopian consensus that, despite its roots in punk, its exponents ended up sounding more like the inheritors of the whiny singer-songwriters than anything else.

We're now in a political and cultural situation in which the hegemonic common sense is that freedom and collectivity are absolutely antithetical. George Gilder, the economic libertarian and moral traditionalist, has written a futurist book, *Life After Television*, about how digital technology will replace television with the interactive computer, or "teleputer" as he calls it, and he sees this technology as eliminating the centralization of broadcasting and thereby "demassifying" culture. He looks forward to no more common culture, no lingua franca or shared images at all, only millions of individuals making their individual transactions with other individuals or their machines. In this version of history, the crowd will simply disappear. But pop music is inherently an offense to this notion, even when appearing to promote it. So long as pop music exists, so will the crowd as idea, memory, and potential.

Dark Carnival

Manhattan is the Rosetta stone of the twentieth century.
—Rem Koolhaas

Back in 1875, ten years after the Civil War had demolished half of the U.S. and twenty-five years before the turn of the century that Ralph Waldo Emerson so ardently seemed to strive toward, during the period in American history that brought us American self-identity, reconstruction, "the role of the Negro," the "woman" question, the "Irish" question, the "Jewish" question, the "Indian" question, taxation, civilization and its emerging discontents, and so on, the American poet and theorist wrote an essay that prefigures much of the discourse around "originality" in late-twentieth-century culture. In "Of Quotation and Originality," Emerson was trying to come to grips with a cultural inertia that he saw in the literature of his day. The central premise was that people's minds were too burdened with the weight of previous creative work; they only took elements from the past and reconfigured them to their own taste in their present day. But Emerson, being the creative individual that he was, tried to look beneath the surface of this kind of cultural saturation. He wrote, "Our debt to tradition through reading and conversation is so massive, our protest . . . so rare and insignificant—and this commonly on the ground of other reading or hearing—that, in large sense, one would say there is no pure originality. All minds quote. Old and new make the warp and woof of every moment. There is no thread that is not a twist of these two strands."

Through love, I have reached a place
where no trace of Love remains,
Where "I" and "we" and the painting of existence
have all been forgotten and left behind

Now who can know where I am,

here where no knowledge, no opinion can be found.

Here even Love is bewildered

and the intellect is crazy, talking nonsense.

Totally impoverished, I have no wealth,

no identity no self—

Free from faithfulness and faithlessness

a stranger to myself and all acquaintances.

Yet only for this can I still be blamed—

that a cry comes from me,

Out of grief for Nurbakhsh I say,

"You have gone. How is it that I know not where?"

   —Javad Nurbakhsh, *In the Paradise of the Sufis*

Two years later—December 6, 1877, to be exact—in a similar region of the world, Thomas Edison invented the first prototype of the phonograph—the "talking machine," also called the "memory machine"—by recording the human voice onto a tinfoil roll. The linkage between Emerson and Edison is more than just serendipitous. Edison always viewed Emerson as his lifelong mentor. In his biography about the inventor's life, *Edison: Inventing the Twentieth Century*, Neil Baldwin wrote about their relationship as being a kind of rough-and-tumble trade-off between the pragmatic, take-no-shorts inventor and the lofty poet. For Baldwin, Edison's initial discoveries and deployments of his mechanical and electric devices led him in time to invention, which was for him a way of trying to deal with America's expansionist urges. In a way, Edison viewed his invention of the phonograph as a method of having access to the past—something that would make it more than just a phantasm of collective memory. He liked to compare himself to the turntables he invented. "I am," he would jokingly say when he would boast about his technical efficiency, "like a phonograph." But the prosthetic relationship between voice and memory is not new. It has haunted human identity for centuries. In this way, the phonograph is as old as the human voice, and perhaps implicit as a phenomenon in human communication.

Recording the voice proposes an ontological risk: the recorded utterance is the captured sound that returns as the schizophonic, hallucinatory presence of another. Today, the voice you speak with may not necessarily be your own. The mechanization of war, the electronicization of information, the hypercommodification of culture, and the exponential growth of mass media all produce a machinic/semiotic hierarchy of representation, a locale in which the human mind acts as a distributed network: a place where consciousness becomes an object of "material memory." The spread of global networks has created a sense of telephony unprecedented in human history: the complete integration and simultaneous representation of the human world as a single, conscious entity based on the implosion of geographic distance or cartographic failure. The mesh of sound, symbol, and sentiment of electronic music is another way of speaking, another fusion of *techné* with *logos* (Greek for *word*), deploying them both in the sociographic space of one's environment.

It is not so much a new language as a new way of pronouncing the ancient syntaxes that history and evolution have given us, a new way of enunciating the basic primal languages, which slip through the fabric of rational thought and infect our psyche at another, deeper level. Could this be the way of healing? Taking elements of our own alienated consciousness and recombining them to create new languages from old, thereby reflecting the chaotic, turbulent reality we all call home, just might be a way of reconciling the damage rapid technological advances have wrought on our collective consciousness. As Glenn Gould writes in "The Prospects of Recording":

The most hopeful thing about this process—about the inevitable disregard for the identity factor in the creative situation—is that it will permit a climate in which biological data and chronological assumption can no longer be the cornerstone for judgments about art as it relates to environment. In fact, this whole situation of individuality in the creative situation—the process through which the creative act results from, absorbs, and re-forms individual opinion— will be subjected to a radical reconsideration.

For Emerson, as with Edison, the notion of re-creating and reproducing text wasn't a mechanical issue, it was a psychological realm riddled with the paradoxes that always seem to follow culture wherever it goes. Today we operate under a recombinant aesthetic that even one hundred years ago was beginning to take shape. In 1875 Emerson wrote, "The originals are not original. There is imitation, model, and suggestion, to the very archangels, if we knew their history. The first book tyrannizes over the second." Today we have an entire youth culture based on the premise of replication (the word *replication* is derived from *reply*), a milieu in which much of what is heard, seen, and thought is basically a refraction of the electronicized world that we have built around ourselves.

Emerson's critique of how text is absorbed closely parallels one of the first recorded copyright disputes in Western history. In sixth-century Ireland, Saint Columba made a copy for himself of a manuscript of the Latin Psalter (one must remember that in Ireland, Christianity was an import, and almost all of the manuscripts were copies), and the original "owner," Finnian of Druim Finn, protested. The king at that time ruled that "as the calf belongs to the cow, so the copy belongs to its book." The two disputing parties went to war, and the "copyright violator" won, and, of course, held on to the book (see *Scientific American*, July 1996). Both Emerson and Saint Columba parallel the thoughts and observations of one of the original Structuralist thinkers, Giambattista Vico, whose notion of "poetic wisdom" informed much of his thoughts while he was writing his book *The New Science*, a folio that acted, as Donald Phillip Verene puts it, as "a theater of memory." Verene describes the role of sound in Vico's work as a kind of zone of aberration, a place where many of the cultural motifs that "the ancients" used were able to be passed down through time in a process of continuous cultural combat between the elements of the new and old. For Verene, the New Science is:

a place within which the universal structures of the human world are brought together with its particulars by the bonding of philosophical and philological thought into a single form of mentality. These two kinds of truth are held together in a way such that one cannot be grasped without the other. . . . The reader confronts an order of contents wherein the logic of what is to be discussed is not evident. Instead there is a collage of topics such as wisdom, giants, sacrifices, poetic logic, monsters, metamorphoses, money, rhythm, song, children, poetic economy, . . . natural law, duels, . . . legal metaphysics, barbaric history. One encounters the scenery of the human world.

Vico adumbrates what he calls "the physics of man," a place where human value structures continuously evolve and change in response to the underlying myths that hold their cultures together: "Philosophers and philologians should [be concerned] in the first place with poetic metaphysics; that is, the science that looks for proof, not in the external world, but in the very modifications of the mind that meditates on it. Since the world of nations is made by men, it is inside their minds that its principles should be sought" (*Principles of a New Science*, 1759). Vico always refers to myths as the underlying forces driving the unconscious impulses of culture. Earlier in his explorations of cultural transformation and his "physics of man," he posits "contests of song" as a way of transferring the values of society. "The civil institutions in use under such kingdoms," he writes of "the ancients," are in a way always mediated by the way they engage the culture that generated their "auspices." He continues:

[*The civil institutions*] *are narrated for us by poetic history in the numerous fables that deal with contests of song . . . and consequently refer to the heroic contests over the auspices. . . . Thus the satyr Marsyas, . . . when overcome by Apollo in a contest of song, is flayed alive by the god, . . . the sirens, who lull sailors to sleep with their song and then cut their throats, [and] the Sphinx, who puts riddles to travelers and slays them on their failure to find the solution . . . all these portray the politics of the heroic cities. The sailors, travelers, and wanderers of these fables are the aliens.*

The receiver gave out a buzz of a kind that K. had never before heard on a telephone. It was like the hum of countless children's voices— but yet not a hum, the echo rather of voices singing at an infinite distance—blended by sheer impossibility into one high but resonant sound that vibrated on the ear as if it were trying to penetrate beyond mere hearing.

—Franz Kafka, *The Castle*

Emerson, like Vico before him, argues for a kind of respectful synthesis at the core of how culture evolves and changes. Midway through his essay, he quotes Goethe, who as far as we know was probably quoting someone else:

"Our country, our customs, laws, our ambitions, and our notions of fit and fair—all these we never made, we found them ready-made; we but quote them." Goethe frankly said, "What would remain to me if this art of appropriation were derogatory to genius? Every one of my writings has been furnished to me by a thousand different persons, a thousand things: wise and foolish have brought me, without suspecting it, the offering of their thoughts, faculties, and experience. My work is an aggregation of beings taken from the whole of nature. It bears the name of Goethe."

Today's notion of creativity and originality is configured by a postmodern discourse characterized, one might say, by velocity: it is a blur, a constellation of styles, a knowledge and pleasure in the play of surfaces, a rejection of history as objective force in favor of subjective interpretations of its residue, a relish for copies and repetition, and so on. We inhabit a cultural zone informed by what Gilles Deleuze liked to call a "logic of the particular," a place where the subjective, multiple interpretations of information lead us to take the real as a kind of consensual, manufactured situation.

We live in a time when the human body is circumscribed by a dense locale of technological sophistry, a place where the line dividing the organic and inorganic elements that form the core essence of human life is blurring. Unravel the distortions of the present day: sampling is like sending a fax to yourself from the sonic debris of a possible future; the cultural permutations of tomorrow, heard today, beyond the corporeal limits of the imagination. Do you get my drift?

Shape can be offensive . . . The shadow is larger than the tree . . . soon man shall be . . . must be free . . . The look is always fixed. It must be unhooked . . . Stop time! Gauge the pace of your breath . . . turn the moon around. Then rewind your hearts.

— Linton Kwesi Johnson, "John de Crow"

The West encounters the notion of "imaginal hypertext" in Giordano Bruno's "memory palaces," which mirror previous spaces conceived by Augustine and later spaces evoked by Deleuze and Félix Guattari. In his *Confessions*, Augustine treats memory as a personal space where "the Divine" acts as a receptacle for the memories one has accrued in life. Bruno was burned at the stake by the Papal Inquisition for heresy because he believed the world and the self are intertwined in a kind of semiotic unity. For him, human existence was a holistic, all-embracing search for identity in a transcendent culture of heterodoxy.

Bruno's work, like a DJ mix, was intended to be ranged over and through: much of it, like Vico's, was fragmented and involuted, mainly a kind of exploration of textual slippage: his style of writing was to be explored, traversed, with the same sense of physical movement as walking through the streets and byways of the urban landscape. Through verse, image, and aphorism, he tried always to synopsize memory as a space open to the world, completely generated through humanity's engagement with its environment. Bruno's "hermetic" thinking refers to other medieval and historic characters, but he is obsessed with heterodoxy, with using the surface elements of perception to search for the underlying unity of the world. He wrote in the "Dedicatory Epistle" in *On the Composition of Images, Signs, and Ideas* about a kind of unified field of perception, what contemporary thinkers like Deleuze and Guattari would call a "morphogenetic field," or a place where all is flux, and human expression rests on a kind of associative action, rather than on the rationalist notion of categorical thinking:

It is that sort of eye which sees all things in itself, and is likewise in all things. By this sublime method, we could be like that sort of eye, if we could discern our species' substance so that our eye could perceive itself, our mind enfold itself. Then it would be as possible to understand all as it would be simple to do all. However, the nature of things in composition and that possess the body does not permit this. For its substance abides in movement and quantity, even if by itself it neither moves nor is moved.

Bruno uses the common medieval notion of the eye as mind (this was common also in Renaissance neo-Platonist philosophy). He intended to say that the mind does not analyze itself, that rationality ends where it begins. So where from there? What textual jumps, what shock-cuts in the text?

[skip/fade/enter/delete]

From this play of night, light, and leather, can I let myself take identity? Equipped with contradictory visions, an ugly hand caged in pretty metal, I observe a new mechanics. I am the wild machinist, past destroyed, reconstructing the present.
—Samuel Delaney, *Dhalgren*

The African-American conceptual artist and philosopher Adrian Piper, in her essay "Xenophobia and Rationalism," critiques much of what Western society has viewed as "rational" through the agency of Immanuel Kant's notion of the "sublime" as a starting point for the recognition of culture, perceptions, and art. In his seminal essay "Critique of Pure Reason," Kant writes:

The transcendental concept of reason is none other than that of proceeding from a totality of conditions to a given condition. Now since only the unconditioned makes the totality of conditions possible, and conversely the totality of the conditions is itself always unconditioned; so a pure concept of reason in general can be explained through the concept of the unconditioned, so far as it contains a basis of the synthesis of the condition. . . . Concepts of pure reason . . . view all experiential knowledge as determined through an absolute totality of conditions.

What intrigues Piper so much about Kant's openness to "anomaly" is the sense that the "total" groundwork of knowledge is always in search of new aspects of information; she "remixes" Kant's idea of, as she puts it, "xenophilia":

So Kant is saying that built into the canons of rationality that structure our experience is an inherent disposition to seek out all the phenomena that demand an inclusive explanation. When applied specifically to the transcendent idea of personhood, this disposition to welcome anomaly as a means of extending our understanding amounts to a kind of xenophilia. That is, amounts to a positive valuation of human difference as intrinsically interesting.

Piper's critique of Kant's notions of "synthetic reason" and its relationship to xenophilia configures the known by recasting previous information, just as Emerson described in "Of Quotation and Originality."

In "Representative Men" (1850), an essay that fascinated Edison, Emerson expounded a system of thought based on the idea that "every material thing has its celestial side, has its translation through humanity, in the spiritual and necessary sphere where it plays a part as indestructible as any other." The inventor for Emerson was someone who "began [his/her] lessons in the shipyards and dissecting rooms" and who could go from there and derive notions that would move the inventor into "the dim spirit-realm." In this place, Emerson felt that the inventor would find that "nature is always self-similar repeating to herself in successive planes" of perception built upon aggregate "units" and "particles." Tracing Edison's view of the "metaphysical," Baldwin posits:

Thomas Edison was equally at home exploring possibilities in metaphysical "realms beyond" as he was in the absolutely grounded world of material phenomena. . . . It naturally followed that when he was in the last decade of his life, Edison returned with deep preoccupation to existence after death. In so doing, he tapped once again into a long, speculative tradition, inaugurated by Gottfried Wilhelm von Leibniz . . . , the Leipzig-born philosopher, mathematician, and statesman, and the foremost intellectual theologian of the seventeenth century.

Much of Leibniz's work was based on the belief that the universe was composed of an infinite number of spiritual force or energy monads (Greek for *units*), a kind of divine plan of ratios made of fragments ranging in size and importance from God to the hosts of angels that he used to guide his plans. Emanuel Swedenborg borrowed heavily from Leibniz with his idea that every being in the universe had a kind of harmony or correspondence with the "divine plan" or "heavenly sphere." (We must not forget here that *rational* is derived from *ratio*, and the notion of repetition is implicit in this world view.)

Today, we are informed by a kind of textuality of the postrational, or a milieu where the "text" of the natural has been displaced by its human-derived interpretations, a place where Lautréamont's description of beauty as "the chance meeting of an umbrella and a sewing machine on a dissecting table" and Arthur Rimbaud's idea of poetry as a "systematic derangement of the senses" hold sway.

In his essay "Text, Discourse, Ideology," Roland Barthes defined *text* as "the phenomenal surface of the literary work; [it is] the fabric of the words which make up the work and which are arranged in such a way as to impose a meaning which is stable and as far as possible is unique." Perhaps even this definition is in serious doubt. He writes, "Text takes part of the spiritual glory of the work, of which it is the prosaic but necessary servant. Constitutively linked with writing (the text is what is written), perhaps because the very graphics of the letter—although remaining linear—suggest not speech, but the interweaving of a tissue (etymologically speaking, 'text' means tissue) . . . the text is a weapon against time, oblivion, and the trickery of speech, which is so easily taken back." And, in his essay "The Pleasure of the Text," he announced the end of the text as a stable object for linear reference: "That is the pleasure of the text: value shifted to the sumptuous rank of the signifier."

The word: Flow. Say it.
Roll it on your tongue. Spit it out. Swim in it. Caress it.

Illocutionary acts of speech, language as a stream of performative sounds, sounds as the end-product of a series of gestures marked by ellipses of silence, places of disappearance on the fabric of the body . . . the poly-phonic, hungry gaze of a culture of repetition, and so on, and so on. . . .

Performativity is a source of discourse that cuts across the terrains occupied traditionally by the history of medicine, film studies, art history, philosophy, psychoanalysis, literary theory, and fiction. This discourse attempts to find an artistic or cultural pretext for each of the expositions of performance. These days there seems to be some sort of confusion as to what is "live," what is performance—what is valid. There are corollaries, axioms of previous migrations of meaning that somehow never seem to reach the dense locale of late-twentieth-century youth culture, a place where many of the issues that drive the discourse of both cultural criticism and philosophy tend to be generated.

[skip/fade/enter/delete]

No philosophy transcends its age.
— G. W. F. Hegel

I begin my conclusion with an excerpt from Samuel Beckett's play *Krapp's Last Tape.* The essay unwinds, the tape spool rolls, reality takes on a shim-mering tinge, a kind of fractal distortion at the edge of your perception.

Theater directions: abstract pain, frozen silence, torn ligaments embed-ded with digital-audio-tape ribbon, scenes from Alain Robbe-Grillet's nouveau roman *Last Year at Marienbad* mixed with footage from Los Angeles riots in 1994, and Islamic fundamentalists protesting in Pakistan in 1997 are projected on the walls of woven fabric behind the actor. The tape begins to play, the curtains rise: (*pause*) He suddenly bends over machine, switches off, wrenches off the tape, throws it away, puts on the other, winds it forward to the passage he wants, switches on, listens staring front.

TAPE: . . . gooseberries, she said. I said again I thought it was hopeless and no good going on, and she agreed, without opening her eyes. (Pause.) *I asked her to look at me and after a few moments*—(pause)—*after a few moments she did, but the eyes just slits, because of the glare. I bent over her to get them in the shadow and they opened.* (Pause. Low.) *Let me in.* (Pause.) *We drifted in among the flags and stuck. The way they went down, sighing, before the stem!* (Pause.) *I lay down across her with my face in her breasts and my hand on her. We lay there without moving. But under us all moved, and moved us, gently, up and down, and from side to side.* (Pause.) *Krapp's lips move. No sound. . . . Krapp motionless staring before him. The tape runs on in silence.*

Whether performance comes to you via tribal ritual, medieval passion plays, the experimental spectacles Leonardo da Vinci staged in front of bemused spectators for his "river pageants," the Futurists' notion of a "Synthetic Theater" (a place where "synchronism" was the all-pervading motif), or performance artists like Q*Bert, Joan Jonas, Stelarc (whose body was controlled for performance pieces by needles electronically connected to the world wide web), Robert Morris, Yves Klein, Wu-Tang Clan, KRS-One, and Robert Wilson, there is one thing that you will probably notice immediately: there is a sense that all of these things can be, and usually are, expressions operating on many levels, in many fashions. I write to you from a milieu in which creativity rests for the most part in how the previous expression of others is recontextualized, a place where there is no such thing as "an immaculate perception." Sampling as the digital equivalent of *feng shui*? Sampling as a kinaesthetic theater of memory? Sampling as the structural inheritor of Mikhail Bakhtin's "chronotopic" literary explorations?

In the ecology of narratives, recycling myths is a very old game, a dance between presence and absence. Perhaps this is what Claude Lévi-Strauss spoke of when he called the "primitive mindset" that of a "bricoleur." Sociographic expression—sound writing—mirrors the sense of continuous inscription and reinscription of text that occurs when the needle (the focal point of sound), electricity, and the refractive characteristics of crystalline structure (the diamond on the tip of the needle) are put into action, when you press *play* on the cassette deck you use to make a mixed tape, or ride the fader on the mixing board. *Soniture. Écriture.* Sound and the electric imagination in youth culture as the manifestation of language as total text. Or, as Toni Morrison puts it in *Playing in the Dark*: "The imagination that produces work which bears and invites rereadings, which motions to future readings, as well as contemporary ones, implies a shareable world and an endlessly flexible language."

Replication as differentiated from mere reproduction. Replication as it stands derived from *reply*: the copies transcend the originals, the original is nothing but a collection of previous cultural movements. Flow. . . . The turntable's needle in DJ culture acts as a kind of mediator between self and the fictions of the external world. With the needle, the DJ weaves the sounds together. Do you get my drift?

No footnotes
No bibliography
No references
Just straight up text . . .

This essay is dedicated to the memory of Phillis Wheatley.

Romance

Love Only Knows

In the late seventies, when I was working as a songwriter in Nashville, playing music and writing rock journalism, I would get together with my friends Ernie and Jim a couple of times a week to write pop tunes. We would gather in the office-studio of Ernie's publishing company on Nineteenth Avenue South and try to finish at least one song per session. To facilitate this pace, we would each bring song-related fragments to every session—things we could use for raw material. Since I write lyrics quickly and do good "title," I usually brought lyric hooks; Jim usually brought guitar licks and melodic hooks; and Ernie (whose day job, which was a night job, was playing bass and singing back-up for George Jones) usually came in with weird bass lines. Amazingly enough, we could nearly always hammer these fugitive materials together into a song that sounded, you know, like a song.

On the afternoon I want to tell you about, we began with a standard bag of trash. Ernie had this pseudo-disco bass line he had appropriated from an old Commodores record. Jim had constructed a nice progression of what he called "Don Henley" chords (lots of inversions and 9s in the bass), which underpinned a little call-and-response melodic idea, for which, as often happened, I had a compatible lyric hook appropriated from my loquacious grandmother, whose standard response to nearly everything was "The Lord only knows . . . ," etc. My title hook, "Love Only Knows (What Touches the Heart)," was one of those psalmic-to-secular transformations that are typical of American songwriting, especially in songs where "love" is conceived as a state of grace. "You've Lost That Loving Feeling" is the classic Nashville example.

These days, I suppose, our process of appropriation and reassembly would be called "sampling." At that time, we just called it songwriting, because, except for Ernie's drum machine and eight-track, we just used

Peter Fischli and David Weiss, *Mick Jagger and Brian Jones Going Home Satisfied After Composing I Can't Get No Satisfaction*, 1981 regular musical instruments and our voices. Even so, it only took us about five minutes to shape Ernie's bass line, Jim's melodic idea, and my title hook into a George Martin–type melodic release to which I appended a Frank Loesser–type lyric that (in style) began and ended with the title:

Love only knows / What touches the heart

Love only knows / What we feel,

Whether the dream / Falls apart at the seams,

Or it's real / And it grows

Love only knows

Having written this chorus, we now wrote a bridge that opened up the structure with a modulation and relaxed the note-lengths. We put some lyrics to the bridge, and that was that. We had a nice little psalmic, theatrical, danceable, American love song. The rest was filling in the blanks. Structurally, the song took a Beatles-type song-shape, which is essentially a show-tune song-shape without the verse; so the song went chorus/chorus/bridge/chorus, etc. with the title hook in the first and last line of everything. Then, since this structure treats the melodic release of the song (the chorus) as a verse and begins with it, we altered the lyrics of the succeeding choruses to make them more verselike, to introduce some personality and narrative. After this, Ernie, who was the best singer in the room, made some suggestions to make the lyrics more singable, suppressing some sibilants and dentals, so the noise would move more easily from the front to the back of the singer's mouth. While Ernie and I were tuning the lyrics, Jim tricked up this nifty little Amos Garrett–type guitar lick to tie the lyric melody into Ernie's bass line.

At this point, we typed the rhythm parts into Ernie's little drum machine, laid down the basic tracks on the eight-track in the office, added some Muscle Shoals harmonies and background sha-la-las, and played back the board mix. This was always the amazing part for me, the magic part of songwriting, because there it was, in the world: a singable, danceable, American pop song, complete with hooks, licks, and chops, that did not exist two hours ago. It was *really* there, and *nobody wrote it!* I didn't write it; Jim didn't write it; Ernie didn't write it; neither did my grandmother, or Don Henley, or the Commodores, or the Beatles, or George Martin, or Amos Garrett, or Frank Loesser, or Rick Hall, or Les Paul, or anybody. But we all had a part in it. This was always the amazing part, that feeling of being completely inside the culture, of having the ambient materials of the culture flow through your consciousness to some collective end. It was almost like sleepwalking, or like being *in the zone* in a basketball game, and, for me at least, and for Ernie and Jim as well, it was a good and interesting feeling, but only a temporary one.

We all had friends who devoted their lives and efforts to writing songs that put them *outside* the culture. We even did this ourselves, occasionally, because the three of us had grown up outside the culture and still lived there. When we left that room, we would be back outside again, living outsider lives, but in that moment, playing back that little pop tune, we were totally in the middle of it, part of something ineffable and enormous. The "I" in the song we had written was none of us, as writers, singers, or listeners, and yet it was all of us, and the song was just *out there*. Sometimes, in fact, a song we wrote would be so *out there* that we couldn't believe we had written it ourselves. So for the next week or so, we would play other people's songs and play our song for other people to see if we had inadvertently stolen it—or, rather, to see if the stuff we had actually stolen actually constituted theft. The best songs, of course, sounded *exactly* like they had been stolen, and if they weren't stolen, that meant you were really, perfectly "in the pipe," as surfers say.

In this sense, writing songs the way we wrote them, which is the way films and TV shows are written, is a *very* seductive activity—all that speed, craft, heart, skill, technology, and collaboration making something out of the collective consciousness that speaks directly to the body of the republic. The sheer power of being able to participate in it is quite literally stunning. This is why I have always felt that this culture is fortunate to have so many *outside* people engaged in this most *inside* of activities—in writing songs, movies, and TV shows—because outside people never stay inside, if they wish to retain their sanity. They must continually step outside the narcoleptic coma of normative culture and ask questions. These questions, well asked and well answered, must ultimately reform, redeem, and inflect our normative blend of memory and expectation.

Throughout this period in my life, in fact, I was perpetually bombarding myself with questions, wondering about the process. Mostly I wondered why there were so many love songs. More specifically, I wondered why ninety percent of the pop songs ever written were love songs, while ninety percent of rock criticism was written about the other ten percent. My own practice complied with these percentages. When I wrote songs, alone or with cowriters, I wrote love songs—happy ones and sad ones, mean ones and sweet ones, hip ones and square ones: hundreds of them. When I wrote about music, I wrote about other things, mostly about music history, politics, drugs, hanging out, and playing the guitar.

Why? I wondered—and I wondered all the time, because it's disquieting to be doing something and not know why you're doing it. I came up with a provisional answer on a cool, windy afternoon in the *zócalo* of a little town on the slopes above Mexico City. I was sitting in a shady arcade with my old friend Brownie, who isn't called that anymore, since he is presently in the Federal Witness Protection Program. We were down in Mexico on a nefarious errand that doubtless contributed to Brownie's uncomfortable accommodation with the Feds, but on this afternoon, nothing very nefarious was going on. We were just sitting at a little table, shooting nothing but the breeze and enjoying the air. Brownie was drinking a beer. I was drinking coffee. At one point, Brownie reached over and touched my arm, nodding at something in the square behind me. I turned around and beheld a perfect Latin American tableau.

On the edge of the curb, on the other side of the square, three people were standing in a row. There was boy of about seventeen, wearing a cheap black suit, a white shirt, and a narrow black tie. Beside him was a beautiful girl of about the same age, in a white lace dress, and, beside her, a duenna in full black battle-regalia with a mantilla over her hair. The duenna was a large woman, and looked for all the world like Dick Butkus in drag. The three of them had been about to cross the street into the plaza. Now finding their way blocked, they were just standing there, at a loss, lined up on the curb with two dirt-brown dogs fucking in the street in front of them.

It was a scene deserving of Murillo. The boy was biting his lip, full of antic life but holding onto his composure, trying not to grin at the ludicrous spectacle. The girl had lowered her eyes demurely to gaze at the tips of her black patent-leather shoes. The duenna was discombobulated, agitated. Her eyes were darting about. First she would glare at the offending canines, who showed no signs of stopping, then she would glance sideways at the young couple, policing their responses, then she would scan the square with her social radar, hoping against hope that no one was *seeing* them seeing brown dogs fucking. Brownie and I, being gringo assholes, were cracking up, and suddenly it occurred to me (probably because I had written a nice melody that morning) that these kids, having a duenna and a lot of other structure besides, did not require a wide selection of love songs. Then, perversely, it occurred to me that the dogs didn't need any love songs at all.

That was my answer. We need so many love songs because the imperative rituals of flirtation, courtship, and mate selection that are required to guarantee the perpetuation of the species and the maintenance of social order—that are hardwired in mammals and socially proscribed in traditional cultures—are up for grabs in mercantile democracies. These things need to be done, but we don't know how to do them, and, being free citizens, we won't be *told how* to do them. Out of necessity, we create the institution of love songs. We saturate our society with a burgeoning, ever-changing proliferation of romantic options, a cornucopia of choices, a panoply of occasions through which these imperative functions may be facilitated. It is a market, of course, a job and a business, but it is also a critical instrumentality in civil society. We cannot do without it. Because it's hard to find someone you love, who loves you—but you can begin, at least, by finding someone who loves your love song. And that, I realized, sitting there in the *zócalo* with Brownie, is what I do: I write love songs for people who live in a democracy.

I'll Have to Say I Love You in a Song

Listen. They're playing our song.

When I'm far away from you my baby
Whisper a little prayer for me my baby
And tell all the stars above
This is dedicated to the one I love . . .

I want to dedicate this special moment to all the songs I've loved: to the ballads that gently submerged me in the waters of deep reflection, and to the rockers that made my blood rush like a warrior's as they blasted through the windows of my car. Here's to the sad songs, so accurate in reading the cracks etched into my heart. Here's to the angry ones, whose sonic violence has given me a language of rage and liberation. Here's to the songs I've shared with others, raising my voice and hands in family feeling as friends bellowed along off-key. And here's to the ones I would never share, whose chart-topping popularity cannot convince me that they speak for anyone but me.

Here's to "Your Song" and "Annie's Song," "Another Love Song," "Another Sad Love Song," and "Another Somebody Done Somebody Wrong Song." I salute the complicated kitsch and plain insight of the Top 40, which introduces most of us to the songs we greedily claim, and then keeps giving them back like surprises, like trinkets of affection. I embrace karaoke, the newest way to fall in love with and marry a song, with no prerequisites beyond a lot of pluck—or a few vodka tonics. I hope that you have had a song, have known the delight of making something personal from the fruits of a billion-dollar industry, and that in doing so you've discovered one or two simple things about yourself. And I vow that I will never forget my songs, although if you asked me to name them all right now, I probably couldn't, there have been so many. Yet sometimes, when I'm walking past the fragrance counter in a department store, one floats toward me, and I am restored, knowing that the song holds my secrets safe as it carries them everywhere on the unsuspecting air.

Without a song, the day would never end
Without a song the road would never bend
When things go wrong a man ain't got a friend
Without a song

I run into my upstairs neighbor in the hallway; I'm carrying a record under my arm. It's Aretha Franklin's *Sparkle*. "Oh, great!" he says. "'Givin' Him Somethin' He Can Feel!' That's Mary Kate's and my wedding song." I compliment him on his and his wife's good taste, but he demurs. "We didn't really have a song," he admits. "The DJ just asked us, right before our first dance, what he should play. He had this one, so we picked it." His matter-of-factness makes me laugh. How many songs, I wonder, are ours for a moment, and then sent back into the ether for anyone else to pick up? If my song then becomes your song, do we share it? I remember my sister-in-law grabbing me and her bridesmaids at her wedding reception when Sister Sledge's "We Are Family" came on the P.A. system. "It's our song!" she shouted, a little drunk on all the champagne and attention. For that moment it was, but is it now?

I have never shared a song with one other "special" person, unless you count my high-school crush Dominic Driano, who would listen with me to America's "Sister Golden Hair" over and over in his parents' Volvo, although he wouldn't kiss me or take me to the prom. I doubt Dominic, now a happily married lawyer somewhere, remembers "Sister Golden Hair" as our song, especially since neither my hair nor his even approached golden. My longtime boyfriend Eric told me years ago that "Right Now" by the Go-Betweens was his song with his college girlfriend Mary, but just this week he sheepishly admitted that she probably never knew he thought of it that way. And for years I had refused to listen to the Go-Betweens, out of jealousy.

Perhaps the real essence of having a song is having it to yourself. All I have to do is think for a few minutes to come up with a list of my songs. My first was "Yesterday," chosen because of its dolefulness (I was an unhappy prepubescent) and its seeming revelation of the soul of Paul McCartney, my first grand passion. I played "Yesterday" enough to drive my parents nearly mental, and screamed at my little brother when he'd sing it off tune. As a teen, I did things for my songs—I grew my hair long to be more like the heroine of Bruce Springsteen's "She's the One" and boycotted the colors blue and brown because I didn't get the fascist reference in the Clash's "Working for the Clampdown." Later came more aesthetically motivated choices: Brian Eno's "I'll Come Running to Tie Your Shoe," "Andalucia" by John Cale, and Brian Wilson's perfect moment, "Caroline No." I didn't keep my hair long for that one. I must have grown up somewhere along the way. But I still loved it, made my friends shut up while I played it, and felt that somehow, although it was hardly clear how, it spoke for me.

I don't really feel like I own songs this way anymore, though I still acquire new favorites. The difference for me, I think, is in the discourse about music that preoccupies me, which is now essentially a professional one. As a critic, I am encouraged to distance myself, even in matters of passion. I assess my feelings carefully and can be persuaded, at times, to rethink my judgments. My love for music has become adult, aware of itself. Rarely does it make me feel undone and commanded. Which is why, although I have been known to listen to Ron Sexsmith's "Secret Heart" obsessively, and I shouted out for it when I saw him play at a small local nightclub, it isn't my song.

Secret heart, what are you made of?

What are you so afraid of?

Could it be three simple words

Or the fear of being overheard?

What's wrong? Let her in on your secret heart . . .

Despite the introspection with which we choose our songs, when we mention them, we usually mean the ones we share with a chosen few. The ritual of song-sharing is embedded in our culture, in the first dance of the newly married couple and the last dance on the high-school prom floor. The membership in a song clique expands outward from these dyads, carrying the intimacy of romance into other contexts. Friends get weepy at college reunions when the DJ plays "We Are the Champions," or whatever song drew them together in their boozy, blithe youth. Sororities and street gangs make these choices official, emblazoning treasured lyrics across yearbooks and leather jackets. Sometimes life perverts the metaphor: the tabloids tell of disturbed teens who enact suicide pacts to the tune of "Free Bird." Moral arbiters shake their heads, disgusted and awed at the power of song.

At its most intense, that power can go beyond the private world to feed whole movements. Those moments when songs have emerged as anthems form the soundtrack to our American history of oppression and liberation, from the spirituals that inspired African-American emancipation, to the updated versions of those refrains that nourished civil-rights activists, to such secular transformations as Helen Reddy's "I Am Woman" or Gloria Gaynor's "I Will Survive," which buoyed the hopes of the sexual revolution of the seventies. Today, hip-hop stars the Fugees reach back into that history, opening their sets with "Lift Every Voice and Sing," the Negro National Anthem. And Public Enemy, another hip-hop group well aware of the power of song as communal vernacular, symbolically links black and white radicals by quoting Crosby, Stills, Nash, and Young's hippie jeremiad "For What It's Worth" in the hit "Who Got Game," reviving the older song's message to serve a new hoped-for revolution.

Mostly, though, songs exchanged do not travel quite so far. They become part of a personal economy of meaning, shining innocently, like rings bought at the local discount jeweler, their value coming in the giving. Although only in modern times have all songs seemed to be love songs, popular music has functioned as a form of communication between sweethearts for centuries. In 1557, law-book printer Richard Tottel published a miscellany that included odes from Sir Thomas Wyatt to his unfortunate paramour, Anne Boleyn; the book proved very popular, and Shakespeare quoted one of its ditties in *Hamlet*. Eighteenth- and nineteenth-century opera, that most romantic of musical forms, takes as a central theme the thwarted attempts of lovers to make their intentions clear—how many heroines fall fatal victim to some tragic misunderstanding, with the last notes of the aria ringing out their true feelings as they drop to the floor? In early America, religious and patriotic music dominated the public sphere, but love ballads like "Aileen Aroon," carried over by immigrants, warmed the home hearth and inspired popular composers as they developed the arts of musical theater and burlesque. By 1868, the romantic import of a tune had become so crucial to its success that composer Henry Tucker constructed a tale about how his beloved, departed— and, in fact, fictional—wife served as inspiration for his song "Sweet Genevieve." Tucker was never caught in his lie, and the song became a bestseller.

We do not want our hearts to lie, but the fact is that our songs inevitably do—whether Henry Tucker ever embraced a Genevieve, whoever purchased his sheet music probably hadn't, and so, in grasping the emotions of Tucker's words and melody, he or she involved himself in an elaborate sleight of heart. Suzanne Langer, in her 1951 treatise *Philosophy in a New Key*, calls music an "unconsummated symbol," and although she is writing about music without words, her phrase applies to pop songs as well, since their words are usually so oblique or clichéd (or occasionally poetic) that they elide specific meaning. Music, Langer explains, does not capture particular emotions so much as show modes of feeling, crude moods—such as "joy," "anger," "love"—which we refine within the process of reception. The listener must form an erotic bond with music for it to have meaning. Listening, linking these sounds and words to memories and unarticulated hopes, she converts songs that naturally belong to no one into personal possessions. But she is also possessed by it, penetrated, and whenever she hears it next it will arouse a similar set of emotions, even when she doesn't want it to. If she has shared this experience of aesthetic and emotional consummation with someone else, that person, too, will always be present when she hears it.

The song is ended, but the melody lingers on.

You and the song are gone

but the melody lingers on

Have you ever been haunted by an ex-song, like an old boyfriend you always wish you'd run into, but whom you walk across the street to avoid? Dinah Washington, who recorded the Irving Berlin tune cited above in 1961, near the end of her life, is not the only one who's had this experience. Olivia Newton-John played the mood for country sap in her seventies hit "Please Mr. Please": "Don't play B-17," she whispered," "It was our song, it was his song, but it's over." Helen Forrest, singing with the Henry James Orchestra, gave "I've Heard That Song Before" a wistful, worldly reading, as if she were ready and willing to go back down the garden path. Aretha Franklin, on the other hand, told her version of this story and transformed it. On "Don't Play That Song Again," from her overlooked 1970 masterpiece *Spirit in the Dark*, Franklin begins by conforming to the ballad's wistful if up-tempo mood, but as soon as the second verse comes she's turning it around. Relating a tale that bears close resemblance to Franklin's own struggles with her ex-husband, Ted White, she seizes on each word and gives it a good shaking up, and the defiant chorus of "You lied!" frees her from both the memory and the song itself. By the song's end, she has exorcised the ghost that bedeviled her by filling the space it still occupies with a new spirit—her own.

Not everyone possesses Aretha's gift for swooping in on an emotion, claiming it completely, and then flying past it under her own power. The more common image is of Humphrey Bogart, his tight face cringing when he hears those first few notes he's so humiliatingly failed to forget. "Play it, Sam," he says, utterly giving up his cool, set adrift on memory bliss. The scene has been parodied so many times that it's become the signpost for romantic overindulgence. But what's indelible about it is the nature of the pain in Bogart's eyes. His need to hear "As Time Goes By" is a junkie's hunger; the song both soothes and poisons him. This is the power we can give these bits of treacle, these silly love songs—the authority to stop us in our tracks. The song that brings a memory stands in the way of our inconsiderate progress through life, it forces us to be still for a moment, and because listening to it is an experience in itself and not only a memory, it confuses time. This madeleine bites us, and backward we go, into all the possibilities that never were.

> **I know it's kind of strange**
> **Every time I'm near you**
> **I just run out of things to say**
> **I know you'd understand**
> **Every time I try to tell you the words just came out wrong**
> **So I'll have to say I love you in a song**

"As Time Goes By" serves another purpose in *Casablanca*, as a kind of mystical communication between the scattered lovers played by Bogart and Bergman. The song says what the two of them can't find words to share; it acts as a bridge and a catalyst. Cameron Crowe updated this notion in his excellent teen flick *Say Anything*. John Cusack, as a lovesick and slightly lunkish kick-boxer, woos the honors student played by Ione Skye by showing up outside her bedroom door and silently holding aloft a boombox pouring forth Peter Gabriel's "In Your Eyes." The scene's meaning is obvious: Cusack's feeling is so great that he cannot speak for himself, but he can resort to a higher power—that of the pop song—to get his point across. In 1957, sociologist Donald Horton charted this function of pop in an essay entitled "The Dialogue of Courtship in Popular Song." Horton's point was that young people are inarticulate and confused, and that songs serve as "mutual messengers" between couples; furthermore, they help explain the up-and-down course of love to the lover herself. Horton's theory seems to correspond to fact, with one problem: nobody really wants to think of Peter Gabriel as a higher power. True, some people find uncharted depths within banal phrasings, but I believe most are like Stella, one of the interviewees of Charles Keil's "Music in Daily Life" project, who explained her love for country star John Conlee by saying, "He sings meaningful, corny songs." Stella knows Conlee's lyrics are hackneyed; the wisdom they give her is profoundly connected to their corniness.

What we really seek in a song we share is a more graceful expression of our own tied tongues.

Pop songs aim to be semiarticulate; it's the best use of their form. Their words must say just enough to stick. Writers who strive for more, like Springsteen or Bob Dylan, often find their songs' catchphrases lifted out and their meanings changed. Some can be more complicated and controlling in the music, but here, too, it's a riff or a chord progression that's usually memorable, a brief interjection within the sound's flow. Pop's artists arrange these half-revelations with profound grace, so that the listener can then complete them. If a song is too specific, too insistent in its meaning, it becomes a novelty; just try to think of making "Don't Cry for Me Argentina" or "Harper Valley P.T.A." your song. To enter into the circular economy of meaning that gives art its emotional power, a song needs to give you space to make your own conclusions. It needs to need you. "The pleasure of pop," Simon Frith writes, "is that we can 'feel' tunes, perform them, in imagination, for ourselves." Or as Wayne Koestenbaum explains about listening to opera, the pop of another century: "Listening is a reciprocation: grateful for what the ear receives, the throat responds by opening."

For all the languages we've developed, the codes we've shared and broken, people are not eloquent at heart. We stumble; we don't know what to say. Pop songs give us a way to give up the fight and be quiet for a while. We are glad to let Peter Gabriel or the Shirelles speak for us, and gladder still that in many ways what they say is as silly and hopelessly short of the mark as what we would have said. "I'm not running a glue factory to patch up fragmented lives," wrote the great songwriter Doc Pomus in a journal during his last years. He must have known what use people were making of his songs, how the sentiments he'd boiled down could flow into the gaps between desire and satisfaction. He may have feared that those plain sentiments would never stick. He needn't have worried. They do endure, these songs we make our own, not because they put us back together but because they honor the moments in which we blissfully, willingly, come apart.

Oh I know that the music is fine, like sparkling wine

Go and have your fun

Laugh and sing, but while we're apart don't give your heart

To anyone

And don't forget who's taking you home

And in whose arms you're gonna be

So darlin', save the last dance for me

Freedom Songs, Love Songs

For all my musical life, I've heard the urging in music, urging for equal rights, urging for peace, most of all urging for love, be it in rock 'n' roll, r & b, salsa, blues, classic blues, or jazz . . . be it textual or nontextual.

In the sixties, my mother and father were in a group called the Freedom Singers. They traveled all over the country singing freedom songs to educate the masses and help desegregate this country. There was nothing romantic about it to me, as I look back on it. In fact, it scares the shit out of me to think about my mother driving around the country in the early sixties in a car with three other black people with nothing but music in their bodies as weapons. But, romance was happening. My mother, Bernice Johnson Reagon, and my father, Cordell Reagon, got together during this time, and they got married, and shortly thereafter I was born. You don't have to be singing romantically themed music for romance to prosper, you just need to be in the atmosphere of powerful music.

I grew up in a household of freedom singers. When we moved to D.C. in the seventies, my mother started the group Sweet Honey in the Rock, which carried on with the business of singing freedom songs. I knew one day I would sing freedom songs, too. But boy, was I shocked when my mom wrote this song called "Hey Man."

Hey man, what you doin' in here.
I don't remember letting you in.
Hey man, how'd you get in here.
You're in my heart without consent . . .

That just blew me away as a kid, 'cause I'd always heard her singing, "I ain't gonna let nobody turn me around . . ."

Sweet Honey sang more love songs, and at the concerts people got just as excited about the love songs as the freedom songs. That was an important

Young people chanted "Freedom" and clapped their hands in rhythm outside the church during Medgar Evers's funeral on June 18, 1963 era for me. I realized the need for love in struggle, and the importance of having love in your heart even as you fight for anything. Love is revolution.

Sweet Honey was in my house, but my mother was open to diversity. Musically, anything I got my hands on was cool as long as it didn't oppress anyone. I couldn't play Randy Newman's "Short People," 'cause people were jumping off of buildings and stuff when that song came out, and my mother is very short and she hated that song. She did not see the humor in it. I said, "Mom, it's like an Archie Bunker thing, you know, Archie's always saying bad things, but they show the two sides." She didn't go for that. And, I think because the theme may have been too hot for a nine-year-old, I couldn't play that song, "Louie, Louie." The one about "She was black as the night, Louie was whiter than . . ." Couldn't sing that one either.

When I was three, it was the Temptations' "My Girl." Then, moving on up a little bit more, it was the Fifth Dimension's "Stoned Soul Picnic." Yes, I know it was written by Laura Nyro. Then my singing training began when I heard Michael Jackson and the Jackson Five. I wanted Marlon to be my boyfriend because he could dance and he was the cutest one. But, sorry, I wanted to sing like Michael. Note for note, I would sing, "Maybe tomorrow, you'll change your mind, girl . . ." And then I'd also sing, "Maria, hey, hey, hey, hey, hey, Maria." Today as I listen back to Michael Jackson, I am amazed at how a ten-year-old kid could be so passionate and committed to the music and its themes without having the life experience, and I think, What was Michael really singing about?

Later, it was the rock 'n' roll band Kiss. I thought they were completely sexy. I liked the song "Love Gun." Led Zeppelin was one of my favorite bands. My high-school band covered the "Lemon Song." It was some years later, when I was studying blues music, that I understood what the "lemon" was. I loved to sing "Whole Lotta Love." When Robert Plant sang "Way down inside," I thought he meant it in a spiritual way. Then a theme started to develop with "every little inch of my love," and I thought maybe it wasn't so spiritual after all.

Parliament also got major product in my community. It always made the teachers at school nervous when we'd dance to Parliament. But, at the same time, Earth, Wind & Fire's "Reasons" would stop any party and have people slow dragging and kissing, no matter who they were. Slow dragging is very slow and intimate and juicy, and we were doing that in the seventh grade. We thought we were grown. We were not grown.

All these songs throughout my life do a little something to me on the inside. It's not really about "Oh, I've got to have sex." No. It's a change in temperature. A calm secret. My girlfriend found it one Valentine's Day. She put all the elements together. She woke me up and told me to keep my eyes closed. She said she had called an old friend of mine and asked her to sing me a special song. I opened my eyes and Chaka Kahn was on the videotape singing "My Funny Valentine." There it was, that feeling. I've heard many people sing that song, and only Chaka Kahn's version does that something to me. So perhaps the romance in music and its effect on you have a lot to do with who is singing as much as what's being sung.

Now I sing, tour, and release records. I have a band and people—thank you God—come to hear me sing. I have two versions of a song called "Darling." One is slow. It goes, "Darling . . . I am captured by your spell this morning." The other one is in a Jamaican rub-a-dub style with the same melody going over it. With the first one, people get cozy and kind of sigh, and when I do the second one, people get a little nasty and dance up close to each other.

My favorite sexy song to sing is "Mr. Conductorman," a blues from the thirties. It makes me feel that same feeling I get when I listen to Chaka Kahn, except it is going out through my voice. My aura feels different, and I float as I sing it. It's a zone. I can get it almost any time I sing that song. It talks about being left by your baby and having to leave town and go to another baby down south. I never sing it the same way twice.

I got up this morning and heard the old train whistle blow.
I got up this morning. I heard the old train whistle blow.
I thought about my baby. I sure didn't want to go.
Please Mr. Conductorman, please take my last dime.
Please, Mr. Conductorman, please take my last dime.
My baby's in trouble, waiting, and I just can't waste no time.

Toshi Reagon at the "Stars Don't Stand Still in the Sky" conference, February 1997

No matter how I participate, either as a listener or a singer, I like the way a song can cut across all prejudices, how a song can change your mind. I know sometimes it only lasts for the length of that song, but I like that raw power. When I sing something and it feels sexy or romantic to folks, I like how people don't care how I look or how they look, or what sex I am or they are. Music will do that. The whole idea of going to see a show with any kind of good music being played is romantic, baby. People who won't look at you on the street, all of a sudden, they're trying to get your phone number.

People just care about how they feel. And, it makes them feel good. This element in music is so accessible to anybody, and its tentacles touch the senses. Some songs tingle less once you've experienced them in different atmospheres, say a music video or during a shitty date. Some songs do more once you've seen them performed live. Some songs I've never paid attention to get special meaning after I hear them with my girlfriend. Some music I refuse to involve in a relationship because I like it so much I don't want to have a hard time listening to it if we break up. No Bob

Marley during sex. No Prince during sex. And no Joni Mitchell during sex. Those are like my root music: I have to have them in my life all the time. If we break up I'll have a hard time listening to them, and I ain't having that.

The coolest thing about the aspect of romance in music is how it belongs to the individual. No matter who you are, music can give you vulnerability, or godlike power, give you the mushy "Wow, man, this is so cool we're together" vibe, or give you the "I just have to be alone with this song" thing. And there are the many other ways we may want to describe the relationship between music and the person involved. It's yours. It's whatever you want. It's whatever you need.

Simon Reynolds

Ecstasy Is a Science:

Techno-Romanticism

Insofar as it exalts feeling and privileges intensity, you could say that the message of rock is: BE HERE NOW. For rock was born when British art-school types and American bohemians projected romantic notions onto black American music, notions like the pursuit of a systematic derangement of the senses, visionary transports, the cult of unreason, the impulse to become godlike. On a more mundane level, by exalting impulse, instinct, the free flow of energy, and desire, rock opposes bourgeois virtues—deferral of gratification, moderation in all things, restraint, prudence—which were all anathema to Romanticism. This utopian streak in the rock imagination has evolved over the decades to reach the point where it is increasingly expressed in the discourse of science and technology.

Rather than drawing on the Romantic poets or renegade philosophers such as Friedrich Nietzsche and Aleister Crowley, as did their precursors in the sixties, contemporary artists are more likely to employ ideas and images derived from genetics, cybernetics, chaos theory, or astrophysics. The shift might be characterized as a shift from a visionary discourse to one of virtuality, in which music works as a machine for creating a NOW-consciousness. The supreme example of this is rave culture, where the combination of volume, syncopated rhythms, psychotropic lights, and illegal intoxicants interfaces with the nervous systems of the audience to form a sort of Dionysus-machine—Dionysus being the god of intoxication. In *The Birth of Tragedy*, Nietzsche writes of the "Dionysiac rapture" that arises through "the influence of those narcotic potions of which all primitive races speak in their hymns." He identified as Dionysian the stirrings "which in medieval Germany drove ever-increasing crowds of people singing and dancing from place to place."

Written in the 1870s, *The Birth of Tragedy* presents science and technical knowledge as opposed to the mythopoeic and orgiastic spirit of Dionysian art. Rave is a modern resurgence of this medieval St. Vitus's dance or *tanzwuth* (dance mania), mediated and intensified by technology. In rave, the Dionysian paroxysm becomes part of the program: regularized, looped for infinity.

The idea of the Dionysian first entered rock culture in the late sixties. Jim Morrison imbibed a heady cocktail of cultural intoxicants: ideas from Nietzsche, William Blake, Arthur Rimbaud, Charles Baudelaire. Morrison was also one of the first rock 'n' rollers to make a cult of the Native American Indian. This was a typical Romantic maneuver of projecting desired and envied qualities onto allegedly primitive cultures: intimacy with nature, warrior masculinity, a sense of the sacred—and one that Byron got to one-hundred-fifty years before Jim, when he wrote of feeling as free as "a Cherokee chief."[1] In this respect, the Doors fit neatly into the general anti-industrial, antiscientific tenor of West Coast psychedelia, which included the pastoral yearnings of the Byrds, Quicksilver, the Grateful Dead, Jefferson Airplane, and so forth. But because the Doors' brand of Romanticism was darker than the back-to-nature idyllics of the flower-power era, Morrison and company are generally felt to have more in common with more urban and nihilistic bands of our own era: Morrison's death-wishful poetry parallels the hunger for oblivion in the Velvets' "Heroin" and the Stooges' "Death Trip."

Although Iggy Pop was influenced by Morrison, the Stooges had a more futurist take on the Dionysian quest. Iggy has said the band was partly inspired by the pounding, throbbing clangor of Detroit's automobile factories. A perverse identification of libido with the military-industrial complex gradually emerges in the Stooges' music. Their third album, *Raw Power*, opens with "Search and Destroy," in which Iggy warns, "look out honey, I'm using technology" and describes himself as a street-walking cheetah with a heart full of napalm.

Several years after *Raw Power*, Iggy described this phase of the Stooges, during which he was supercharging his nervous system with huge amounts of drugs: "Rather than become a person singing about subjects, I sort of sublimated the person, and I became, if you will, a human electronic tool creating this sort of buzzing, throbbing music."[2] The title track of *Raw Power* is a hymn to elemental dynamic energies for which Iggy is the conduit. A cocktail of amplified electric guitars, amphetamines, adrenalin, and primal death drive, raw power "has not got no place to go," "it don't want to know," "raw power, it's laughing at you and me." Impersonal and intransitive, raw power is a kind of force field in which the individual is suspended and in which subjective consciousness is wiped clean away, replaced by what the Stooges called the O-mind. The O might be Oblivion or Norman Mailer's apocalyptic Orgasm; either way it's a sublime vacancy, the point at which self-aggrandizement and self-annihilation fuse. In his autobiography, *I Need More*, Iggy says:

I'm sure the constant exposure to amplifiers and electric guitars, and hearing my own voice amplified, has altered my body chemistry, in which, after all, the life lives. . . . I feel so umbilically connected to the thing itself, the process is far more important than the result. It is the proximity of the electric hum in the background and just the tremendous feeling of buoyancy and power. . . . I was really determined to use the noises on myself, as if I were a scientist experimenting on himself, like Dr. Jekyll or the Hulk.[3]

Heavy metal took the Stooges' fusion of Romanticism and Futurism even further. The term "heavy metal"—originally a nineteenth-century military term referring to heavy artillery—first appeared in rock as the line about "heavy metal thunder" in Steppenwolf's "Born to Be Wild." This hymn to the grandiosity of breaking the speed limit as you hurtle down the freeway is notable for phallic/militaristic lines like "fire all of your guns at once/explode into space," while the chorus "like a true Nature's child/we were born, born to be wild" describes a godlike feeling of wanton omnipotence. Strangely, this feeling of being Nature's child is entirely enabled by such products of Western industrialism as Harley-Davidsons and the interstate highway system.

The true inheritors of the Jim Morrison and Iggy Pop Dionysian tradition, however, are the Young Gods, a Swiss cyberpunk band who sample guitar riffs from Motörhead and Metallica and orchestral bombast from Richard Wagner and Ludwig van Beethoven. Like Morrison, Young

Gods singer Franz Treichler is influenced by the usual Romantic suspects—Blake, Nietzsche, etc.—and is obsessed with Native American tribes. (He goes one better than Jim in the shaman credentials, however, in that he's half–Amazonian Indian). But there's one crucial difference between the Young Gods' bacchanalia and that of their illustrious ancestors: the Young Gods' music is cyborg rock, an uncanny blend of the machinic and the feral. The digital, sampling side of the band in its early days was handled by Cesare Pizzi, an ex-paratrooper who once worked measuring the vibrates of gib cranes and airplanes on military airfields, and later had a job as a computer technician for Reuters.

This idea of a nonmusical technician being such a crucial member of an ostensibly romantic, neoprimitivist band as the Young Gods seems odd, but it parallels the rise of the engineer in dance music to the status of auteur. In today's dance music, the domain of creativity is vested in sound-in-itself—the timbre and penetration of a bass tone, the sensuous feel of a sample-texture: the realm of the engineer. Modern dance music demands that we start thinking of the engineer as poet, or as an "imagineer," someone who implements a vision using the studio and digital technology.

The figure of the engineer-poet first emerged in black music. Dub-reggae pioneer Lee Perry talked of his Black Ark studio as a living thing, an entity with which he interfaced himself. Another stellar dub-reggae producer, Hopeton Brown, called himself "Scientist," and declared "Dub is really . . . a masterpiece of the engineering—engineers using the recording equipment to bring about musical changes." Similarly, the U.K.'s leading dub producer is Mad Professor, whose name also plays on the idea of the crackpot scientist, the boffin in the sound-laboratory. In Detroit, another producer-based black-music culture emerged in the mid-eighties, drawing inspiration from Kraftwerk's cyborg fantasies and from Alvin Toffler's notion of the "techno rebels," renegades who embraced technology as a means of resistance against the corporate powers that mass-produced these new machines.[4] And so techno-pioneer Juan Atkins described himself as "a warrior for the technological revolution." Meanwhile, at the New York house club the Paradise Garage, DJ Larry Levan worked with engineer

Richard Long to custom design the sound system; he developed a science of bass and treble that worked on the drugged bodies of his mostly gay and black audience.

The fetishism of science in dub reggae, Detroit techno, and house then infected white popular music via British rave culture. In the last few years, the word "science" has become a major buzzword in the rave scene: examples include the titles of albums, like Omni Trio's *Haunted Science*, A Guy Called Gerald's *Black Secret Technology*, Fatboy Slim's *Better Living Through Chemistry*; as well as the titles of EPs, like DJ Krust's "Genetic Manipulations"; the names of artists, like Droppin' Science, Twisted Science, the Chemical Brothers; and the names of clubs, like PM Scientists and the Science Lab. In addition, a U.K. compilation and New York's first jungle retail store are both called Breakbeat Science, which describes the intricacy of rhythm programming in jungle, where breakbeats from early seventies funk are sampled, chopped up, resequenced, and processed, all within the virtual space of the computer to infinitesimal degrees of complexity. The word "science" fits because there's nothing romantic or rock 'n' roll about the *process* of making this music, little scope for spontaneity or intuition. Breakbeat science is incredibly time-consuming, tricky, and it involves an almost surgical precision. Like gene-splicing or designing a guided missile, it's not much fun, but the results can be spectacular.

How does this scientific imagery relate to romanticism? Well, jungle emerged from rave culture, which fused late sixties psychedelic utopianism with the postdisco music that came out of Chicago and Detroit. As in the sixties, the fuel for utopianism was a pharmacopoeia of mind-altering substances. What's striking about rave culture is that European youth took Rimbaud's ideal of "systematic derangement of the senses" and really systematized it. Rave became a gigantic psychosocial experiment, with millions of kids modifying their own neuro-chemistry. By 1991 the average teenage raver was a connoisseur of poisons, adept at mixing and matching them to achieve bliss by any means available.

This "street knowledge" (to borrow the title of a track by Nasty Habits) often expressed itself in the discourse of science, as in the track by Bizzy B entitled "Ecstasy Is a Science" or the band Kaotic Kemistry, whose debut

EP's sleeve depicts the ingredients for a typical night of Dionysian revelry: a joint, a line of speed, and a handful of Ecstasy pills. On the *LSD* EP is a track called "Illegal Subs," a pun on illicit substances and sub-bass levels so dangerous they *ought* to be outlawed. The track also samples a Nation of Islam orator hailing her African-American audience—"you are the people of chemistry, the people of physics, the people of music, the people of rhythm"—transforming her oratory into a tribute to rave's "chemical generation" (to use Irvine Welsh's famous phrase).

Scientific experiments can also produce cataclysmic results. On the sleeve of 4Hero's "The Headhunter," three mysterious, cloaked figures stare aghast at a gang of grotesquely misshapen mutants. The band's Dego McFarlane explained that the cartoon was a self-mocking scenario of 4Hero as "B-movie scientists. . . . The experiments get out of hand, he . . . takes the serum . . . and messes himself up. . . . We started off at about 120 b.p.m. and around 'Headhunter' it was getting towards 140 b.p.m. Going to that speed was causing deformations in the music."

Rave music literalizes Walt Whitman's trope of "the body electric"; using both high-tempo music and drugs, these kids remake their nervous systems, supercharging them with artificial energy. Drugs like speed and Ecstasy work by increasing the flow of certain neurotransmitters, chemicals that conduct electrical signals within the brain. Whitman's "body electric" was a product of the nineteenth-century excitement about the discovery of electricity, which many regarded as the élan vital or life force. Another product of this convergence between Romanticism and science was Mary Shelley's *Frankenstein, or, A Modern Prometheus*, the first cyborg fantasy, with Dr. Frankenstein using his mastery of chemistry and other natural sciences to achieve godlike powers. In rave, kids play the roles of both Frankenstein and the monster, experimenting on their own nervous systems. In 1991 there was actually a hardcore rave anthem called "A Modern Prometheus" by the Hypnotist.

The Prodigy has emerged from the British rave scene to take that Promethean quest into the American mainstream. Starting as a hardcore rave outfit, the Prodigy cleverly reinvented themselves as a sort of cyber-rock group. With their titanic self-assertion and appetite for destruction, songs like "Firestarter," "Hyperspeed," "The Heat (The Energy)," "Fuel My Fire," and "Breathe" exalt primal dynamic forces. Singer Keith Flint describes the Prodigy as "buzz music"; as with the Stooges, it's all about raw power, the rush, an intensity without object or objective. But this is a painstakingly constructed simulacrum of rock bacchanalia, drawing on the studio science of techno and hip hop. The musical genius behind the band is another engineer-poet, Liam Howlett. While the music's mode of construction is doubtless dreary, the end result expresses the same Dionysian impulses as the Doors, Steppenwolf, the Stooges, the Young Gods; and it sounds remarkably like rock music. This is Techno-Romanticism, and its motto could be Aleister Crowley's boast, "Our method is science, our aim is religion."

Notes

1. George Gordon, Lord Byron, quoted in Bertrand Russell, *A History of Western Philosophy and Its Connection with Political and Social Circumstances from the Earliest Times to the Present Day* (New York: Simon and Schuster, 1945), p. 748.

2. Iggy Pop, *I Need More: The Stooges and Other Stories* (Princeton: Karz-Cohl, 1982).
3. Ibid., p. 64.
4. See Alvin Toffler, *The Third Wave* (New York: William Morrow, 1980), pp. 149–54.

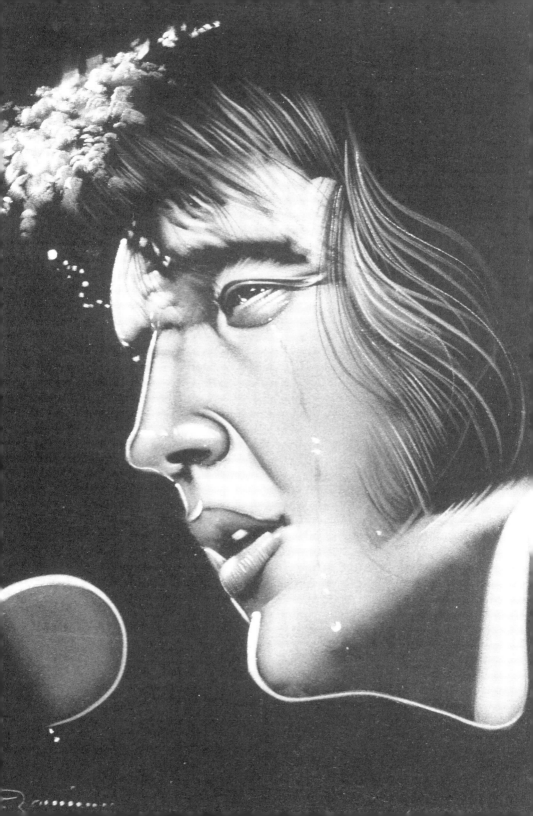

Ralph Rugoff

Between a Hard Rock and a Velvet Elvis:

Fatal Attractions in Rock Iconography

Icons, at least pop icons, almost always seem to embody a fatal attraction between medium and subject, as in the case, say, of Andy Warhol's sloppy silkscreens and Campbell's soup cans. Velvet painting and Elvis Presley make up another such fatal pairing (Elvis portraits being the current all-time bestseller in that medium), just as on a more mainstream level, rock 'n' roll and Las Vegas constitute yet another, assuming Las Vegas can be considered a multidimensional medium as well as a place. It takes two to tango, as they say, and fatal attractions like these suggest that whenever an image or institution strikes a resonant cultural note, a good romance is part of the picture.

That Elvis should be king in the world of velvet art, in this, its soft twilight hour, follows some logic that seems at once inexplicable and inevitable, just as his name sonorously, yet discreetly, echoes the word *velvet* itself. Call it the Velvis Effect. The attraction is apparently so powerful that it transcends the celebrity factor: Miguel Mariscal, owner of Tijuana's leading velvet art gallery, once told me that his young customers no longer even know who Elvis is, they simply like his image and buy it.

Since hearing this, I have wondered about this fatal attraction between Elvis and painting on velvet, and the complementary elements that support it—the set of ties that bind them together. Undoubtedly, part of the attraction is the volatile character of velvet as a surface, which lends itself to the singer's iconic schizophrenia. Slight changes in illumination, or even currents of air, can significantly alter the appearance of a velvet painting, and this shiftiness redeems even the most banal images, lending them movement and even a kind of unpredictability, as each viewing situation yields a modest metamorphosis. What better medium could there be, then, for a performer whose identity was so profoundly split that even the U.S. Postal Service was forced to issue, not one, but two commemorative stamps to satisfy fans of both the Younger and the Elder Elvis, the Pelvis and the Blob, the Nashville and the Vegas personae? (Not surprisingly, there is more than one velvet Elvis; in fact, at least four or five different incarnations are popularly available, including the traditional *Blue Elvis*, where the singer appears with a tear under his eye; a macho Elvis sporting leather jacket and studded wrist bands; and a younger, androgynous, and vaguely lascivious model.)

But the romance between Elvis and a fabric characterized by a short, soft, dense warp pile was not, it turns out, love at first sight. Back in the sixties, when Tijuana galleries such as Mariscal's helped spearhead a velvet revolution by exporting hundreds of thousands of velvet paintings into the United States (Kmart was a major distributor), images of Tahitian landscapes, Vargas-style nudes, and sad-eyed clowns dominated the velvet market, along with morbid portraits of Jesus Christ.

It is the latter that provide a clue to Presley's velveteen apotheosis. With their glowing wounds, black-velvet Jesuses mix equal doses of religiosity and horror in a gothic concoction, and often appear alarmingly vivid. This is largely due to the cheap theatrical magic of the medium's low-tech holography, which, when seen under the right light, can be surprisingly effective. (Like the late Elvis, velvet painting cannot be seen in direct daylight, which completely subdues the secretive depths of unpainted black pile, and thereby precludes the subject's theatrical leap off the picture plane.) The gaudy whorishness of velvet painting, which gives its favors freely, also adds a wiggy intensity to its subjects: Vargas nudes and fleshy Christs jump out at the eye with the same hallucinatory force.

Exaggerating the power of these spectacular effects is the unpainted background of black fabric, which lends an otherworldly or ghostly aspect to many velvet portraits. Heads and bodies appear to be floating in a depthless space, as if lost in some vast interstellar darkness. One of the advantages of black velvet is that you do not have to paint shadows, or for that matter, black hair: Elvis's coiffure is typically rendered with a couple of highlights on a patch of unpainted fabric. The flesh is thus seamlessly linked with the unmarked void, and in this way black-velvet painting presents itself as an interface between our earthly existence and some other, unanchored dimension. It is a medium's medium.

This macabre nocturnality lends itself to memorial portraiture. In the late sixties and early seventies, paintings of Martin Luther King, Jr., John F. Kennedy, and Robert Kennedy—the holy trinity of assassination victims—topped the velvet charts. And as for Presley, Mariscal's gallery (like those of his competitors) did not begin selling the singer's portrait until after his death. As the proprietor straightforwardly explained to me, "We mainly paint dead guys."

An Elvis head floating in black space hits a decidedly ghostly note, yet the tactile appeal of velvet also sets up a tension between the hand and eye, allowing for images that appear sensual and ghostly at the same time, while effectively evoking the young Elvis's raw sexuality. As a material, velvet reeks of tactile charms: they make bags out of canvas, but evening dresses out of velvet. Like fur, it conjures a lush animal sensuality (it seems only apt that the word should also denote the soft, vascular skin that envelops and nourishes the developing antlers of young deer).

But the medium seems best suited for representing Presley's late-sixties transformation into a nocturnal icon: the lost and lugubrious Elvis, sleepless and pudgy; the Elvis with a crooning balladeer's voice in which depth and soulful authority battled with rhetorical bloat, tinged with gospel sheen, and a rolling depth that—all appearances taken into account—conjured a dark, oily eroticism, and behind those curtains, the Big Ugly—the great unseen and exotic vastness of death.

Should we be surprised if fatal attractions inevitably conjure fatality itself? (Here lies a piece of the romance, I suspect, between Warhol's imperfect silkscreening and the immaculate and virgin soup cans he portrayed.) Yet if the velvet Elvis is essentially a dead Elvis, an Elvis from beyond, it is not as a ghoul that he appears in this medium, but as an unembraceable memory. Of course, for fans of the early Memphis Elvis, the star was already merely a memory of a dear departed one during most of his lifetime. Whenever someone changes drastically, as Elvis did, relationships come to an abrupt end, just as with death; indeed, John Lennon famously quipped that rock 'n' roll itself had died when Presley entered the U.S. Army and publicity shots showed him as a happy soldier, shorn of sideburns and rockin' attitude. The death of his early incarnation seemed to hover in the background of Presley's later career, haunting it like the ghost of his stillborn twin, tainting the Elder Elvis with an aura of mortality, which may partly account for his image's irresistible union with black velvet.

It may also explain why, in contrast to the black-velvet Jesuses that typically appear alarmingly lifelike, the Elvis portraits are generally executed in either a monochrome blue tint or a tasteful grisaille, casting the singer in distinctly Platonic hues. It is not Elvis, but the memory of Elvis that is commemorated and conjured, a spectral, haunted figment that velvet, with its tactile promise, imbues with palpable presence, as well as a melancholy Latin nostalgia for things lost in the inevitable transformations of life.

A fatal attraction, like any good romance, involves a conspiracy of compatibilities and complementary contradictions. It is also, even if obliquely, tinted with the idea of death, and in the duet of Las Vegas and rock 'n' roll, mortality notes come into play in numerous ways. As visual environments, Las Vegas's megaresorts may be stimulating, dynamic, and humorous, but as a group they exude the air of a garish morgue, a wax museum of embalmed exoticisms and cartoon memories. This is why the "new" theme-park Las Vegas is supposedly family-friendly—culturally speaking, it is as safe as a cemetery.

Which makes it a perfect candidate for the capitol of rock 'n' roll. Not that rock is dead so much as that it, too, has become a family affair, rather than the cultural property of teenagers. To put it slightly differently, rock's audience has grown older as the teenage population has expanded to include both ten-year-olds and fifty-year-old baby boomers. Rock 'n' roll, then, is essentially a kind of family playpen for a culture in which the generation gap no longer exists, as adolescence is the norm.

It was Presley himself who, with the marketing of Graceland, pioneered the concept of rock 'n' roll as a tourist destination. That notion finds its most full-blown current expression, not in Cleveland's Rock and Roll Hall of Fame and Museum, but in Las Vegas's Hard Rock Casino and Hotel, which, as a nineties monument of rock iconography, seems far more pointed and "relevant" than a hall of fame, just as Vegas makes a more apt contemporary home for rock than does Cleveland.

The fatal attraction between Las Vegas and rock also involves, as do many romantic attachments, a shared sense of humor. In comically conjuring ancient Egypt, medieval England, or the South Seas, Las Vegas's multimedia resorts allow us to laugh at the impossibility (or the death) of the exotic in our age of overexposure. Much of rock 'n' roll today often seems to engage a similar project—it plays at rebellion, but with a knowing self-consciousness, as if real revolutionary activity were now as much of an impossibility as voyaging to unknown and exotic locales.

Visitors who check into the Hard Rock Casino and Hotel are greeted by a monumental welcome sign, executed in fake-bronze, 3D lettering, which hangs above the reception desk: "Here we are, now entertain us— Kurt Cobain." That Cobain is not in much of a position to be entertained these days may leave you wondering if this isn't in unusually bad taste, even by Vegas standards, but at least it seems deliberate: the sign's doleful solemnity effectively conveys a sepulchral atmosphere.

Perhaps we're meant to think we've died and gone to rock 'n' roll heaven. Or that we're visiting a mausoleum of the gods: around the corner from the check-in area, a Nirvana window display features one of Kurt's guitars, some grungewear, a newspaper headline announcing his suicide, and whatever notes this week's pilgrims have inserted behind the glass. The only thing missing is the shotgun with which Cobain blew his brains out, but maybe that would be overkill.

Mistah Kurt, he dead, but he can still entertain us—that's the main point. Of course nobody really dies in Vegas, home of the eternally living legends, yet at first glance rock 'n' roll appears to have been snugly embalmed here—the "hard" in Hard Rock could easily be mistaken for a reference to rigor mortis. The resort's casino and lobby areas are a tomb of artifacts, with displays showcasing not only Beatles and Stones memorabilia, but also more morbid curios, such as a piece of the plane in which Otis Redding crashed.

Other exhibits camp it up: opposite a Sante Fe–style installation featuring a selection of flowery jackets supposedly worn by Jimi Hendrix, the "AeroSmithsonian" presents aerodynamic guitars and Steve Tyler's gaudy stage gear. In addition to slot machines for the rainforest, there are "Anarchy in the U.K." models, replete with graphics lifted from the Sex Pistols' *Never Mind the Bollocks* album. If you have ever believed in the symbolic purity of your musical heroes, you cannot help but feel that something sacrosanct, some pure rebellious spirit that seemed like it could change the world—or your little corner of it, anyway—has been terminally corrupted. At least that is the impression you get wandering around this unique casino-museum, where you would naturally expect to find Bon Jovi's sequined jumpsuit, but where a glass case containing Courtney Love's dress and guitar comes as a bit of surprise—ditto for leather jackets belonging to "underground" heroes like Joey Ramone and Iggy Pop, not to mention relics from blues giant John Lee Hooker, including his hat, Kaye guitar, and amp.

Las Vegas is famously a city of costumes, with hotel staff forced to dress like extras in campy Hollywood period films. As you peruse these glassed-in exhibits, the realization gradually dawns that everything here is also a type of costume, including the custom guitars, which are flared and painted to suit each performer's whims. Whether you are taking in "The Soul Case," which houses matching orange, double-breasted suits worn by the Temptations, as well as Smokey Robinson's green, velvet, matador-style tuxedo, or admiring displays of punk couture, it is hard to avoid concluding that pop is really a kind of costume drama—that it may have as much or more to do with dressing up as with teenage alienation.

This is not merely a matter of a sartorial subgenre, encompassing out-rageous examples from *Sgt. Pepper's* and the New York Dolls to Parliament Funkadelic and Kiss. On the contrary, every pop outfit, including a minimalist torn T-shirt and jeans, embodies a fantasy ethic. Even groups like the Band, whom nobody at the time considered a costume act, dressed thematically—in their case, wearing clothing that made them look like refugees from a Klondike gold rush. From contemporary rapper and grungewear to the West Texas monastic look of ZZ Top and the spandex and hair extensions favored by old-time heavy metalists, the pop world comprises an apparel phantasmagoria, as giddy in its own way as the excesses of Las Vegas burlesque shows.

Thus you could argue that the Hard Rock Casino is what rock 'n' roll has usually been all about—show biz and glitz. In so many words, this was what John Lydon told a *Los Angeles Times* reporter at the hotel's opening gala, and while it may seem a typically cynical comment from the leader of a band some still see it as a high point of countercultural protest Lydon's remark also points to a less acidic truth: it's not that rock has always been about selling out, but simply that its brand of costume theater is not ill-suited to the fantasy milieu of Vegas. Even much of punk, after all, was slightly cartoony: with their identical haircuts and lobotomized demeanor, the four Ramones looked like a group of grown-up and inter-changeable chipmunks; the Sex Pistols, meanwhile, conjured the campy theatrics of prowrestling with stage names like Johnny Rotten and Sid Vicious. James Brown's famous cape routine (his cape-and-crown set, by the way, are on display in the hotel's "Soul Case") was inspired by the foppish wrestler Gorgeous George, while ornamented attire belonging to Prince and Madonna would look right at home in the nearby Liberace museum.

The flash roots of rock, once buried beneath the "authentic" posturing of sincere singer-songwriters and nihilist screamers alike, are resurfacing for all to see. Forget about the rare pop drag act, like RuPaul: far more telling is the emergence a few years back of Tony Bennett as an MTV star, or the singing duet of Bono and Frank Sinatra. Once reviled by any self-respecting rocker as avatars of a corrupt show-biz establishment, old-time Vegas superstars are now embraced with the understanding that their faded glamour has a certain camp value, and that, more importantly perhaps, all performers are united by shared theatrical rituals. Not that this is a recent development: for all its satire, even Sid Vicious's trashing of "My Way" was partly an homage; today's pop performers are far less alienated from their historical antecedents.

While purists may moan that rock 'n' roll has been theatricalized and debased by advertising as well as by MTV and corporate control of the recording business, the Hard Rock Casino tells another story. Commercial rock and pop was always theatrical, always rooted in fantasy. For the true believers among us, and the followers of rock prophets and poets, this may be a rude awakening, but in Las Vegas it makes perfect sense. Out in that desert-rimmed island, rock 'n' roll is just another fabulous motif, which—like ancient Rome or the Wild West—can set people dreaming while they crank those slots, and the velvet ghost of Elvis cries "Viva Las Vegas!"

Arlene Stein

Rock Against Romance:

Gender, Rock 'n' Roll, and Resistance

Recently I watched the PBS series on the history of rock 'n' roll for a second time. The first time I saw the documentary, I was captivated by the story of how white male youth found a vision of a different way of life in black rhythm and blues. Music often transgresses social boundaries that otherwise seem impassable. As the PBS series clearly illustrates, white kids in this country appreciated black music, enacting a kind of cultural desegregation even before the legal barriers separating the races were lifted.

This time, while watching the documentary, I imagined myself as a young girl listening to the music of my youth. I tried to re-create the reactions I'd had to rock 'n' roll and think through its gender politics. In doing so, I couldn't help but reflect on the ways girls and women have often been understood in relationship to rock. The dominant image—at least for those of us who grew up in the sixties and seventies—is of Beatle-crazed girls and swooning groupies—uncritical, desiring masses. In the feminist take on this story, female rock fans are engaged in the affirmation of a fantasized, omnipotent masculinity. When *Ms.* asked in 1974, "Can a Feminist Love the World's Greatest Rock 'n' Roll Band?" Robin Morgan replied that feminists who listened to the Rolling Stones had adopted a "male style" that would destroy the women's movement.[1] Female rock fans are, in other words, dupes of men, prisoners of lust, or both. I, for one, couldn't find myself in any of these images.

I came of age in the early seventies, in a towering Bronx apartment building filled with working- and lower-middle-class people united only by their mutual envy of those who had more. During this transitional moment of gender relations, images of female rage filled the media, and talk of feminism was in the air. Some of this talk had trickled down to my world. Mothers, like mine, who had become full-time housewives, were encouraging their daughters to go to college and pursue careers. Still, the codes of femininity that valued catching a man over all else were pervasive in the culture at large. We girls were expected to enjoy "love comics," syrupy tales of fawning girls waiting for their knights in shining armor, or love ballads sung by clean-cut crooners.

From an early age I knew that love comics and teen crooners were not my cup of tea. My mother served as an example of what was in store if I lived by these codes of femininity: a woman whose visions of bliss clashed with the reality of a failed marriage. At the same time, many of my fantasies of rapture involved my favorite female English teacher—those knights in shining armor were nowhere to be found. Little that I saw around me in popular culture fit with these desires and fears—until, that is, I found rock 'n' roll. Rock spoke of the alienation I felt from my parents and their world. It put me in touch with an image of a different way of life, and gave me a space to imagine alternative visions of gender.

As the psychoanalyst Ethel Person suggests, men and women pursue self-realization through passionate quests. For women, "the passionate quest is almost always predominantly interpersonal in nature, and generally involves romantic love, while for men," she says, "it is more often heroic, the pursuit of achievement or power." This gendered dichotomy—in which "men favor power over love and women achieve power through love"—is reflected in mainstream popular culture, and encapsulated in the romance narrative.[2] For second-wave feminists, romance was a form of ideology, a myth that kept women down. As Shulamith Firestone put it, "Romanticism is a cultural tool of male power to keep women from knowing their condition." Women, she says, "may be duped, but men are quite conscious of this as a valuable manipulative technique."[3]

More recently, feminist cultural critics have attempted to reclaim romance as a hidden pleasure of femininity—reconsidering romance novels, sixties girl-groups' lyrics, even love letters—cultural forms earlier renounced as evidence of women's entrapment—to be examples of female resistance.[4] Early feminist critiques of romance, which ignored how women actually feel and think about the popular culture they consume, were somewhat simplistic. Nonetheless, while it may offer women private pleasures, the romance narrative suggests that we can only achieve self-realization through merger with an Other, and by valuing private achievements over public power. Romance remains a central trope of hegemonic femininity.

So instead of rehabilitating romance, what I'd like to do is reclaim rock 'n' roll, or at least explain how women have used rock as a form of resistance—often in relation to the discourse of romance. Twenty years ago, Ellen Willis proclaimed the pleasures—and paradoxes—that rock held for female fans. "Music that boldly and aggressively laid out what the singer wanted, loved, hated—as good rock 'n' roll did," wrote Willis, "challenged me to do the same, and so even when the content was anti-woman, antisexual, in a sense antihuman, the form encouraged my struggle for liberation."[5] Yet the emerging history of rock focuses upon how its modes of performance embodied male rebellion; missing is an explanation of how and why young women, in Alice Echols's words, "harnessed rock's subversive and rebellious possibilities"—if not as active participants in the production of the music, then surely as consumers and fans.[6]

What meanings does rock embody for female fans? They are certainly masculinist meanings, but they are not *simply* that. The meanings of rock are complex and contradictory. As the last ten years of media analysis has suggested, they are not easily "read" from song lyrics. Rather, the gendered meanings of music, and the meanings of music in general, emerge in relation to an audience, and in a particular historical context. Audiences "use" music creatively, often in ways that go against their intended meanings. Indeed, in an age when feminism was barely visible in the culture at large, rock 'n' roll helped me to place myself outside of the narrow definitions of femininity I saw around me.

Pleasure and Power

Music, writes critic Simon Frith, allows us to participate in "imagined forms of democracy and desire." Twenty years after feminist critiques of rock first surfaced, Frith is responding to the brave new world of globalization, cultural fragmentation, and "active" audiences. Our experience of music, of music making and music listening, he says, "is best understood as an experience of self-in-process."[7] Frith describes how he has found pleasure in black music and gay music, or female music, though he clearly does not identify as black or gay or female. Music, he suggests, knows no borders. It can be enjoyed by all, regardless of race, or religion, or gender.

Music, in its purest sense, *is* fundamentally a democratic art form, at least in principle. But relations of power shape the contexts of production and reception. Music offers possibilities in fantasy that few of us can actually realize in our daily lives. But where hierarchies rule, those pleasures are always connected to inequality. So, for example, in contemporary America, white kids listening to black music, getting off on its rhythms and identifying with it, means something rather different from black folks listening to "white music." For white people, an identification with black culture is at least partly about the fantasy of surrender, of identifying across the racial divide, with the Other. Black folks get off on white music too. But a black person who appreciates opera, or other white (particularly high) cultural forms, is identifying with power. Much the same is true of girls' attraction to rock 'n' roll.

Girls' fiction and magazines convey the belief that the most important goal in life is to fall in love.[8] Romance permits a transcendence of the mundane through the rapturous embrace of love. It is through the romantic quest that the inner experiences and needs of individuals are mutually recognized and validated, and through which, potentially, both individuals are transformed. But this transcendence is founded upon inequality: in the standard romance narrative, boys/men become empowered sexual subjects and girls/women emerge as little more than sexual objects.

If the romance myth is predicated on female passivity, it also assumes heterosexuality. It can never admit that girls may in fact be aroused by other girls, or even that two girls might prefer each other's company to the company of boys. Indeed, it is the pursuit of the male fantasy object that sets females against each other. As Angela McRobbie describes British girls' magazines, "No story ever ends with two girls alone together and enjoying each other's company." They cancel out completely any possibility other than the romantic one between girl and boy. Indeed, that admission would threaten the central tension that drives the narrative.[9]

If girls' popular culture proclaims that self-realization comes through the merger with a (male) Other, boys' culture is its antithesis. The images available to boys and young men—in television, magazines, and pop music—emphasize separation, autonomy, and power. Rock 'n' roll exemplifies this quest. Rock, Simon Reynolds and Joy Press write, is "fueled by a violent fervor to cut loose." The born-to-run impulse of the Rolling Stones, the warrior comrade in arms (the Clash), the omnipotent (the Doors, gangsta rap) are all "ways in which the male rebel has dramatized himself against the feminine."[10] A classic example from the sixties is the Who's song "A Legal Matter," where the hero feels his willpower enfeebled by the "household fog" of furnishings, baby clothes, marriage, and the like. As Reynolds and Press suggest, throughout the sixties, "male wildness is dramatized against female domestication."

This isn't to say that romantic narratives don't make their way into rock 'n' roll. Indeed, as Reynolds and Press argue, the psychedelic tradition—including such performers as Pink Floyd, Brian Eno, along with today's ambient techno music—engages in a mystical identification with the feminine. This rock tradition speaks of "longing to be enfolded and subsumed," exemplified by oceanic and cosmic imagery. But the *dominant* trope of rock emphasizes separation, not surrender.

Rock as a discourse, a way of knowing the world, operates, then, largely in relation and in opposition to the traditionally female value of relationality—epitomized by the romance narrative. While romance values merger with an Other, rock glorifies separation. Through rock 'n' roll, girls have been able to resist the cultural idealization of hegemonic femininity. Rock has offered girls and women a vision of power, an alternative to the romance "script"; girls' attraction to rock 'n' roll, then, has a lot to do with gender transgression. As a teenager, I think I knew this intuitively. I didn't want to be confined to boys, marriage, and babies. I wanted more. Given the choice between dependence and autonomy, romance and rock 'n' roll, I chose the latter.

Ambivalent Pleasures

A preoccupation with romance was certainly reflected in the popular culture of my youth. Girls' magazines such as *Seventeen* carried (and still do carry, to some extent) the following message: girls must devote their lives to the quest for romance, for the "right" boy. She must go to all lengths to catch him. This search for rapture is inevitably accompanied by enormous anxiety and a loss of autonomy. Will he find me attractive? Will he still love me tomorrow? Popular culture told us to be obsessed with finding, falling in love with, and keeping boys, and to dream about rather than participate in life.

I was, instead, devoted to bands from what was then called "the British Invasion." My friend Lisa and I snatched up the records of the Who, the Rolling Stones, and the Kinks. We sneered at our friends who preferred more acceptable mass-culture creations like the Monkees or the Partridge Family. In high school we sometimes cut class early to head downtown to see our favorite bands, waiting on line for hours to buy tickets. When the Who played Madison Square Garden in 1974, Lisa and I managed to score two tickets. For months I waited in anticipation of that night, our first live show. The concert itself was rather disappointing—the pot smoke was so thick we could barely see, our seats were so far from the stage that we could hardly hear. But in a way, it didn't really matter. We were there for the experience.

What did I identify with in this music? The Who was a rather odd choice for a fourteen-year-old girl. *Quadrophenia*, perhaps my favorite Who album, was the ultimate paean to male teen angst. It told the story of Jimmy, an alienated working-class lad who gobbles up amphetamines to escape his claustrophobic family. In search of salvation, he flees to the seaside and enters the world of mods and rockers, and drugs, sex, and rock 'n' roll. This is a classic male dream of escape.

For me the appeal of the music was less about the expression of desire than the formation of an identity. I was a good girl who wanted to be bad. Loud, rhythmic music produced by scraggly young men put me in touch with an image of a different way of life, one that was a long way from home. For me, the pleasures of rock were integrally related to identification with a sense of power that was only available to boys, and the feeling that through that music, I was subverting those gender barriers at least a little bit. Like those British lads, I felt trapped within the shabby gentility of the aspiring middle class, captive in my parents' home. When Roger Daltrey had the gall to sing "Why don't you all just f-f-fade away?" and fantasize himself as a snotty-nosed teenager on a train to Brighton, I was carried along with the ride—even if in reality I lacked the means of escape. Listening to it was a kind of protofeminist act, enacting a secret rebellion at a time when a more overt rebellion was out of the question. During hot summer nights, Lisa and I went to shows in Central Park at least three times a week. At times we weren't even picky about what we went to see. We wanted to luxuriate in the aggressive loudness of the music. We wanted to get out of the house and away from the watchful eyes of our hyperprotective parents—even if our fathers dutifully drove their cars to pick us up after the shows were over, shattering our illusions of teenage rebellion.

The dominant "reading" of girls and rock 'n' roll suggests that they are less interested in the music than in dreaming about their favorite male performers. Using this line of argument, some have suggested that the early Beatles appealed mainly to girls, and that when rock 'n' roll got heavier, and headier, more "male"—with the rise of the Rolling Stones, and others—girls lost their interest in it. This doesn't describe my experience. I loved loud, thrashing rock 'n' roll. I wasn't one of those girls who stared dreamily at my favorite male rock stars, imagining that one day I'd fall into their arms. Anyway, Pete Townsend, my favorite member of the Who, wasn't much of a heartthrob.

I didn't necessarily want to be a guy, or even want to date one, but I did fantasize, perhaps unconsciously, about possessing their power. If my embrace of rock was at least partly a revolt against my mother, it was also a revolt against the gender system that trapped her. Seventies mass culture, filled with sugary-sweet images of functional families in consumerist ecstasy, or teenage girls and boys enrapt in romantic bliss, was, I believed, downright disingenuous. In choosing rock over romance, the Who over

The Who, circa 1965

teenybopper idols such as Bobby Sherman, I was resisting normative expectations of how girls are supposed to be. Rather than buy into the cultural idealization of female dependence, I opted, in fantasy if not reality, for autonomy.

Rock glorified masculinity and simultaneously suggested that it was fraught with contradictions; it reinforced hegemonic notions of gender and revealed that they were a lie. From the mid-sixties on, even as they cockily strutted their stuff, male rockers like Mick Jagger toyed with androgyny and sex-role reversal, wearing lipstick and feather boas and carrying on rudely with their bandmates. David Bowie turned this subversion into an art form, flaunting sexually ambiguous alter-egos such as Ziggy Stardust and Aladdin Sane. I loved it. Rock 'n' roll gave me a space to imagine alternative visions of gender when there were few other possibilities for resistance. It also spoke to my own budding lesbianism.

But at the same time, I knew, deep down, that my favorite performers— Pete Townsend, David Bowie, and the rest—weren't really singing to me. Rock 'n' roll, in its classic form, was produced by and for young men. As

Reynolds and Press point out, female rock fans were "written out of the rock 'n' roll script." At one point, sometime after the mid-seventies, I became very conscious of this fact, and of my love of rock. I hid my Rolling Stones records for fear of being branded with the charge of "false consciousness." I tried, with little success, to listen to feminist folk, or "women's music," but it failed to move me. In distancing itself from the romance narrative, feminist music relinquished the power of rock, retaining a rather passive, traditional conception of femininity. The most exciting music, as Ellen Willis observed, was really for the boys.

Faced with this ambivalence, in order to enjoy the music, the female rock fan learns to change the pronouns of lyrics in her head, imagining herself in the role of the active, knowing male subject. Or she simply denies her femaleness. She is forced to choose between male values of autonomy and female values of dependence. This is a familiar dilemma, as described by feminist theorist Jane Flax: women can either "be loved and nurtured and remain tied to the mother, or be autonomous and externally successful, and be like a man."[11]

Changing Femininities

Young women who are looking around for cultural representations that reflect their experiences are in a less conflicted position today than girls of my generation twenty years ago. They are no longer forced to choose between a discourse of romance that glorifies surrender and a discourse of rock that idealizes autonomy. They have a much greater variety of different images of gender available to them.

A new crop of artists are using the conventions of rock to rewrite the romance script. Gone are the blissful images of romance; a new reflexivity about romance is central to the most interesting music emerging today. Many of these artists, including Polly Jean Harvey, Hole, and Liz Phair, struggle with the pleasures and perils of relationships with the opposite sex. A recent song by the Columbus, Ohio, band Scrawl contains the word-string: "He cleaned up/she took him back/he fucked up/she kicked him out" repeated over and over at an ever-increasing pace. Critic Gina Arnold recently wrote, "If I were a boy and I found out that my girlfriend was listening intently to Scrawl's *Travel On Rider*, I'd take a good, long, hard look at my relationship, and try to figure out what was bugging her."[12]

Other performers rewrite the romance narrative to overturn compulsory heterosexuality. k.d. lang and Melissa Etheridge have become lesbian cover girls. Ani diFranco's sexual ambiguity—which teeters across the boundaries of identity, as she sings of love, lust, and failed relationships with both men and women—has won her a huge following. Bands like Bikini Kill, Team Dresch, and Luscious Jackson embody an empowered female sexuality that takes its cue from Madonna but dispenses with her contrived postures. Even the Spice Girls, for all their bubble-gum appeal, are more than simply bimbos who sing. Clearly, in terms of a small but growing sector of popular music, the dominant gender codes, including passive stereotypes of femininity, are withering away—along with the hegemony of romance and its glorification of women's surrender.

In mass-produced girls' fiction, a similar pattern is evident. "The girl is no longer the victim of romance," writes McRobbie. "She is no longer a slave to love. . . . There is love and there is sex and there are boys, but the conventionally coded metanarratives of romance, which could only create a neurotically dependent female subject, have gone for good." McRobbie suggests that patterns of meaning which were once emblematic of the experience of teenage femininity (i.e. romance) have disappeared. They are being replaced by a more "diffuse femininity," one which "has been cut loose from the firm underpinning provided by romance."[13]

How can we explain the ferment that is now taking place in rock 'n' roll, and the unprecedented entry of a new generation of savvy, sophisticated female performers and fans? Perhaps by looking at how feminism has changed—and is changing—our culture. On the heels of the feminist movement, female performers and fans have become commercially important properties and markets, giving both musicians and fans new power. The artists are not necessarily self-proclaimed feminists. Indeed, many are explicitly not. Polly Harvey, among the most angst-filled of the bunch, is a case in point. But in some ways, that's irrelevant. For the very existence of these artists is made possible by feminism. Girls do not want to be represented in a humiliating way. They are not dependent on boys for their own sense of identity.

Young women coming out as lesbians today are much more likely to see their sexuality as inherently acceptable, even respectable, than did women of my generation. They can learn about lesbian lives in women's studies courses, feminist fiction, and, increasingly, in mass-produced popular culture, such as the television show *Ellen*, or the music of the Indigo Girls. They do not feel a sense of loyalty to feminist or women's culture, as did many women of my generation. When I recently asked a nineteen-year-old what music she listens to, she replied, "I like mainstream women's music the best." Rather than listen to out-lesbian musicians recording on alternative record labels, she prefers to listen to women musicians who make use of lesbian/feminist imagery but perform for a mass audience. This may explain the recent popularity of the Lilith Fair, the roaming festival of mainstream girl pop, featuring the likes of Sarah McLachlan, Sinead O'Connor, and Erykah Badu. Young women today have a much greater sense of entitlement than we did; they believe that they deserve to be represented in mainstream culture, and they're making it happen.[14]

We're certainly not "talkin' about a revolution" here. For every empowered young woman, there are many others who suffer from material and other forms of deprivation. The recording industry is, for all intents and purposes, still in the hands of men. But things are changing, slowly—but significantly. In the world of popular music, a growing number of female performers have been able to use the system to their advantage, openly incorporating gender rebellion into their art. Consequently, young women looking for popular culture that reflects their lives are no longer caught between two unsatisfying alternatives: a world of romance that embodies female dependence and a world of rock 'n' roll that glorifies male separation. They have a greater variety of images of femininity available to them.

If this story poses a challenge to the emergent narrative of rock history that makes female rebellion relatively invisible, it is also a rejoinder to the feminist view that rock and feminism are necessarily at odds. Certainly rock 'n' roll in its classic form embodies male values of autonomy and separation. But for many female fans, rock has also been a source of gender rebellion. Increasingly, this rebellious spirit is reflected in the music itself, and future histories of rock 'n' roll will certainly include artists such as Polly Harvey, Sleater-Kinney, and Hole. But even before the recent wave of "women in rock," some of us used rock to enact a secret gender rebellion. The history of rock should also include the story of girls like me, whose lives were saved by rock 'n' roll.

Dedicated to Lisa Kramer.

Notes

1. Robin Morgan, quoted in Karen Durbin, "Can a Feminist Love the World's Greatest Rock 'n' Roll Band?" *Ms.* (October 1974), pp. 24–27. See also Simon Frith and Angela McRobbie, "Rock and Sexuality," in *On the Record: Rock, Pop, and the Written Word*, ed. Simon Frith and Andrew Goodwin (New York: Pantheon, 1990).

2. Ethel Spector Person, *Dreams of Love and Fateful Encounters* (New York: Penguin, 1988), p. 267.

3. Shulamith Firestone, *The Dialectic of Sex* (New York: Morrow, 1970), pp. 166, 150.

4. See, for example, Janice Radway, *Reading the Romance: Women, Patriarchy, and Popular Literature* (Chapel Hill: University of North Carolina, 1984); Tania Modleski, *Loving with a Vengeance: Mass-Produced Fantasies for Women* (New York: Methuen, 1982); Barbara Bradby, "Do-Talk and Don't-Talk: The Division of the Subject in Girl-Group Music," in Frith and Goodwin.

5. Ellen Willis, "Beginning to See the Light," in *Beginning to See the Light* (New York: Knopf, 1981), p. 99. For more recent contributions to the feminist conversation about rock, see Gillian Gaar, *She's a Rebel* (Seattle: Seal Press, 1992), and the essays collected by Evelyn McDonnell and Ann Powers in *Rock She Wrote* (New York: Delta, 1995).

6. Alice Echols, "We Gotta Get Outta This Place: The Sixties," in *Cultural Politics and Social Movements*, ed. Marcy Darnovsky, Barbara Epstein, et al. (Philadelphia: Temple University Press, 1995), p. 123.

7. Simon Frith, "Music and Identity," in *Questions of Cultural Identity*, ed. Stuart Hall and Paul du Gay, (London: Sage, 1996), pp. 109, 123.

8. Angela McRobbie, "Romantic Individualism and the Teenage Girl," in *Feminism and Youth Culture* (London: Macmillan, 1991), p. 131.

9. Ibid., p. 101.

10. Simon Reynolds and Joy Press, *The Sex Revolts* (Cambridge, Mass.: Harvard University Press, 1995), p. xv.

11. Jane Flax, "Mother-Daughter Relationships," in *The Future of Difference*, ed. H. Eisenstein and A. Jardine (New Brunswick, N.J.: Rutgers, 1985), p. 37.

12. Gina Arnold, "Fools Rush In," *East Bay Express*, 27 December 1996.

13. Angela McRobbie, "Shut Up and Dance: Youth Culture and Changing Modes of Femininity," in *Postmodernism and Popular Culture* (London: Routledge, 1994), p. 164.

14. See Arlene Stein, *Sex and Sensibility: Stories of a Lesbian Generation* (Berkeley: University of California Press, 1997).

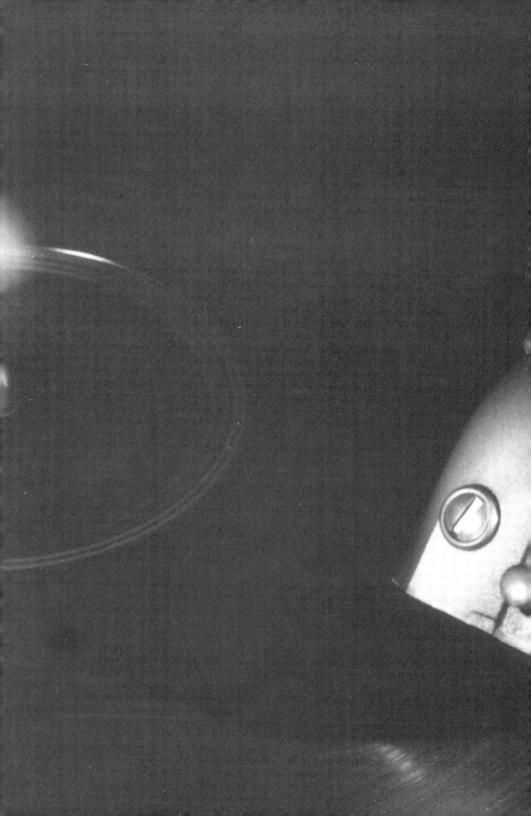

History and Memory

Keeping Time

In the popular imagination, music narrates history. American history, a particular yet evocative narrative, certainly has its soundtracks—a blues guitar for the post-Depression era, Janis Joplin's wail or Jimi Hendrix's purring guitar for sixties riots and peace rallies, or Madonna's spirited cheer for eighties tawdry materialism. Music can also provide a sound-track for a more personal experience. "Some people mark time by the cycles of the sun, the moon, or, say, national holidays," writes Donna Gaines. "Rock fanatics mark time by their 'Bowie phase,' or when they 'went hardcore.'"[1] Ubiquitous three-minute pop songs invent images, tell stories, and become mythological—music to live by.

Inspired by a trip to the Rock and Roll Hall of Fame and Museum shortly after its opening in 1995, this section on "History and Memory" takes as its focus the chronicling of music history. The museum carries out its assignment to archive rock 'n' roll, not only by ordaining the famous, but also by amassing thousands of objects, an entrenched museological practice. The resulting displays at the museum attest to recent desires to construct an overarching narrative, with mythic consequence, that empowers popular music as a seminal recorder of twentieth-century American culture. Among their treasures are newsreels that track censorial assaults on music, stage costumes that broke dress-code barriers, and tattered napkins where immortalized lyrics were first written.

History and memory are infused in these objects. On the glass cases distancing the objects from our touch, our image is reflected, enabling our metaphoric inhabitation of the garments and items,[2] so that we can narcissistically see ourselves as participants in the timeline, or link some quality of our personal identities to the whole matrix of social organization. This reflection is welcome because we want to believe our individual experiences and actions are as meaningful, conspicuous, and effective as those embodied by these hallowed relics.

Meg Handler, *Graceland, Tribute Week*, 1996

The zeal to inscribe history within the discourse of popular culture is not unfamiliar: as Martin Beck describes, "the emphatic declaration of the end of history within postmodern discourses" coincides with its appearance everywhere in the field of popular music. In the past ten years, popular music archives, or containers of "collective memory, filled with frozen historical moments," like the CD boxed sets of Robert Johnson or the Doors, became an obsession.[3] Hard Rock Cafés have proliferated around the globe, adorned with historical rock 'n' roll artifacts; various documentaries on the history of popular music have been produced; and style, along with its attendant behavioral phenomena, is now continuously recycled—the most recent being the rebirth of swing, witnessed in Gap commercials as well as the new swing clubs. History is being manufactured, commodified, and ravenously consumed; the postmodern, end-of-the-millenium production of history is a capitalist enterprise, dependent on the fashion industry's market economy.

Within this same sphere, the seemingly paradoxical baby-boomer conviction that rock 'n' roll was conceived in the spirit of a counter-cultural idealism is sustained, albeit with progressively less and less vigor. Music can be, as Anthony DeCurtis has aptly portrayed it, both as "safe as milk and a clear and present danger."[4] Perhaps the cultural longings to retrieve that lost, insubordinate, yet optimistic, past can be concretized by capturing time, storing time within audio archives, the written word, or display cases of gathered and ordered memorabilia. A newly "authentic" narrative comes to the rescue and compensates for the loss of that sanguine past; these archives and collections serve as memorials, dedications to the spirit of revolution and upheaval. One part of the curatorial struggle at rock's new museum, as Robert Santelli describes it here, has been to reconcile history and myth, and to question patterns of iconization. But, inevitably, narratives evolve through these compilations; history and myth are inescapably intertwined—which doesn't mean that their signified meanings are simply fictional accounts, nor are they unified or singular.

"Historical research has always led . . . to myth," Marina Warner has said. "Even the most immediate and intense emotional upheavals pass

Jamie Reid, *Old Queen*, 1977

through a mesh of common images and utterances, which are grounded in ideas about nature and the supernatural."[5] Audiences remember, re-create, or imagine those moments of transgression and creation through individual experiences grounded within a larger social arena. The multiple and layered conventions of the society in which music is generated and heard filter its style and promotion, often reinforcing the most common stories and representations—the rebels, the villains, the sex gods and goddesses, and the heroines and heroes. Imagined dialogues with the past, like the one Jessica Hagedorn evokes between Jimi Hendrix and his scions Rocky Rivera and Elvis Chang, propose to clarify our present relationship with history, and both teach us to sift through mythic cultural structures and encourage counternarratives that are simultaneously personal and collective—two domains that are entangled, not oppositional, especially in pop-cultural annals.

Since the sixties, there has been a dual effort to summon manifold subjects of history and to acknowledge the power the image holds. As Barbara O'Dair describes here, that historical endeavor is long overdue within the field of music criticism. The icons that are assembled through popular music, she argues, are not only, or not necessarily, mystifications. During adolescence, that period of fierce socialization, when popular culture seems to hold its most intensive grip, these icons can recount new stories—new paradigms—which may help to instigate positive identification across gender, racial, class, and even aesthetic lines, and which will, hopefully, broaden the structural and political dimensions of identity at its most formative stage. It is somewhere in the blurring of these lines—that liminal zone—that things get edgy. Somehow, for example, Bob Marley's song "Get Up, Stand Up," generated from within a specific political context and utilizing an explicit aesthetic style, manifests a universalized rallying call for human justice.

For there are no eternal myths, since, as Roland Barthes has shown in his classic study *Mythologies*, myths always have a "historical foundation" and cannot "evolve from the 'nature' of things." The task, then, for contemporary artists, critics, and historians is to engage in some intense "memory work," as Paul Gilroy calls it, without slipping into the murky puddle of nostalgia, wherein sentimentality and uncritical emotion belie memory. For nostalgia feeds on desire, destined never to achieve its goal, which is to close the gap between the symbolic and *lived* experience. It is that closure that should be the purpose of any more comprehensive project of remembrance. The questions we should be asking are: what, in fact, are the contemporary uses of the past, what symbolic representations are invoked, why, in what contexts, and how do these metaphorical constructions repress alternative inscriptions of cultural mythologies. Out of the revelations might emerge firmer, less arbitrary, historical foundations. History should be thought of as a ground from which the present can be continually re-evaluated.

Notes

1. Donna Gaines, in an unpublished statement in an online discussion that took place on Dia's website during February 1997.

2. Dan Graham has made a similar argument regarding the effect of store-window display on consumers. See Dan Graham, "Notes on 'Video Piece for Showcase Windows in a Shopping Arcade' (1976)," in *Video—Architecture—Television: Writings on Video and Video Works 1970–78* (Halifax, N.S.: The Press of the Nova Scotia College of Art and Design, in association with New York University Press, 1979), pp. 53–54.

3. Martin Beck, "Pop, Inc.," an unpublished essay submitted to the online discussion cited above.

4. Anthony DeCurtis, preface to *Present Tense: Rock & Roll and Culture* (Durham, N.C.: Duke University Press, 1992), p. xii.

5. Marina Warner, foreword to *Six Myths of Our Time: Little Angels, Little Monsters, Beautiful Beasts, and More* (New York: Vintage Books, 1994), p. xviii.

Robert Santelli

The Rock and Roll Hall of Fame and Museum:

Myth, Memory, and History

Depending on your point of view, the Cleveland-based Rock and Roll Hall of Fame and Museum is either the music's official house of history—the place where one can find proof of its artistic and cultural merit—or a triangular-shaped glass temple that has more to do with myth and mass consumption than the real story of rock 'n' roll. Ever since this museum dedicated to the music and its abiding culture was conceived more than a decade ago, the debate over whether it was a good idea or a bad one has kept many a critic and music historian engaged in vigorous discourse.

The skeptics' fear that institutionalizing rock 'n' roll would kill the music's present and future and trivialize and compress its past into neat, carefully packaged modules was not to be taken lightly, even by the museum's proponents. After all, rock, by its very nature, has always been chaotic, incorrigible, and anti-institutional. Together the music and its culture represented the antithesis of establishment and order. The spirit of rebellion and deconstruction found in much of the best rock 'n' roll helped make the music a significant force in American arts and culture in the postwar years. Attempting to explain the inexplicable and control the uncontrollable—in a museum, of all places—was nothing less than an assault on rock's most primal and sacred roots. Or so naysayers railed.

No one explained, mind you, how rock's integrity would be violated if a museum dedicated to preserving and interpreting its history were to be successful. No critic came forth with any anarchic alternative worth recalling. If anything, a few of the loudest skeptics seemed soured by the possibility that some of rock's creative juices could run dry due to an exhibition, say, on punk rock that might attempt to explain the phenomenon, trace its origins, archive the music, and categorize its artifacts. But no one ever said how or why that would happen. I can recall a thought I had in the early nineties when first confronted with anti–Rock Hall criticism: I

Gene Vincent's leather jacket

Bee Gees' jacket

wondered if hanging contemporary art in a gallery discouraged the visual artists who viewed the work or, instead, inspired them.

What the curators faced when confronted with the daunting task of developing a rock 'n' roll museum with a particular point of view and an arching vision of its past and present was not unlike what virtually every other curatorial department faces, whether it puts together a small display or a major exhibition. These questions inevitably arise: What are the most relevant artifacts? How are issues of representation resolved? How does one avoid the problem, as Peter Wollen describes it, of condemning the museum visitor "to a world in which we can see everything but understand nothing."

Yet, such questions were a bit more problematic for the Rock Hall. That there had never been a museum, or any institution for that matter, dedicated to the history of rock 'n' roll music and culture meant that there were no reference points to examine or road maps to follow. As a member of the curatorial team that assembled the artifacts and created the exhibits for the September 1995 grand opening, I can attest to the frustrations we encountered in going it alone. But being the first to create a museological plan regarding rock 'n' roll also meant we could only be original in our conceptual designs and curatorial ambitions—and, at least to a certain degree, be free to make mistakes.

It wasn't just museological questions we faced. Rock 'n' roll, not even a half-century old, does not possess a historiography. The late Robert Palmer, one of rock's most astute observers, wrote that the history of rock 'n' roll is almost "as unruly as the music itself" and that "any attempt at a definitive overview is . . . an exercise in wishful thinking." In place of a rock 'n' roll historiography is a myth-plated story of the music and its most famous artists that is often shallow, vague, fractured, exclusionary, and nonrevisionist. Much of rock's history has been penned by writers with only a cursory grasp of methodology and few tools either to intellectualize this complicated pop-art form or to separate fact from faction, fantasy from reality.

Joe Walsh's T-shirt

This dearth inspired one of the museum's earliest goals, which was not just to preserve rock 'n' roll history, but to identify it. The curatorial team attempted to build a rock 'n' roll historiography where none had existed previously, one that would create a basic foundation from which future discourse on the music could be launched. Special exhibits, the permanent collection, interactive displays, and educational programs would all serve to complement such a canon.

What all this meant is that the Rock Hall's curatorial and education departments actually became part of the historical process. Curators, most obviously in the narratives and texts they wrote to accompany the exhibits, in the interactive modules such as "Five Hundred Songs That Shaped Rock and Roll," and in the kind of artifacts exhibited and the space accorded each display, created the museum's own history of the music. The danger in all this was that curators could conceivably manufacture false history. Without any standard historiographical reference, there was no way to know for sure if we had gone too far, forging, for example, our own ideas on rock's role as a countercultural force in the sixties, or assigning values to certain artifacts, or giving one artist too much credit and another too little in shaping the music. Even more important, how could we be certain that we separated myth from truth, when so much of what passes as standard pop-music history is suspect? Given the importance of myth in rock history, should myth be accorded a place in the museum? Where? And how? These questions the staff wrestled with before the museum opened, and continue to wrestle with today.

When artifact collection earnestly began in January 1994, some eighteen months before the museum's opening, it was hoped that the exhibits we'd create would at least define a shared rock 'n' roll experience. But it didn't take us long to conclude there is no such thing. Jim Henke, the museum's newly appointed chief curator, assembled a team of music journalists to act as consultants, most of whom he had worked with or who had worked for him when he was music editor at *Rolling Stone*. Each consultant brought his or her ideas and experiences in rock 'n' roll to the curatorial meetings, held in Cleveland and New York. We quickly found out that

Tom Petty's hat

each of us owned entirely different interpretations of events, artists, and albums, despite the fact that we were all approximately the same age—late thirties to early forties—had made rock 'n' roll our lives in some capacity, had been at many of the same major concerts, knew intimately the so-called classic-rock works, and believed that the music had a profound impact on American culture in the second half of the twentieth century.

If we didn't share a collective pop-music memory, there was no reason to believe museum visitors—with their diverse ethnicity, gender, race, class, and geography—would possess one. This meant that it was impossible to create an encompassing, shared experience at the museum. Rock 'n' roll, like America itself, is a multicultural, multidimensional maze. The museum, it was agreed, ought to reflect this.

In an essay entitled "Beyond Belief: The Museum as Metaphor," Ralph Rugoff wrote that "if a museum can disrupt our sense of distance from the objects it displays, it might not serve to isolate the past so much as to link it to our current experiences." The Rock and Roll Hall of Fame and Museum might have used such a statement as one of its main missions. Unlike an art museum, for instance, that might offer its patrons a fifteenth-century Italian painting exhibition, the Rock Hall has no such distant past to celebrate and to interpret. Rock 'n' roll was born in the early fifties, a direct offspring of the union of black and white music and black and white culture. Its roots are nearly all in the twentieth century. Many people who visit the Rock Hall were alive when rock 'n' roll was conceived, and they matured into their teens as the music evolved into a force with increasing sociological and cultural impact. In short, rock 'n' roll became the soundtrack of the baby-boom generation and, to a lesser degree, post-boomers and Generation Xers who, like their older brothers and sisters or parents, believe that the music offers something much more than sheer entertainment and physical release: from rock, it was possible to retrieve political, sociological, artistic, and even spiritual wisdom. Rock fans expected their music to be vital and relevant to their lives, and for many it was—and still is.

Michelle Phillips's boots

Many visitors to the Rock Hall experience a unique personalized and emotional connection that that they might not feel at, say, a museum featuring medieval painting. The typical fortysomething visitor to the Rock Hall has lived the music and loved it, and even if he still doesn't, nostalgia makes him think he does. He comes to the museum with uncommonly strong expectations; he is empowered with the belief that because he went to the Woodstock music festival in 1969 he is a vital part of the history of sixties rock and a personal or "living-history" extension of any sixties rock or Woodstock exhibit the Rock Hall might present. Many of these kinds of visitors come, not to broaden their understanding of rock, but rather to validate it.

An encounter with one woman during the Rock Hall's exhibition on sixties music and culture called "I Want to Take You Higher: The Psychedelic Years" demonstrated the power and personification of myth in rock history. She had been to Woodstock, lost her virginity there, and had what she called "a quasi-religious rock experience" at Yasgur's farm. She argued that the exhibition did not stress enough the importance of Woodstock. She called the fest "the most imporant achievement" in rock 'n' roll history and had no intention of hearing or viewing anything to the contrary. She left the exhibition disappointed, even disgruntled, muttering that the curators were "too jaded to really understand rock 'n' roll."

The Woodstock festival was a high-water mark in sixties rock history since it showcased the relationship the music had with the period's counterculture, and, in sheer size and numbers, it was the largest music event of the decade. Woodstock also set the music industry in a frenzy to sign new bands and take advantage of the vast new commercial potential of rock. But the Woodstock festival contained few classic performances; the proof can be found in the pair of less-than-overwhelming soundtrack albums that followed the film documentary. At the concert site, the sound was bad, and with the rain, the mud, the poor sanitary conditions, and the scarcity of food and water, it was far from the "garden" that Joni Mitchell sang about in her song "Woodstock."

Yet, thanks, in part, to the media, which hyped Woodstock like it had hyped Beatlemania five years earlier, the mythmaking machinery was revved up almost immediately after the fest. From that mercenary frenzy came the idea that those who had gone to upstate New York that August witnessed the birth of the Woodstock Nation, participated in the ultimate celebration of hippie values, and made sure peace and love triumphed over hate and greed. What was perceived to have happened at Woodstock was far more embracing than what actually happened. Woodstock's representation in "I Want to Take You Higher" focused on the facts of the event and its musical makeup, in effect deconstructing much of the festival's mythological standing.

But when myth is deconstructed at the museum, some visitors feel a bit cheated or disappointed. The average first-time visitor spends nearly four hours perusing the exhibits, watching the films, and engaging in its interactive displays. More than seeking additional knowledge about rock history and culture, a majority of museum visitors want, first and foremost, to be nostalgically entertained—or so indicate the responses to surveys the museum has conducted since its opening.

The inevitable intrusion of nostalgia undoubtedly impacts the Rock Hall experience. Some fans who visited the museum during its maiden year were disappointed because their favorite artist was not represented. There was little concern that the artist in question might have made little or no significant contribution to rock history other than a one-shot hit record. Nevertheless, these fans expected, even demanded, that their favorite artist be included in the rock 'n' roll story.

One of the Rock Hall's initial exhibition strategies not only challenged the intrusion of nostalgia but sought to deconstruct notions of identity that might lead to nostalgic diversions at the expense of the significance of artifacts on display. Since so much of rock 'n' roll is visual, many stage costumes were on display for the museum's grand opening. The answer to the question of what to hang these costumes on proved elusive. To create lifelike mannequins, imitating exact facial features, might make the figures, in the eyes of the visitor, more meaningful than the clothes, and thus was never seriously considered. Merely presenting the costumes on hangers seemed void of any connection to the artist or the music. The display strategy ultimately settled on was to present the costumes on mannequins whose faces only vaguely resembled the artist. This middle-ground approach eliminated idol worship, the kind one would find at a wax museum. But too many museum visitors thought the Rock Hall's design staff had simply done a bad job at re-creating the faces of the artists!

In order to challenge further conventional myths within rock history and keep issues of nostalgia in check, the curatorial staff opted to take a postmodernist view of representation and narration for the museum's opening. As opposed to presenting a chronologically linear history of rock 'n' roll with exhibits outlining the music's origins in the early fifties and culminating with ones pertaining to rock in the nineties, the Rock Hall exhibits instead subverted the visitors' expectations of an easy-flowing, nonchallenging walk through rock history. An exhibit on the nineties Seattle music scene sat across from one on the blues, a fashion exhibit followed one on antirock reactions from the establishment in the fifties. An exhibit on the Allman Brothers Band demonstrated its importance as a musical unit minus theatrical histrionics, like those that made Alice Cooper's shows so exciting in the early seventies; yet an Alice Cooper exhibit, complete with stage props and costumes, was positioned just a few feet away, as if the two were somehow thematically linked. Such a chaotic, "unruly" approach to rock history was spectacularly effective in breaking apart myth and convention and challenged the visitor to rethink his view of rock history—perhaps the museum's most important accomplishment at this point.

The Rock and Roll Hall of Fame and Museum is now an established cultural institution, and a major tourist attraction in downtown Cleveland. It remains controversial, while problems of representation, myth, and history continue to be resolved. It will always be different things to different people, but, underneath the swirling criticism and the acclaim, the museum acknowledges that rock is a living, breathing music form that routinely reinvents itself. Not only does its story continue to unfold, but so does its very definition of itself. The same can be said of the Rock and Roll Hall of Fame and Museum—and that's a good thing.

Barbara O'Dair

Across the Great Divide:

Rock Critics, Rock Women

I. Making Greatness

Two years ago, I edited a book of essays by women called *The Rolling Stone Book of Women in Rock: Trouble Girls*. Early in the process, my partner, Rolling Stone Press editor Holly George-Warren, suggested that the outline do away with the notion of "greatness." Rather than designating fifty or so important rock women on whom to focus, she wondered if it might be wiser to try to document many more, with the idea of finally giving voice to a silent history.

After serious consideration, I decided that we'd do better identifying a generous handful of women than calculating legions who have toiled without credit. A finite group, even an elite one with recognizable names and faces, might ultimately tell more about the meanings of gender and stardom, and sexual double standards. But I understood what my partner was getting at. "Greatness," as it had come to be defined, hadn't done much for us lately.

We'd been inspired to do *Trouble Girls* for this very reason, among others: steeped as we both were in the mostly male culture of *Rolling Stone* (although neither of us at the time an editor on the magazine), I for one wanted the opportunity to get something different on record. And luckily, for the most part, the process of making the book was free from interference. It was only after the book was sent to press that a number of events unfolded that were maddening enough to convince us that the book represented a fly in the ointment of the establishment, which would apparently go to great lengths to wrest back control. Upon seeing the finished version of our book, *Rolling Stone* editors announced they would produce a tribute issue to "Women in Rock" as part of the magazine's thirtieth-anniversary celebration. They then requested that Random

Grace Jones at the New York Disco Convention, September 1977

House push back the publication date of *Trouble Girls* eight months to coincide with the special issue, which among other things required us to update a good deal of our material.

Not only were Holly and I not invited to consult on the issue (though we each did contribute a couple of Q&A's in the end), most frustrating, *Trouble Girls* was not even mentioned in the editor's introduction to the special issue. Still, after the issue briskly came and went, as bi-weekly periodicals do, the idea of having produced a book from under the roof of one of the book's implicit main targets was tickling, and immensely gratifying. Plus, we had a shelf life.

II. The Act of Canonization: A Little Evidence

Trouble Girls eventually came out in November 1997. The two previous years had seen a number of similarly themed books, among them an anthology of women's rock criticism, *Rock She Wrote: Women Write About Rock, Pop, and Rap*, edited by Evelyn McDonnell and Ann Powers; Lucy O'Brien's critical history, *She Bop*; Amy Raphael's collection of interviews, *Grrrls: Viva Rock Divas*; and Simon Reynolds and Joy Press's *The Sex Revolts: Gender, Rebellion, and Rock 'n' Roll*. Prior to this flurry, only a few books had been devoted to the topic of women in rock: Gillian Gaar's 1992 *She's a Rebel: The History of Women in Rock and Roll*, the eclectic *Signed, Sealed, and Delivered: True Life Stories of Women in Rock* by Sue Steward and Sheryl Garratt in 1984, and 1980's *Rockabye Baby* by Aida Pavletich.

Most of the new women-in-rock titles received a brief flush of attention upon publication, then quickly beat a retreat to the specialty shelves. On the other hand, *The Rolling Stone Illustrated History of Rock and Roll*, originally published in 1976, continues to hold considerable status, along with *The Rolling Stone Encyclopedia of Rock and Roll*, as the definitive rock resource. The latest version of the *Illustrated History*, updated in 1992, contains just three chapters devoted to a single woman who has made significant contributions to rock 'n' roll, namely, Aretha Franklin, Janis Joplin, and Madonna, the last of which was added for the new edition.

On the other hand, male bands and individual male artists—from the Beach Boys to U2, from Elvis Presley to Michael Jackson—received closer to 100. Survey chapters such as "Motown" and "The Evolution of the Singer-Songwriter" sweep in major artists such as the Supremes and Joni Mitchell. Two chapters—"The Girl Groups" and "Women in Revolt" (about punk and post-punk rock women)—are devoted exclusively to women's creation of and/or participation in a genre, but in the latter chapter artists as diverse as Patti Smith, Chrissie Hynde, and Sinead O'Connor are lumped together.

Rock women have met similar fates in other notable books. Blues scholar and former *New York Times* critic Robert Palmer (who died in 1997) contributed a companion volume to a 1995 PBS series entitled *Rock & Roll: An Unruly History*. The critic's work has been hailed by rock scribes who have valued Palmer's passion for and expertise in a broad pop-music spectrum, encompassing both rock's roots and contemporary art-rock masters. "Masters," by the way, is the operative word here: *An Unruly History* was written with virtually *no significant references* to women's contributions to the genre (check the index, if you're curious). While Patti Smith and Debbie Harry get cursory mentions (these two fare better by association in Greil Marcus's chapter in the *Illustrated History*, "Anarchy in the U.K.," in which he writes, "[Punk] was . . . the first such movement in which women played a significant, even defining role"), it's clear that Palmer's history isn't quite unruly enough to mess with guitar-god obsession. (Even an homage to Sonic Youth almost completely ignores cofounder Kim Gordon in favor of her husband, Thurston Moore.)

Perhaps the most instructive example of pop-music history's selective memory comes in considering rock crit's most sacred text: Marcus's brilliant 1974 book *Mystery Train: Images of America in Rock 'n' Roll Music*. Widely and deservedly regarded as *the* classic study of rock 'n' roll and the first to introduce rock's mythic proportions, *Mystery Train* combines musicology, social history, and cultural analysis to illuminate some seminal characters in rock: "ancestors" Harmonica Frank and Robert Johnson and "inheritors" the Band, Sly Stone, Randy Newman, and Elvis Presley—all, you might notice, men. Though written during a period in which radical feminism flourished, Marcus's book effectively creates a prefeminist canon of its own.

In *Mystery Train*, Marcus writes that the performers he selected appealed to him because:

These men tend to see themselves as symbolic Americans; I think their music is an attempt to live up to that role. Their records dramatize a sense of what it is to be an American; what it means, what it's worth, what the stakes of life in America might be. This book, then, is an exploration of a few artists, all of whom seem to me to have found their own voices; it is rooted in the idea that these artists can illuminate those American questions and that the questions can add resonance to their work.

In 1974, these were radical ideas, as Marcus wrote: rock was not just "youth culture, or counterculture, but simply American culture." We usually now take for granted that rock provides a cultural history. Are we ready, however, for women to carry that much meaning?

After all, by Marcus's account, his rock heroes, the ones who tell what it is to be an American, are men. "American" implies American men; these men transcend gender to represent all Americans. About which women in rock could we say: She "dramatize[s] a sense of what it is to be an American; what it means, what it's worth, what the stakes of life in America might be"? For starters, Aretha Franklin, Madonna, Courtney Love. But what woman truly transcends her gender to become a representative American, as opposed to a representative American woman? Women are instead relegated to a subset of "American." The female experience is rarefied, extraordinary, and ironically, less meaningful. The female qualities the culture traditionally prizes seem to be definitively at odds with the rock experience and lifestyle we admire.

We know female performers have been active throughout the rock era: Big Mama Thornton, Etta James, Ruth Brown, Janis Joplin, Joni Mitchell. These and many other rock women have avid fans, and their commercial impact is recorded on the charts. The version of "history" that is documented, however, in *The Illustrated History*, *Mystery Train*, *An Unruly History* and elsewhere tells a different story: it's not necessarily the result of a vast conspiracy to write women out of history, but something deeper, more unsettling—a lack of passion for or connection with women.

Our best and most prolific historians and critics, in fact, appear to be looking for rock to fill a need: that is, to provide role models and forefather figures for themselves and men like them, to be a mythic masculine force. Because rock criticism and history have been almost completely written by males, critics' and historians' failure to identify across, not race or class, but primarily *gender* has caused a serious imbalance in rock's record.

III. Girls Will Be Boys and Boys Will Be Girls . . .

At two-and-a-half, my daughter Charlotte always takes the protagonist's role at play, which—surprise—is usually male. It's no big deal for her to pretend she's Littlefoot the Longneck, boy dinosaur; I get to be the side-kick, who is often female. Leadership, not gender, is what matters; in my daughter's world, she is always the protagonist. We, her parents, are helpers.

Similarly, even by adolescence, I had not outgrown the gender blindness that actually saved me as a girl. As I wrote in the introduction to *Trouble Girls* in evaluating the appeal of male rock stars to me as a young teen:

It was not only sex but a sex-and-gender twist that attracted me to many of my early rock heroes, Mick and Keith, Hendrix, Bowie, Bolan, Marvin Gaye. I objectified these heroes and identified with them, across gender and race, not to mention life experience, with their androgynous play as much as their macho poses. I include myself among the legions of female fans who empowered male rock stars for embodying our own wild desires: to my uncomfortably feminized being, these guys were infinitely more attractive than most of the crooning moon maidens who appeared to be the other main event, or the shadowy female figures, perfect but unknowable, found on the back of a motorcycle or naked under a bearskin rug. . . . Because of Tina [Turner], Janis Joplin, and Grace Slick, I remained oblivious to the gender discrepancy in what I had come to think of as my lifesaver. Still, in almost every instance, it came more naturally to want to be Mick than Marianne, Dylan than Baez, Bowie than Joni.

As a fan, identifying across my gender was easy and fun. For men, it appears not so. As much as rock 'n' roll can engage men in conventional masculine behavior, it can also free them from conventions without thoroughly threatening their sexual identity. The male rock star can serve as a vehicle for provocative sexuality, or androgynous sex play, or grand emotion—so-called feminine attributes. But while male fans and critics may say it's okay for Mick Jagger to wear eyeliner or Kurt Cobain a dress, identifying with actual female rockers appears to be a much greater leap for most men to take. It's interesting to note, for instance, that the male fans Joni Mitchell and Madonna boast seem to be disproportionately gay.

Only in my twenties did it become important to me to find women (and images of women) who represented the strength and daring I looked for in myself: Madonna, Slits, Raincoats, Bush Tetras; later, Lucinda Williams, Breeders, Liz Phair, Courtney Love, and Hole. My hankering for them grew in direct proportion to my reluctant acknowledgment of the social limitations placed on me solely because of my gender.

Stories become myth, and heroes become icons, when they express both the personal experiences of the storyteller and the larger world of human experience. The fact that women have very few cultural touchstones at their disposal makes a strong case for including not just women rockers but also women writers, documentarians, inventors, fantasists, historians, and critics in the pantheon. Stories take on weight as they are reiterated. Without individuals with a stake in these stories, the stories fade away, become footnotes, errata, cultural detritus.

We may now be making our own iconic cultural history, one that seeks to explode old myths (see Carol Cooper on Billie Holiday), review them (Deborah Frost on Patti Smith, Sue Cummings on Karen Carpenter), create them anew (Carola Dibbell on women in punk), or probe the very notion of historical interpretation and its versions on the road toward iconization (Terri Sutton on Janis Joplin). Now a substantial group of women have the opportunity to challenge the rock hierarchy with their own stories that express female experience while eschewing stereotype. Several years ago, Frost penned a record review of Hole's *Pretty on the Inside* in which she wrote, "Courtney Love may be the logical by-product of what happens when the myths of Madonna are crossed with the cult of Patti Smith." Evident in this statement is a keen sense of history and influence, the kind that would also inform the tracking of Madonna back to Debbie Harry, and Sheryl Crow to Chrissie Hynde.

But if only women write about women, will only women listen? Although more than a few asked, I chose not to include men among the contributors to *Trouble Girls* because I wanted the book to have two purposes: to champion women in rock with smart, critical, and historical essays, and to do so by employing women rock critics, who had yet to make their lasting mark (although that is changing, with more women music editors, critics, and reporters). As I made my assignments, my thinking was not primarily that women could tell women's stories better (though it's hard to beat direct experience), but that it was important to raise the profiles of women writers as well as performers. And, next time, and for maximum effect, I would seriously consider assigning simply the best critics—male or female—to the task.

Greil Marcus wrote of his subjects, "They are more ambitious and . . . they take more risks than most. They risk artistic disaster (in rock terms, pretentiousness), or the alienation of an audience that can be soothed far more easily than it can be provoked . . ." Couldn't, after all, the very same words be said about Madonna, Lucinda Williams, Liz Phair?

Music for Gangsters

and (Other) Chameleons

In the seventies and eighties, I led a nine-piece band called the Gangster Choir. As a woman and a poet, I wasn't taken too seriously by most club owners and knucklehead A&R types, who asked the kind of questions that made me want to tear my hair out in utter despair: *What kind of music do you play? Who's your target audience? Do you actually sing?* In spite of these obstacles the band performed at the usual downtown venues: Mudd Club, Danceteria, CBGB's, Armageddon, Squat Theater, and the Underground, to name a few.

Pop music, rock music, funkadelic, punkadelic, psychedelic, jazz fusion, acid house, gangsta rap, Bali-ghali, bhangra-jangra, hip-swaying, knee-bending, nitty-gritty, soul music—call it what you will. The Gangster Choir defied categories. The band's surreal name embraced contradiction and ambiguity, a bit of glorification and romantic identification with the rebel/outlaw/outsider. And there the connection to "gangsta rap" begins, takes a sharp left turn, and probably ends. I don't want to get too academic and analyze it to death. The Gangster Choir's musical and literary influences could be traced to Sly Stone, the original Last Poets, those early Amiri Baraka recordings, which feature Baraka declaiming to the sweet "baby-baby" of a doo-wop chorus, the dissonant, menacing funk of Miles Davis's "Live Evil" period, the jangly rhythm guitars and tight horn sections of James Brown, the flash and showmanship of Patti Labelle, and the movies of Jean-Luc Godard. And why not? In the fifties and sixties, in the Philippines and in America, I grew up on a vibrant mix of Perez Prado and Motown, Frank Sinatra and Eartha Kitt, lush Douglas Sirk melodramas, and a tradition of melancholy Philippine love songs known as *kundimans*. My family, along with most people we knew in Manila, listened to and appreciated a wide variety of music, without worrying about distinctions and categories.

Filipinos are the ultimate outsiders: hybrid and resilient masters of eerie mimicry and witty appropriation. We are tropical chameleons, elegant dancers, and funky, soulful musicians. It's not for nothing that the best bands in Asia—the ones who can segue smoothly from perfect covers of Prince's naughty "Kiss" to Debbie Boone's super-schmaltzy "You Light Up My Life"—are Filipino.

My novel *The Gangster of Love* is a story about the sometimes redemptive and sometimes destructive power of rock 'n' roll. It is also about the coming of age of a young poet and wannabe musician named Rocky Rivera. Along with her fierce mother, Milagros, and her dreamy, manic-depressive brother, Voltaire, Rocky emigrates to America—from the Philippines of Ferdinand Marcos's dictatorship to the freewheeling, politically charged Bay Area of the seventies. She falls in and out of love with a guitar player named Elvis Chang, starts a band with him, moves to New York in the eighties, then returns to the Philippines to make peace with her dying father.

The novel is haunted by the musical spirits of Jimi Hendrix, Sly Stone, and Miles Davis. Writing it provided much-needed catharsis and honored the memory of my "real-life" band. The Gangster Choir came together in my San Francisco garage back in 1975 and disbanded in New York City after a farewell performance at the Kitchen exactly ten years later. The band never managed to land a record deal, but it drew an astonishing group of musicians that came and went over the years. Julian Priester, Butch Morris, Vernon Reid, Linda Tillery, Makoto Horiuchi, Bugsy Moore, Laurie Carlos, Steve Bernstein, Paul Shapiro, Pheeroan AkLaff, etc. etc. All left their indelible mark. When we were good, we were very, very good, and very much of our time was spent grappling with complex combinations of spoken word, music, rhythms, and the very notion of improvisation and "performance." As I write this in 1998, a lot of people take dancing to words for granted, but back then, those dazzling innovations were what we aimed for. In spite of our bumbling attempts to create something "new," to break down musical and social barriers, we were also acutely aware of the political contradictions inherent in making art and making commerce.

I sometimes miss the reckless days of rock 'n' roll band life. Not the bickering, ego-crunching, sexist, rope-a-dope paranoia part of it, but the delicious, exhilarating, creative, and divine part. Connecting to an audience—even for a brief, fleeting moment—could be heaven on earth. And hell, too.

This excerpt from *The Gangster of Love*, in which Rocky Rivera and Elvis Chang confront the ghost of Jimi Hendrix, is intended as a sort of defiant celebration of rebel music and the many strange ways of becoming American.

[*Interior of an empty nightclub. Midafternoon. A tape loop of "Voodoo Chile" plays on the soundtrack. Elvis and Rocky are kissing passionately, ensconced in a booth. Sitting across from the kissing couple is a bemused Jimi Hendrix, as he looked in 1970, the year he died. Black Western gear and a silver conch belt studded with turquoise, black sombrero, and sunglasses. A bib stained with wine and vomit is tied around Jimi's neck.*]

Elvis: Listen to your own words. "Oh, the night I was born, the moon turned a fire red." You were in sync with the times, but ahead of it too. Before you, there was no one. Maybe Chuck Berry. Maybe Little Richard. I was into Chuck Berry, just like every other guitar player in the world. I memorized all his licks. And that jagged chunka-chunka thing in all them James Brown classics. Juicy horn riffs.

Jimi: Maceo.

Rocky: That groove on "Cold Sweat." You know it?

Jimi: Say, beautiful. Of course I know it.

Rocky: [*trying to appease him*] I meant "you know it." Like you *know* it. Not you don't know it? Know what I mean? [*pause*] Why are you wearing that bib?

Jimi: To protect my shirt, ha ha.

Rocky: Now it's my turn to be offended.

Jimi: Sorry, beautiful. I'm feeling blue. Desolate and blue. [*He looks around the room indifferently.*] Nothing's changed.

Rocky: Take off those glasses. Let me see your eyes.

[*Jimi takes off glasses slowly.*]

Listen to the wail of your feedback, so fierce against the drummer's desperate flailing and bashing. What was his name?

Jimi: Noel. [*puts glasses back on*]

Rocky: Whatever. He can't keep up. He's drowning. The song winds down, the song's about to end. Hey, it was Mitch Mitchell on drums, wasn't it?

Jimi: You mean *whomever*, don't you? God, I am so bored with that song! Keyboards like a funhouse circus, the bass thumping. Aren't you sick of it? And I'm singin' so earnestly! They never said I *couldn't* sing, but shit. I hate *earnest*. God in a roomful of mirrors. Music is strange like that. Do this old man a favor and *turn the goddam song off!* [*pause*] Nothing interests me here. It's all about money.

Elvis: Three things to remember, old man. *Uno*, we can hardly afford to rehearse. *Dos*, hindsight is easy. *Tres*, Rocky is saved.

Jimi: Put anything else on. I don't give a fuck. Funkadelic! Prince! The Art Ensemble of Chicago!

Rocky: I was fourteen years old when you died. My brother was seventeen. He wanted to play guitar like you so bad, it paralyzed him. [*pause*] If you listen carefully, the "Voodoo Chile" melody is exactly the same as "Catfish Blues."

Jimi: I loved being taken care of. All I wanted to worry about was music. Those Europeans gave me carte blanche. "What is it you want to do, Jimi?" they asked me. "Would you like to present a big work, or something intimate for forty people?" [*laughs, pleased with himself.*]

Rocky: If you listen carefully, "Voodoo Chile" follows "Catfish Blues."

Jimi: Are you accusing me of plagiarizing? Do this old man a favor and turn that fucker off! [*looks around the room, agitated.*] Garçon! Garçon! Goddamit, where's service when you need it, *s'il vous plaît.*

Rocky: I believe we're in the South Bronx.

Elvis: [*embarrassed*] Sorry. We'll come back later. [*gets up to leave, but Rocky pulls him back into his seat.*]

Rocky: [*to Jimi*] We're in London, eternally twenty-seven years old, in honor of you. Why are you afraid? This is a beautiful song. *You wrote it.*

You sang it. Before you, there was no one. Accept your role in history. Flames bursting out of your skull. Salvation funky. Redemption funky.

Jimi: Redemption? [*laughs*] I sure as hell can't relate to that, sister.

Rocky: Why are you wearing that bib?

[*Jimi chuckles. Rocky climbs up on the table and starts to dance wildly. Just as abruptly, she sits back down.*]

Jimi: "Not enough grease." "Too much grease." These kids, they're like piranhas gnawing at me. I got tired of being critiqued. Do I play like the white boys? Do I fuck too many white women? I always wanted some of that white boy money. What a dilemma. Shit. I'm just a country boy.

Elvis: I'm just a country boy, too, Oakland country. My pop taught me to love the blues. Sounds just like Chinese music, he said. He gave me my name, didn't he? And I took a lotta shit for it.

Jimi: Your father named you after a clown and a thief. You know what Elvis the Pelvis once said? "Ain't nothin' a nigger can do for me but shine my shoes." [*to Rocky*] And what about you, beautiful? Why you try so hard to be a man?

Rocky: You sound just like my mother.

Jimi: Fuck me, then. Save my soul.

Rocky: Let's get one thing straight. You can't fool me. I know all about you. I was fourteen when you died, but I'm not stupid. Did you die with that bib on?

Jimi: Have you any idea how much pussy was thrown at me?

Elvis: [*to Rocky*] Will you quit blaming him for everything? Damn, I wish Sly were here. [*to Jimi*] Sorry about her. She's volatile. [*pause*] Our friend Sly, if he coulda met you, if he coulda jammed with you, he'd've died a happy man.

Rocky: But he didn't. No stairway to heaven for that poor sonuvabitch. Sly was shot full of holes because he was stupid, and now he's burning up in hell.

Jimi: [*to Rocky*] It's a thin line between love and hate, and you sure got a filthy mouth. [*to Elvis*] *Please*. Feel free to call me Jimi. [*to Rocky*] Say beautiful, can you calm down enough to spare this old man one of those Indonesian cigarettes? If I have to listen to this same old tired song all night long—[*pause as he lights up and exhales gratefully*] Ahhh. Smells good, don't it? Like a man's perfume. Sweet fire. [*sheepish*] I've tried cutting down, but it just don't work.

Elvis: You get the joke, right? We did a cover of "Voodoo Chile."

Rocky: Your song.

Jimi: No kidding.

Elvis: It was Rocky's idea to do it. She absolutely loved you, man.

Jimi: [*smiling at Rocky*] Is it true? You absolutely loved me?

Rocky: Still do.

Elvis: She did. We all did. She said, "Face it. We'll never write a song as simple and as good as this one." We always gave you the proper credit. [*Hendrix laughs.*]

Rocky: How come you played dead for so long?

Jimi: I had no choice. Sorry.

Rocky: I throw a party in your honor every year, on the anniversary of your death, which is also the anniversary of our coming to America. You know that? Of course you don't. [*pause*] Has anyone ever asked you if you were Filipino? You look like you might have some of that blood.

Jimi: What blood?

Rocky: *Filipino blood.* Damn, aren't you listening? Haven't you heard a thing I've said? Everybody I love is dead or dying. I have outlived most of my friends. I have a baby—somewhere. [*frantically looks under the table*] Oh my God, where did I put the baby? [*to Hendrix*] Do you have any children? Lookit you, sitting there so sad and sorry and horny. A dirty bib tied around your neck stinking of vomit. Why'd you go and die and have to be so predictable?

Jimi: Thought I was a mystic, thought I was blessed. Thought that was enough. Chewed peyote. Wrote psychedelic poetry. Believed my own press, my cocaine-induced, rainbow warrior, ghetto royalty, gypsy freedom fighter, LSD-laced, corny, cosmicomic mythology. I wasn't as bad as you think, was I?

[*Jimi and Rocky start singing*] I'm a voodoo chile / voodoo chile / voodoo chile / voodoo chile.

I played guitar with my tongue, set it on fire, and the whole world, too.

What more do you want from me? I don't owe you or anyone else an apology, beautiful. The nights were long, the dogs kept howlin'. Like Edith Piaf usedta moan, *Je ne regrette rien.*

[*Rocky leans over and slips off Hendrix's sunglasses before kissing him on the lips. It is a long, meaningful kiss. Elvis picks up Hendrix's burning cigarette and smokes it. He studies their passionate clinch with detached interest. "Voodoo Chile" audio fades up as this last image fades to black.*]

As appeared in the
NEW YORK POST

The man behind the Vanguard

Analogues of Mourning,

Mourning the Analog

Writing in his 1936 book on black music, with his fellow African Americans especially on his mind, Alain Locke, the great sage of the Harlem Renaissance, described the modern black peoples of the Americas as the "troubadours" of the Western world. Sixty or so years later, though we can argue about where the curtain might have come down, I think we can safely say that the era in which that assertion was plausible is over. His choice of that medieval word to identify that special role was poignant even then, and troubadours are an anachronistic presence these days. The forms of entertainment that they traded were bound to expressive conventions lost long ago. Maybe the special period of creativity that Locke's words summon ended with the demise of the phonograph, which was the principal vehicle for so many subversive possibilities in days gone by.

The link between music and black life is no longer what it was. The role and significance of music have been transformed, there's nothing to be gained by denying the full extent of those historic shifts. They mark the passage from an affirmative to a compensatory mode of engagement with music. To put it more bluntly still, the countercultural force of popular music has ebbed, and whatever desperate assertions we might want to make to the contrary, music is no longer the privileged center of black cultural life. It still has a role, but I fear that its importance, though present, is increasingly residual. To mythify music's past dominance as though it still endured is to mystify our cultural history. What response is appropriate? A comprehensive history of that special period in which phonographic technology first made black music into a planetary force remains to be written. But the memory of that time haunts us in the shadow of its demise. Mourning is one of several commemorative practices of memory that should be considered carefully. A variety of mourning is an appropriate response to our new "post-troubadour" predicament,

Anthony Barboza, *Untitled (Office Wall, Village Vanguard)*, 1988 though I wouldn't want our analogues of mourning to be transposed into the self-defeating processes involved in mourning the passing of the analog.

I feel obliged to confess that my own critical standpoint has been shaped by a sense of loss that is my demographic, geographical, and generational affliction, though it hasn't felt like a curse until recently. Lawrence Grossberg has explained some of the reasons why the compulsion to speak in this autobiographical register overwhelms us. I don't want to capitulate to the absurd pressures that dictate a nostalgic relationship to the latter part of that departed Golden Age in which Bob Marley could disclose, without putting his creole authenticity on the line, that his favorite tune was the Beatles' song "All You Need Is Love."

I remember a great parade of black-Atlantic, of black-American, performers flowing through London's musical scenes, beginning in 1969, when I started going out to hear live music at the Saville, the Albert Hall, the Rainbow, and the Roundhouse. More recently, digital audio, stagnation, and what we could politely call recycling have intervened to make live music less pleasurable, and, in my view, less live, than it once was. That fundamental change has brought on an insistent and gnawing sense of loss that gets stronger by the day. This loss involves grieving for a certain fragile, precious relationship between black music and black politics in which the former amended, stretched, and enriched the latter. It encompasses a yearning for a certain quality of engagement and profundity in the music itself—something that I do recall, though I doubt my capacity to recall those joyous nights with the Voices of East Harlem, Curtis Mayfield, James Brown, Jimi Hendrix, Freddie King, Bob Marley, and the rest. It's a sadness provoked by my recollections of a long-vanished ontological depth, a lost ethical flavor in our face-to-face, prevideo transculture. This is something that Kathleen Hanna also seems to identify when she talks about the strange *flatness* of the expectations of her audience. The signature quality of my loss might be defined by the departed vitality of music made and heard in real time. It is a yearning also for a public culture in which the dimensions of art and life in our complex practice as a collectivity dissolve into each other.

This loss is compounded by a desire for a time and space when there might still have been a barrier between the world of entertainment and the world of advertising. This was a time in which I recall, wrongly no doubt, that a sort of folded, interior, antiphonic dialogue between voice and guitar was still a reliable indicator of the well-being of something more than just the health of the individuals who gave voice to it. This was also a moment when it was still fruitful to ask, in a setting provided by a dynamic oppositional mood, that fateful, heroic question: "What did I do to be so black and so blue?" We could ask it transnationally, ask it almost placelessly, ask it in the utopian key that was defined for me as a teenager, by that small, promising window through which the New Minister of the Super Heavy Funk had observed the joyous, transgressive activities of the long-haired hippies and the Afro-blacks partying on the good foot. You might remember that, too. It was adjacent to another promising location: the one from which Sly Stone had surveyed the political debris of the sixties, and made his "Sex Machine" a piece of music without words—a piece of music directed at the awareness that words would never, could never be enough to tell that misanthropic, race-transcending tale. I didn't like the fuzz-bass solo that Larry Graham contributed, but I still like to think about what that extraordinary struggle with the limits of the harmonica means.

Now we Diaspora teens were a long way from sweet-home Chicago, but we too could find ourselves in the traveling truths of the people who had now become darker than blue. And there was something about the classic live recordings of that era: they all invited us, beckoned us, solicited us into that utopian collectivity, especially those of Aretha Franklin (*Live at the Fillmore West*), Curtis Mayfield (*Curtis Live*), and especially, for this discussion anyway, Donny Hathaway's *Live*. Think about the role of the audience, the counterpoint that the crowd supplies, for example, in the live version of Hathaway's "The Ghetto." Think about the claims, the promise, the opportunities that are momentarily opened up when Willie Weeks begins to take his chance in "Voices Inside (Everything is Everything)."

Perhaps we need to recall those possibilities now that the special art of live recording has shrunk to fit the kind of hyperreal niche in which we are told jazz is supposed to dwell. Of course, the crowd was a dynamic participant in those performances. Sometime during the preparation for this conference, a sort of strange and exciting rumor reached me in London that Curtis Mayfield might be involved. I was happy at that prospect because I remember as a kind of epiphany the tour that brought him to London in 1970 or 1971, which was partly recorded on *Curtis Live*. So even though he can't be here in the flesh, I want him to be here in this room. I want to remember him. To put it another way, I want to recover his troubadour spirit, and to commemorate it, not to mourn it. Commemorate it. Commemoration is not mourning, but it is another practice of social memory. I want to commemorate, because an imaginary line between Curtis and James Brown constituted an axis of my nascent U.K. black mindset.

Where, in what we now have to call "the age of Tupac," has all that dignity, that bespectacled seriousness, gone? We need it. How did the hopeful, the open-minded insights of "Mighty Mighty" come to sound so out of season? "In foolishness we've all been caught," damn right! and more of that later. The creative model that Curtis furnished us with worked wonders in other places too. In Jamaica, Bunny Livingstone copied his phrasing, but it was Bob Marley who adapted his political imaginings, his timeliness, and his clear-sighted orientation toward a condition that Curtis had struggled to name on "Future Shock." "As wise as serpents, and as weak as lambs," yes indeed. That was the idea that his fragile voice made manifest. I'm inclined here to overlook many of the problems in the workings of that insurgent, but emphatically prefeminist, culture. Its best qualities look like great strengths when compared to the unmemorable forms that succeeded them, which simulated community for commercial ends rather than the people's cause.

An argument could be made about the periodization of the postmodern in the production of black music, but as a more oblique, "sly" way of raising that problem, figured in the progression involved between conjuring culture and iconizing culture, I want to focus on the question of *memory* in what some might see, rather unexpectedly coming from me, as the Afro-centric spirit of homage to some of the great music makers of the recent past. I want to dwell with and revere the generation that has begun to die out. Their decisive input formed a tradition—yes, a tradition—so powerful that their uneulogized and largely, though not absolutely, unmourned deaths have been bewildering. For every James Jameson on a T-shirt, there are others whose faces remain unknown even if the sounds they made are familiar. When I come to New York, I always think of two of them who passed in the last couple of years: Eric Gale and Richard Tee, members of the generation who took the voice of Ray Charles as their fundamental inspiration. I used to go and listen to them in Mikell's. I want to ask you to join me in remembering them, their art and their achievements: their struggles to create an idiom, to find a form adequate to the task of representing the unrepresentable. I do this also to illustrate a point that has to do with a kind of rapport with the presence of death that seems to have been one of the key characteristics of that tradition of music making.

I don't understand the precise mechanisms linking that rapport to a critique of capitalism and its corrosive reification of our culture, but that culture was always something more than just a matter of life and death, and even if the linking between that rapport and a critique of capitalism was a contingent thing, a fortuitous thing, I still think it's something worth remembering, hanging onto. That sense of the proximity of this art to the heightened awareness of death, loss, and suffering betrays a different system of value or judgment that was not merely incompatible with the indices of the market, but was deeply opposed to them. They co-existed, but the cracks were always there. In recognition of Greil Marcus's great insight, we could take something like the *Superfly* soundtrack as a paradigmatic instance of that conflict between the market and the counterculture/counterpower in its critical relationship to the movie. Of course, in those days, film soundtracks were usually made by one artist or group, and a different relationship between sound and image is constructed by the more memorable albums—*Come Back Charleston Blue* (1972), *Let's Do It Again* (1975), *Sparkle* (1976)—than the sort of fragmentary association in, for example, *High School High* (1996) or *Set It Off* (1996). Strange demographic games are now being played with a different phenomenology

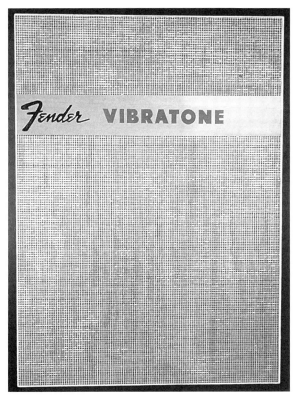

Douglas Wada, *Vibratone*, 1998. Oil on canvas.

of memory. A different ordering of memory has been formed by the total dominance of image over sound.

I also suspect that the long struggle against commodification, which began with the reification of black bodies in racial slavery, is over, too. The artist still known as Prince, bless him, may scrawl that word "slave" on his cheek, but we know he's being paid in full. He derives important benefits from ceding the ownership and control of that well-formed cheek to other folk. We have been forced to yield to the same seductive iconization of a rebel culture by the collusion of its practitioners, their media cheerleaders, their corporate hench people, and their pimps. Though there are performers still around who can swim in those troubled waters—Prince, I guess, among them—most cannot. For my own sake as well as theirs, I want to register a token protest against the destruction of that musical tradition in

the name of its currency in ever-wider markets, against the same fatal collusion in the denial of the form's own rich history, against the systematic
erasure of historic patterns in the relationship between past and present,
because, as you GUI operators out there know, iconization impacts upon
the workings of memory. Icons, like logos, are designed to be unforgettable.
They are simple visual cues; I call them triggers because the poetic language
fostered by the rise of "gangsta rap" is always on my mind. They make
the difficult work of recollection into the simplistic work of association.
Often memory ceases to be work. A society where between thirty-five and
forty percent of adult Americans are functionally illiterate supplies the
context in which we have to think about these techniques of memory and
their service to the industry of marketing.

Musically speaking, the poles between which we must work today—
and I do mean us, a community of commentators—can be represented by
two unsavory, or unsatisfactory, alternatives. On the one hand, there's the
recycling of old ideas, which might look like the continuation of tradition,
but isn't really. Recycling operates without the pleasures that arose from
the initial discovery of the forms. And those who have reaffirmed those
forms have not themselves made any great contribution, nor indeed any
contribution *whatsoever*, to their development. I will call this first stance
the Marsalis option, because it fetishizes technique to produce a sham
authenticity from the hard but beautiful labor involved in mastering that
idiom. On the other hand, there are deskilling, dehumanizing technologies.
Along with disinterest, laziness, and disregard, they have reduced the
whole of that modernist tradition to a lexicon of preconstituted fragments.
This second option I will call the DJ Spooky option, in honor of Paul
Miller's contribution here. That strategy seems to make even the negative
labor of technique redundant. I wouldn't want to accept too swiftly or
casually his suggestion that instruments are entirely obsolete; we are not
yet postinstrumental.

Each of these options has its own characteristic patterns of pseudo-
commemoration. Each promotes an uncomplicated variety of *pastness* to
offset the stress of the immediate. Neither of them is comfortable with
history, and neither of them involves memory work. There seem to be two

urgent areas of memory work that we might want collectively to engage in our discussion. One is actually the memory work involved in the writing of the history of rock: Is it going to be national or transnational? Is it going to be local or translocal? How do those choices factor into what we think rock is? I don't want to give rock to America too quickly—I'd rather think of it as American and something else. It has its own logic of supplementation and accretion. There is clearly a real struggle about the scale upon which that history is to be recovered.

Another thing connected to this issue of American origins is more difficult. I am troubled about the memory work that hasn't been practiced here. This relates to the history of what is too reductively called rock and demands attention to the rockin' romance of "race" and whiteness. Before I came here, I didn't know rock was white, even though it may have "black roots." What that means depends on what kind of roots are being talked about—are they the deep-forest roots of the old arborescent model or the roots found in the jungle, the swamp, and the rainforest? Let's not trivialize the ecological issues lodged in our poetics! The memory work, the official memory of that thing we call rock, local or translocal, should include the explicit sentiments of racism and fascism that have been voiced by people such as David Bowie, Elvis Costello, and Eric Clapton—those things shouldn't be passed over too quickly. Whatever Elvis has to say about the bittersweet genius of the composer Billy Strayhorn, he has also had rather a lot to say about niggers, coons, and monkey music. We should make him face that. The distinguished singer Bonnie Bramlett took a stand on these questions, and I would like to see *that* folded back into the official memory, the memorialization and commemorization processes.

I want to do a roll call, a different roll call than the one that's been done, because I want to suggest that the black participation in rock is more complex than we've let it be. Let's let it breathe and remember, remember these people and the struggles they had and the choices they made: Andy Newmark; Steve Gadd; Mike Bloomfield; Reggie Young (one minute he's playing with Bobby Womack and the next he's playing with Merle Haggard, hiding behind a curtain so people can't see who's playing the guitar); Arthur Lee and Eric Mercury (I never liked anything they did, but I want to affirm their right to exist); Gregory Reeves, Gerald Johnson, and Annie Sampson (the vanguard in that trickle of supposedly hip black bass players and "chick singers" that upholstered the finest products of psychedelia). Where's Ian Levine in the story of house and its dismal offshoots, of how black music became workout music and generic dance music? I want to call the names of Tim Drummond, David Hood, Duck Dunn, Bob Babbitt, Will Lee, and Barry Beckett. Les Back, who has been working on an oral history of the involvement of white musicians in rhythm and blues, told me that Roger Hawkins and Will Lee were once brought together to play on a session. "I thought you were black!" is what they said to each other when they met.

These days, of course, in the planetary-culture industry, there's a trading in blackness going on, which is a different market because blackness often represents a kind of prestige rather than abjection. The shift away from music and toward sports is a decisive way of marking that change. I'm calling for a negative verdict on the culture of simulation that requires music and its pleasures to be moved, to be displaced, from that privileged space acquired at the core of our history, our sociality. Instead they become components in the dubious soundtrack to an even more questionable flow of images: icons.

The disaggregation of the performative moment can be identified as another effect of that fateful change, but there are additional ethical losses involved in the departure from the equilibrium of a performance-centered culture. That development has itself been compounded by political changes, which can be illustrated by the unlikely intergenerational alliance of KRS-One, Gil Scott-Heron, and Nike. Whatever Gil did with "The Bottle," he's now telling us that the revolution *will* be televised after all. He's being paid to tell us that so we'll go and buy those damn shoes.

In addition, the mechanization and the militarization of rhythm are being practiced under the sign of generic dance music. House and its proliferating "technocratic" offshoots culminate in a kind of imprisonment of rhythm. Rhythm is under house arrest. Frail, feeble, and funky humanity has been expelled and the sinuous warmth of real-time bass and drums is largely surplus to requirements. Surprisingly, the phrase "the regression of listening" springs to mind to make some sense of this, for ears are no longer tuned in to the possibility of distinguishing the sampled from the played, the sequenced and quantized from those older but still supple forms of interactivity that characterized music made in a culture of listening for a community of listeners. We should address the end of this version of community: we've lost our *minoritarian*, dissident public sphere. Raymond Williams was prescient about "moving privatization." I'd want to suggest that a culture of loneliness exists there, not isolation or solitude, but loneliness marked by the desire for forms of sociality to which the market provides an inadequate answer.

Spike Lee's symptomatic stardom can yet again usefully encapsulate some wider historical tendencies. How and why was the promotional tour for his film *Get on the Bus* sponsored by the brewers Anheuser-Busch? Spike also announced his unprecedented commercial collaboration with the advertising giant DDB Needham in the formation of a new advertising agency to be called Spike DDB. It is a historic marriage not only for the fact that DDB actually called Spike an "icon" in the press release announcing the new venture but it also provides a corporate imprimatur on the American "urban consumer," who now fixes patterns for selling and using profitable products. The culture industry is prepared to make substantial investments to yield a user-friendly reading or translation of that stubbornly oracular vernacular. The needs of African American and indeed black-Atlantic political cultures can only look parochial when contrasted with that glittering, post-traditional possibility. But in what might be heard as the last gasp of the *Superfly* strategy, Curtis reached out from his wheelchair toward the future with the song "The New World Order," which was then grabbed and folded into the soundtrack of *Get on the Bus*. His voice and moral authority are still potent. It was interesting that Spike had to conscript them as a means to bring the noble past into the service of a regimented and nationalistic present.

Our history, then, from modern racial slavery on down, conveys an important message: the destructive advance of capitalism and its cultural industry demands the liquidation of memory and the colonization of those capacities for recollection that have utopian and oppositional potential. In his unwholesome nineteenth-century raciological inquiries into the idea of nationality, Ernst Renan argued that there was an active contradiction between the demands of nation-building and those of historical study. The nation and its new time involved for him some socialized forms of forgetting and historical error. A kind of orchestrated amnesia supplied the climate in which the nation's novel principles of belonging and solidarity could become attractive and powerful. It would be a tragic irony if the operations of a postmodern, market-savvy black nationalism, currently being supervised by formations such as Spike DDB and, indeed, *Vibe* magazine, required the erasure of a complex cultural history of the period that preceded it, the very period that produced these exciting, communicative opportunities in the first place.

Bibliography

Acker, Kathy. *Pussy, King of the Pirates.* New York: Grove Press, 1996.

Ammann, Judith, ed. *Who's Been Sleeping in My Brain?: Post-Punk Interviews.* Frankfurt am Main: Edition Suhrkamp, 1987.

Arnold, Gina. *Kiss This: Punk in the Present Tense.* New York: St. Martin's Griffin, 1997.

Arnold, Gina. *Route 666: On the Road to Nirvana.* New York: St. Martin's Press, 1993.

Azerrad, Michael. *Come As You Are: The Story of Nirvana.* New York: Doubleday, 1993.

Azerrad, Michael, and Charles Peterson. *Screaming Life: A Chronicle of the Seattle Music Scene.* New York: Harper-Collins, 1995.

Baldauf, Anette, and Katharina Weingartner, eds. *Lips. Tits. Hits. Power?: Popkultur und Feminismus.* Vienna: Folio, 1998.

Bangs, Lester. *Psychotic Reactions and Carburetor Dung.* Ed. Greil Marcus. New York: Knopf, 1987.

Block, Adrienne Fried, and Carol Neuls Bates, eds. *Women in American Music: A Bibliography of Music and Literature.* Westport, Conn.: Greenwood Press, 1979.

Bright, Susie. *Sexual State of the Union.* New York: Simon & Schuster, 1997.

Burchill, Julie, and Tony Parsons. *"The Boy Looked at Johnny": The Obituary of Rock and Roll.* London: Pluto Press, 1978.

Butler, Judith. *Gender Trouble: Feminism and the Subversion of Identity.* New York: Routledge, 1990.

Canetti, Elias. *Crowds and Power.* Trans. Carol Stewart. New York: Viking Press, 1962.

Cantwell, Robert. *Bluegrass Breakdown: The Making of the Old Southern Sound.* New York: Da Capo Press, 1984.

Cantwell, Robert. *When We Were Good: The Folk Revival.* Cambridge, Mass.: Harvard University Press, 1996.

Carey, James W. *Communication as Culture: Essays on Media and Society.* Boston: Unwin, 1988.

Chambers, Iain. *Urban Rhythms: Pop Music and Popular Culture.* New York: St. Martin's Press, 1985.

Chapple, Steve, and Reebee Garofalo. *Rock 'n' Roll Is Here to Pay: The History and Politics of the Music Industry.* Chicago: Nelson-Hall, 1977.

Christgau, Robert. *Christgau's Record Guide: The Eighties.* New York: Pantheon Books, 1990.

Christgau, Robert. *Christgau's Record Guide: Rock Albums of the Seventies.* New Haven: Ticknor & Fields, 1981.

Christgau, Robert. *Grown Up All Wrong: 75 Great Rock and Pop Artists from Vaudeville to Techno.* Cambridge, Mass.: Harvard University Press, 1998.

Collins, Jim. *Uncommon Cultures: Popular Culture and Postmodernism.* New York: Routledge, 1989.

Costello, Mark, and David Foster Wallace, eds. *Signifying Rappers: Rap and Race in the Urban Present.* New York: Ecco Press, 1990.

Crafts, Susan D., et al., eds. *My Music.* Hanover, N.H.: University Press of New England, 1993.

Creekmur, Corey, and Alexander Doty, eds. *Out in Culture: Gay, Lesbian, and Queer Essays on Popular Culture.* Durham, N.C.: Duke University Press, 1995.

Currie, Cherie, and Neal Shusterman. *Neon Angel: The Cherie Currie Story.* Los Angeles: Price Stern Sloan, 1989.

Curtis, Deborah. *Touching at a Distance: Ian Curtis and Joy Division.* London: Faber & Faber, 1995.

Dahl, Linda. *Stormy Weather: The Music and Lives of a Century of Jazzwomen.* New York: Pantheon Books, 1984.

Dannen, Fredric. *Hit Men: Power Brokers and Fast Money Inside the Music Business.* New York: Times Books, 1990.

Davis, Angela Y. *Blues Legacies and Black Feminism: Gertrude "Ma" Rainey, Bessie Smith, and Billie Holiday.* New York: Pantheon, 1998.

DeCurtis, Anthony. *Rocking My Life Away: Writing About Music and Other Matters.* Durham: Duke University Press, 1998.

DeCurtis, Anthony. *Rolling Stone Images of Rock & Roll.* Ed. Fred Woodward. Boston: Little, Brown, 1995.

DeCurtis, Anthony, ed. *Present Tense: Rock & Roll and Culture.* Durham: Duke University Press, 1992.

DeCurtis, Anthony, and James Henke, eds. *The Rolling Stone Illustrated History of Rock and Roll: The Definitive History of the Most Important Artists and Their Music.* New York: Random House, 1992.

Denisoff, R. Serge. *Inside MTV.* New Brunswick, N.J.: Transaction Books, 1988.

Denisoff, R. Serge. *Solid Gold: The Popular Record Industry.* New Brunswick, N.J.: Transaction Books, 1975.

Denisoff, R. Serge. *Tarnished Gold: The Record Industry Revisited.* New Brunswick, N.J.: Transaction Books, 1986.

Dent, Gina, ed. *Black Popular Culture: A Project by Michele Wallace.* Seattle: Bay Press, in association with Dia Center for the Arts, New York, 1992.

DeRogatis, Jim. *Kaleidoscope Eyes: Psychedelic Rock from the '60s to the '90s.* Secaucus, N.J.: Carol Pub. Group, 1996.

Des Barres, Pamela. *I'm with the Band: Confessions of a Groupie.* New York: Beech Tree Books, 1987.

Des Barres, Pamela. *Rock Bottom: Dark Moments in Music Babylon.* New York: St. Martin's Press, 1996.

Douglas, Susan J. *Where the Girls Are: Growing Up Female with the Mass Media.* New York: Times Books, 1994.

Draper, Robert. *Rolling Stone Magazine: The Uncensored History.* New York: Doubleday, 1990.

Early, Gerald. *One Nation under a Groove: Motown and American Culture.* Hopewell, N.J.: Ecco Press, 1995.

Eddy, Chuck. *The Accidental Evolution of Rock 'n' Roll: A Misguided Tour through Popular Music.* New York: Da Capo Press, 1997.

Eddy, Chuck. *Stairway To Hell: The 500 Best Heavy-Metal Albums in the Universe.* New York: Harmony Books, 1991.

Evans, Liz. *Girls Will Be Boys: Women Report on Rock.* London: Pandora, 1997.

Evans, Liz, ed. *Women, Sex, and Rock 'n' Roll: In Their Own Words.* London: Pandora, 1994.

Faithfull, Marianne, with David Dalton. *Faithfull: An Autobiography.* Boston: Little, Brown, 1994.

Ferguson, Russell, et al., eds. *Discourses: Conversations in Postmodern Art and Culture.* Cambridge: MIT Press, in association with the New Museum of Contemporary Art, New York 1990.

Fiske, John. *Media Matters: Everyday Culture and Political Change.* Minneapolis: University of Minnesota Press, 1994.

Fiske, John. *Power Plays, Power Works.* New York: Verso, 1993.

Fiske, John. *Reading the Popular.* Boston: Unwin Hyman, 1989.

Frank, Lisa, and Paul Smith, eds. *Madonnarama: Essays on Sex and Popular Culture.* Pittsburgh, Pa.: Cleis Press, 1993.

Frith, Simon. *Music for Pleasure: Essays in the Sociology of Pop.* Cambridge: Polity Press, in association with Blackwell, 1988.

Frith, Simon. *Performing Rites: On the Value of Popular Music.* New York: Oxford University Press, 1996.

Frith, Simon. *Sound Effects: Youth, Leisure, and the Politics of Rock 'n' Roll.* New York: Pantheon Books, 1981.

Frith, Simon, ed. *Facing the Music: A Pantheon Guide to Popular Culture.* New York: Pantheon Books, 1988.

Frith, Simon, and Andrew Goodwin, eds. *On Record: Rock, Pop, and the Written Word.* New York: Pantheon Books, 1990.

Frith, Simon, Andrew Goodwin, and Lawrence Grossberg, eds. *Sound and Vision: The Music-Video Reader.* New York: Routledge, 1993.

Gaar, Gillian G., *She's a Rebel: The History of Women in Rock & Roll.* Seattle, Wash.: Seal Press, 1992.

Gaines, Donna. *Teenage Wasteland: Suburbia's Dead-End Kids.* New York: Pantheon Books, 1991.

Garofalo, Reebee. *Rockin' Out: Popular Music in the U.S.A.* Boston: Allyn and Bacon, 1997.

Garofalo, Reebee, ed. *Rockin' the Boat: Mass Music and Mass Movements.* Boston: South End Press, 1992.

George, Nelson. *Buppies, B-Boys, Baps, & Bohos: Notes on Post-Soul Black Culture.* New York: HarperCollins, 1992.

George, Nelson. *The Death of Rhythm & Blues.* New York: Pantheon, 1988.

George, Nelson. *Hip-Hop America.* New York: Viking, 1998.

George, Nelson. *Where Did Our Love Go?: The Rise & Fall of the Motown Sound.* New York: St. Martin's Press, 1985.

George-Warren, Holly, and Patricia Romanowski, eds. *The New Rolling Stone Encyclopedia of Rock and Roll.* New York: Fireside, 1995.

Gill, John. *Queer Noises: Male and Female Homosexuality in Twentieth-Century Music.* Minneapolis: University of Minnesota Press, 1995.

Gillett, Charlie. *The Sound of the City: The Rise of Rock and Roll.* London: Souvenir Press, 1983.

Gilmore, Mikal. *Night Beat: A Shadow History of Rock & Roll.* New York: Doubleday, 1998.

Gilroy, Paul. *The Black Atlantic: Modernity and Double Consciousness.* Cambridge, Mass.: Harvard University Press, 1993.

Gilroy, Paul. *Small Acts: Thoughts on the Politics of Black Cultures.* New York: Serpent's Tail, 1993.

Gilroy, Paul. *"There Ain't No Black in the Union Jack": The Cultural Politics of Race and Nation.* London: Hutchinson, 1987.

Goodman, Fred. *The Mansion on the Hill: Dylan, Young, Geffen, Springsteen, and the Head-On Collision of Rock and Commerce.* New York: Times Books, 1997.

Graham, Dan. *Rock My Religion: Writing and Art Projects 1965–90.* Ed. Brian Wallis. Cambridge, Mass.: MIT Press, 1993.

Green, Karen, and Tristan Taormino. *A Girl's Guide to Taking Over the World: Writings from the Girl 'Zine Revolution.* New York: St. Martin's Griffin, 1997.

Grossberg, Lawrence. *Bringing It All Back Home: Essays on Cultural Studies.* Durham, N.C.: Duke University Press, 1997.

Grossberg, Lawrence. *Dancing in Spite of Myself: Essays on Popular Culture.* Durham, N.C.: Duke University Press, 1997.

Grossberg, Lawrence. *Mediamaking: Mass Media in a Popular Culture.* Thousand Oaks, Calif.: Sage Publications, 1998.

Grossberg, Lawrence. *We Gotta Get Out of This Place: Popular Conservatism and Postmodern Culture.* New York: Routledge, 1992.

Grossberg, Lawrence, Cary Nelson, and Paula A. Treichler, eds. *Cultural Studies.* New York: Routledge, 1992.

Guralnick, Peter. *Feel Like Going Home: Portraits in Blues and Rock 'n' Roll.* 1971; reprint New York: Vintage Books, 1981.

Guralnick, Peter. *Last Train to Memphis: The Rise of Elvis Presley.* Boston: Little, Brown, 1994.

Hagedorn, Jessica. *Danger and Beauty.* New York: Penguin, 1993.

Hagedorn, Jessica. *Dangerous Music.* San Francisco: Momo's Press, 1975.

Hagedorn, Jessica. *Dogeaters.* New York: Pantheon Books, 1990.

Hagedorn, Jessica. *The Gangster of Love.* Boston: Houghton Mifflin, 1996.

Hall, Stuart. *Minimal Selves.* ICA Document 6. London: Institute of Contemporary Arts, 1988.

Hall, Stuart, et al., eds. *Culture, Media, Language: Working Papers in Cultural Studies, 1972–79.* London: Hutchinson, 1980.

Hall, Stuart, and Tony Jefferson, eds. *Resistance through Rituals: Youth Subcultures in Post-War Britain.* London: Hutchinson, 1976.

Hay, James, Lawrence Grossberg, Ellen Wartella, eds. *The Audience and Its Landscape.* Boulder: Westview Press, 1996.

Hebdige, Dick. *Cut 'n' Mix: Culture, Identity, and Caribbean Music.* New York: Methuen, 1987.

Hebdige, Dick. *Subculture: The Meaning of Style.* London: Methuen, 1979.

Henderson, David. *'Scuse Me While I Kiss the Sky: The Life of Jimi Hendrix.* New York: Bantam Books, 1996.

Heylin, Clinton. *Bootleg: The Secret History of the Other Recording Industry.* New York: St. Martin's Griffin, 1996.

Heylin, Clinton. *From the Velvets to the Voidoids: A Pre-Punk History for a Post-Punk World.* New York: Penguin Books, 1993.

Heylin, Clinton. *The Penguin Book of Rock & Roll Writing.* New York: Penguin Group, 1992.

Hickey, Dave. *Air Guitar: Essays on Art and Democracy.* Los Angeles: Art issues. Press, 1997.

Hickey, Dave. *The Invisible Dragon: Four Essays on Beauty.* Los Angeles: Art issues. Press, 1993.

Hickey, Dave. *Prior Convictions: Stories from the Sixties.* Dallas: Southern Methodist University Press, 1989.

Hirshey, Gerri. *Nowhere to Run: The Story of Soul Music.* New York: Times Books, 1984.

Holiday, Billie, with William Dufty. *Lady Sings the Blues.* 1956; reprint New York: Lancer Books, 1972.

Kaplan, E. Ann. *Rocking Around the Clock: Music Television, Postmodernism, and Consumer Culture.* New York: Methuen, 1987.

Keil, Charles, and Steven Feld, *Music Grooves.* Chicago: University of Chicago Press, 1994.

Kennealy, Patricia. *Strange Days: My Life With and Without Jim Morrison.* New York: Dutton, 1992.

Kennedy, Pagan. *'Zine: How I Spent Six Years of My Life in the Underground and Finally Found Myself—I Think.* New York: St. Martin's Griffin, 1995.

Kent, Nick. *The Dark Stuff: Selected Writings on Rock Music, 1972–95.* New York: Da Capo Press, 1995.

Kureishi, Hanif, and Jon Savage, eds. *The Faber Book of Pop.* Boston: Faber and Faber, 1995.

Larson, Jonathan, and Evelyn McDonnell, with Katherine Silberger. *Rent.* New York: Rob Weisbach Books: 1997.

Leonardi, Susan J., and Rebecca Pope. *The Diva's Mouth: Body, Voice, Prima-Donna Politics.* New Brunswick, N.J.: Rutgers University Press, 1996.

Leppert, Richard, and Susan McClary, eds. *Music and Society: The Politics of Composition, Performance, and Reception.* New York: Cambridge University Press, 1987.

Lewis, Lisa A. *The Adoring Audience: Fan Culture and Popular Media.* New York: Routledge, 1992.

Lipsitz, George. *Dangerous Crossroads: Popular Music, Postmodernism, and the Poetics of Place.* New York: Verso, 1994.

Lipsitz, George. *Time Passages: Collective Memory and American Popular Culture.* Minneapolis: University of Minnesota Press, 1990.

Longhurst, Brian. *Popular Music and Society.* Cambridge: Polity, 1995.

Lull, James. *Popular Music and Communication.* Newbury Park, Calif.: Sage Publications, 1987.

Lydon, John, with Keith and Kent Zimmerman. *Rotten: No Irish, No Blacks, No Dogs: The Authorized Autobiography of Johnny Rotten of the Sex Pistols.* New York: St. Martin's Press, 1994.

Marcus, Greil. *Dead Elvis: A Chronicle of a Cultural Obsession.* New York: Doubleday, 1991.

Marcus, Greil. *The Dustbin of History.* Cambridge, Mass.: Harvard University Press, 1995.

Marcus, Greil. *In the Fascist Bathroom: Writings on Punk, 1977–92.* New York: Penguin Books, 1994.

Marcus, Greil. *Invisible Republic: Bob Dylan's Basement Tapes.* New York: Henry Holt & Company. 1997.

Marcus, Greil. *Lipstick Traces: A Secret History of the Twentieth Century.* Cambridge, Mass.: Harvard University Press, 1989.

Marcus, Greil. *Mystery Train: Images of America in Rock 'n' Roll Music.* New York: E. P. Dutton, 1975.

Marcus, Greil. *Ranters & Crowd Pleasers: Punk in Pop Music, 1977–92.* New York: Anchor Books, 1994.

Marsh, Dave. *Born to Run: The Bruce Springsteen Story.* Garden City, N.Y.: Dolphin Books, 1979.

Marsh, Dave. *Fortunate Son: Criticism and Journalism by America's Best-Known Rock Writer.* New York: Random House, 1985.

Marsh, Dave. *Louie, Louie: The History and Mythology of the World's Most Famous Rock 'n' Roll Song.* New York: Hyperion, 1993.

Marsh, Dave, and John Swenson, eds. *The New Rolling Stone Record Guide.* New York: Random House/Rolling Stone Press, 1983.

Martin, Linda, and Kerry Segrave. *Anti-Rock: The Opposition to Rock 'n' Roll.* Hamden, Conn.: Archon Books, 1988.

McClary, Susan. *Feminine Endings: Music, Gender, and Sexuality.* Minneapolis: University of Minnesota Press, 1991.

McDonnell, Evelyn, and Ann Powers, eds. *Rock She Wrote.* New York: Delta, 1995.

McNeil, Legs, and Gillian McCain, eds. *Please Kill Me: The Uncensored Oral History of Punk.* New York: Grove Press, 1996.

McRobbie, Angela. *British Fashion Design: Rag Trade or Image Industry?* New York: Routledge, 1998.

McRobbie, Angela. *Feminism and Youth Culture: From "Jackie" to "Just Seventeen."* Boston: Unwin Hyman, 1991.

McRobbie, Angela. *Postmodernism and Popular Culture.* New York: Routledge, 1994.

McRobbie, Angela, ed. *Back to Reality?: Social Experience and Cultural Studies.* Manchester: Manchester University Press, 1997.

McRobbie, Angela, ed. *Zoot Suits and Second-Hand Dresses: An Anthology of Fashion and Music.* Boston: Unwin Hyman, 1988.

McRobbie, Angela, and Mica Nava, eds. *Gender and Generation.* Houndmills, Basingstoke, Hampshire: Macmillan, 1984.

Mekons, *United.* Lakeland, Fla.: Polk Museum of Art, in association with Quarterstick Records, 1996.

Meltzer, Richard. *The Aesthetics of Rock.* New York: Da Capo, 1970.

Mercer, Mick. *Gothic Rock.* Los Angeles: Cleopatra, 1993.

Middlebrook, Diane Wood. *Suits Me: The Double Life of Billy Tipton.* Boston: Houghton Mifflin, 1998.

Mitchell, Tony. *Popular Music and Local Identity: Rock, Pop, and Rap in Europe and Oceania.* New York: Leicester University Press, 1996.

Morris, Meaghan. *Upward Mobility: Popular Genres and Cultural Change.* Bloomington: University of Indiana Press, 1998.

Murray, Charles Shaar. *Crosstown Traffic: Jimi Hendrix and Post-War Pop.* London: Faber & Faber, 1989.

Negus, Keith. *Popular Music in Theory.* Cambridge: Polity, 1996.

Nelson, Havelock, and Michael A. Gonzales. *Bring the Noise: A Guide to Rap Music and Hip-Hop Culture.* New York: Harmony Books, 1991.

Neuls-Bates, Carol, ed. *Women in Music: An Anthology of Source Readings from the Middle Ages to the Present.* Boston: Northeastern University Press, 1996.

O'Brien, Lucy. *She Bop: The Definitive History of Women in Rock, Pop, and Soul.* New York: Penguin Books, 1996.

O'Dair, Barbara, ed. *Caught Looking: Feminism, Pornography, and Censorship.* Seattle : Real Comet Press, 1988.

O'Dair, Barbara, ed. *The Rolling Stone Book of Women in Rock: Trouble Girls.* New York: Random House, 1997.

Palac, Lisa. *The Edge of the Bed: How Dirty Pictures Changed My Life.* Boston: Little, Brown, 1998.

Palmer, Robert. *Rock & Roll: An Unruly History.* New York: Harmony Books, 1995.

Pareles, Jon, ed. *The Rolling Stone Encyclopedia of Rock & Roll.* New York: Rolling Stone Press, 1983.

Pavletich, Aida. *Rock-a-Bye, Baby.* Garden City, N.Y.: Doubleday, 1980.

Perkins, Eric, ed. *Droppin' Science: Critical Essays on Rap Music and Hip-Hop Culture.* Philadelphia: Temple University Press, 1996.

Press, Joy, and Simon Reynolds. *The Sex Revolts: Gender, Rebellion and Rock 'n' Roll.* Cambridge, Mass.: Harvard University Press, 1995.

Raphael, Amy. *Grrrls: Viva Rock Divas.* New York: St. Martin's Griffin, 1996.

Reid, Jamie. *Up They Rise.* London: Faber & Faber, 1987.

Reynolds, Simon. *Blissed Out: The Raptures of Rock.* London: Serpent's Tail, 1990.

Reynolds, Simon. *Generation Ecstasy: Into the World of Techno and Rave Culture.* Boston: Little, Brown, 1998.

Robbins, Ira A., ed. *The Trouser Press Record Guide.* New York: Collier Books, 1991.

Rose, Tricia. *Black Noise: Rap Music and Black Culture in Contemporary America.* Hanover, N.H.: University Press of New England, 1994.

Ross, Andrew. *No Respect: Intellectuals and Popular Culture.* New York: Routledge, 1989.

Ross, Andrew, and Tricia Rose, eds. *Microphone Fiends: Youth Music and Youth Culture.* New York: Routledge, 1994.

Ross, Andrew. *Real Love: In Pursuit of Cultural Justice.* New York: New York University Press, 1998.

Rugoff, Ralph. *Circus Americanus.* New York: Verso, 1995.

Rugoff, Ralph. *Scene of the Crime.* Cambridge, Mass.: MIT Press, 1997.

Santelli, Robert. *Aquarius Rising: The Rock Festival Years.* New York: Dell Pub. Co., 1980.

Santelli, Robert. *The Best of the Blues: The 101 Essential Albums.* New York: Penguin Books, 1997.

Santelli, Robert. *The Big Book of Blues: A Biographical Encyclopedia.* New York: Penguin, 1993.

Savage, Jon. *England's Dreaming: Sex Pistols and Punk Rock.* Boston: Faber & Faber, 1991.

Savage, Jon. *The Kinks: The Official Biography.* Boston: Faber & Faber, 1984.

Savage, Jon. *Nirvana in the Studio.* New York: St. Martin's Press, 1997.

Savage, Jon. *Picture Post Idols.* London: Collins & Brown, 1992.

Schwichtenberg, Cathy, ed. *The Madonna Connection: Representational Politics, Subcultural Identities, and Cultural Theory.* Boulder: Westview Press, 1993.

Selvin, Joel. *Summer of Love: The Inside Story of LSD, Rock and Roll, Free Love, and High Times in the Wild '60s.* Plume Books, 1995.

Sexton, Adam, ed. *Desperately Seeking Madonna: In Search of the Meaning of the World's Most Famous Woman.* New York: Delta, 1993.

Sexton, Adam, ed. *Rap on Rap: Straight-Up Talk on Hip-Hop Culture.* New York: Delta, 1995.

Shuker, Roy. *Understanding Popular Music.* London: Routledge, 1994.

Simone, Nina. *I Put a Spell on You.* New York: Pantheon Books, 1992.

Smith, Jean. *The Ghost of Understanding.* Vancouver: Arsenal Pulp Press, 1998.

Smith, Joe. *Off the Record: An Oral History of Popular Music.* New York: Warner Books, 1988.

Smith, Patti. *The Coral Sea.* New York: W. W. Norton, 1996.

Smith, Patti. *Early Work.* New York: W. W. Norton, 1994.

Spungen, Deborah. *And I Don't Want to Live This Life.* New York: Villard Books, 1983.

Starr, Victoria. *k.d. lang: all you get is me.* New York: St. Martin's Press, 1994.

Stein, Arlene. *Sex and Sensibility: Stories of a Lesbian Generation.* Berkeley, Calif.: University of California Press, 1997.

Stein, Arlene, ed. *Sisters, Sexperts, Queers: Beyond the Lesbian Nation.* New York: Plume, 1993.

Swiss, Thomas, John Sloop, and Andrew Herman, eds. *Mapping the Beat.* Oxford: Blackwells, 1998.

Tate, Greg. *Flyboy in the Buttermilk: Essays on Contemporary America.* New York: Simon & Schuster, 1992.

Toop, David. *Ocean of Sound: Aether Talk, Ambient Sound, and Imaginary Worlds.* New York: Serpent's Tail, 1995.

Toop, David. *The Rap Attack: African Jive to New York Hip Hop.* Boston: South End Press, 1984.

Toop, David. *Rap Attack 2: African Rap to Global Hip Hop.* New York: Serpent's Tail, 1994.

Weinstein, Deena. *Heavy Metal: A Cultural Sociology.* New York: Lexington Books, 1991.

Weisbard, Eric, with Craig Marks, eds.. *Spin Alternative Record Guide.* New York: Vintage, 1995.

Willis, Ellen. *Beginning to See the Light: Pieces of a Decade.* New York: Knopf, 1981.

Willis, Ellen. *No More Nice Girls: Countercultural Essays.* Hanover, N.H.: Wesleyan University Press, 1992.

List of Contributors

Anthony DeCurtis is the author of *Rocking My Life Away: Writing About Music and Other Matters* and editor of *Present Tense: Rock & Roll and Culture*. In addition, he is coeditor of the *Rolling Stone Illustrated History of Rock & Roll* and the *Rolling Stone Album Guide*. He is a contributing editor of *Rolling Stone*, and he holds a Ph.D. in American literature from Indiana University.

Katherine Dieckmann is a writer-director who has made music videos for R.E.M., Vic Chesnutt, Everything But the Girl, and Throwing Muses, among others. Her critical writing has appeared in the *Village Voice*, *Artforum*, *Art in America*, and *Spin*. She recently completed her first feature film, *A Good Baby*.

Chuck Eddy is the author of *Stairway to Hell: The 500 Best Heavy-Metal Albums in the Universe* and *The Accidental Evolution of Rock 'n' Roll: A Misguided Tour Through Popular Music*. He currently writes for *Rolling Stone*, *Spin*, *Request*, *Entertainment Weekly*, the *Village Voice*, the *L.A. Weekly*, and *Boston Phoenix*. He lives in Philadelphia, where he recently acquired a pet guinea pig named Eggplant.

Paul Gilroy teaches at Goldsmith's College, University of London. His books include *Small Acts: Thoughts on the Politics of Black Cultures* (Serpent's Tail) and *The Black Atlantic: Modernity and Double Consciousness* (Harvard University Press).

Lawrence Grossberg is the Morris Davis Distinguished Professor of Communications Studies at the University of North Carolina at Chapel Hill. He writes a lot, talks a lot, listens to a lot of music, and plays a lot with his three-year-old son Zachariah.

Jessica Hagedorn is the author of *Dogeaters* and *The Gangster of Love*. She is also a performer and former leader of the band The Gangster Choir.

Kathleen Hanna is a feminist artist who lives in Durham, North Carolina. For seven years, she was a member of Bikini Kill, the band she references throughout this essay. Currently, she is trying to raise money for several film and video projects and recently released a record called *Julie Ruin*.

Pluto is in the middle of **James Hannaham**'s rising sign Virgo. This means he is a natural born critic.

Dave Hickey is currently Associate Professor of Art Criticism and Theory at the University of Nevada, Las Vegas. He is author of *Prior Convictions*, a volume of his short fiction, *The Invisible Dragon: Four Essays on Beauty*, and *Air Guitar: Essays on Art and Democracy*. He has served as executive editor for *Art in America* magazine in New York and as staff songwriter for Glaser Publications in Nashville.

Karen Kelly is Director of Publications at the Dia Center for the Arts, where she edits books on exhibitions and organizes the Discussions in Contemporary Culture series.

Jon Langford is a founding member of the fundamentalist Leeds punk-rock band the Mekons. He is currently exiled in Chicago, where he paints and performs with the Waco Brothers and a protest disco power quartet called the Skull Orchard.

Greil Marcus is the author of *Invisible Republic*, *Lipstick Traces*, and *Mystery Train*. He currently writes monthly columns for *Interview* and *Esquire*. He lives in Berkeley.

Former *Village Voice* music editor **Evelyn McDonnell** has written for *Ms.*, *Rolling Stone*, the *New York Times*, *Spin*, *Request*, *Option*, and *Swing*. She edited with Ann Powers the anthology *Rock She Wrote: Women Write*

About Rock, Pop, and Rap, and wrote with Katherine Silberger the official history of the musical *Rent*. She published and edited the fanzines *Resister* and *OK Go Now*. Her writing is included in several collections, including *A Girl's Guide to Taking Over the World*, *The Spin Guide to Alternative Records*, and *Girljock: The Book*.

Angela McRobbie is Professor of Communications at Goldsmith's College in London. She is author of *British Fashion Design: Rag Trade or Image Industry?* (Routledge, 1998) and the forthcoming *"Deep, Anonymous Murmur": Essays in Cultural Studies* (Routledge, 1999). She is also a cultural critic, writing regularly for a range of magazines and newspapers.

Paul D. Miller a.k.a. DJ Spooky That Subliminal Kid is a New York–based writer and conceptual artist, who has curated many art events and happenings. His records include *Necropolis, Songs of a Dead Dreamer*, and *Riddim Warfare*.

Barbara O'Dair has edited two collections of essays, *The Rolling Stone Book of Women in Rock: Trouble Girls* and *Caught Looking: Women, Pornography, and Censorship*. She is currently the executive editor of *Details* magazine.

Ann Powers is writing a personal history of bohemianism to be published by Simon & Schuster. She has written for the *Village Voice, Spin, Rolling Stone*, the *New York Times*, and many other publications. With Evelyn McDonnell, she edited *Rock She Wrote*. And she's been kissed by Bono.

Toshi Reagon is a singer-songwriter, multi-instrumentalist, and producer. She has toured extensively in the U.S. Her latest recording, *Kindness*, was released in 1997 on the Folkways label. Toshi lives in Brooklyn.

Simon Reynolds is the author of *Blissed Out: The Raptures of Rock* (London: Serpent's Tail, 1990) and the coauthor (with Joy Press) of *The Sex Revolts: Gender, Rebellion, and Rock 'n' Roll* (Cambridge: Harvard University Press, 1995). "Ecstasy Is a Science" is a by-product of *Generation Ecstasy: Into The*

World of Techno and Rave Culture (New York: Little, Brown, 1998). He is a senior editor at *Spin* and a freelance contributor to the *Village Voice*, and the *Wire*, and operates a website, "A White Brit Rave Aesthete Thinks Aloud," at http://members.aol.com/blissout/.

Ralph Rugoff is a cultural critic and curator living in London. His most recent exhibitions and publications include *Scene of the Crime* (MIT Press) and *At the Threshold of the Visible* (Independent Curators, Inc.).

Robert Santelli was Assistant Curator at the Rock and Roll Hall of Fame and Museum before he became Director of Education in 1995. He is the author of several books, including *The Big Book of Blues* and *The Best of the Blues*. Santelli has taught at Monmouth and Rutgers universities in the American studies departments. His most recent work is a book of essays he edited with Emily Davidson entitled *Hard Travelin': The Life and Legacy of Woodie Guthrie* to be published by Wesleyan University Press. Santelli lives in Shaker Heights, Ohio, with his wife and three children.

Jon Savage is author of *Time Travel: Pop, Media, and Sexuality 1976–96*, *England's Dreaming: Anarchy, Sex Pistols, Punk Rock, and Beyond* and *The Faber Book of Pop*. He is also a regular contributor to *Artforum* and *Frieze* magazines.

Arlene Stein teaches and writes about culture, politics and sexuality. Her latest book is *Sex and Sensibility: Stories of a Lesbian Generation* (University of California Press). She is currently writing a book about the "culture wars" in rural Oregon.

Deena Weinstein is Professor of Sociology at DePaul University, where she teaches courses in sociology of rock, mass communications, and popular culture. She is the author of *Heavy Metal: A Cultural Sociology* and *Serious Rock*, as well as books on sociological theory and complex organizations, and many articles on rock music and sociological theory. She is also a rock critic who contributes reviews, interviews, and features to various rock magazines around the world.

Ellen Willis, who was the *New Yorker*'s first rock critic, directs the Cultural Reporting and Criticism program in the journalism department at New York University. Her articles have been collected in two books, *Beginning To See the Light: Sex, Hope, and Rock & Roll* and *No More Nice Girls: Countercultural Essays*. A third book of essays, *The Radical Imagination*, will be published in 1999.

Photo Credits and Permissions

Cover photograph by Nathan Nedorostek; pages 12, 28–29, 115, 132–133, 160, 173, 214, 228–229, Courtesy Corbis-Bettmann; page 16, © MORIMURA Yasumasa, Courtesy of the artist and Luhring Augustine Gallery, New York; page 30, Courtesy of the artist and Marian Goodman Gallery, New York, photo by Bob Goedewaagen; pages 36, 157, 174–175, 182, 198, Courtesy UPI/Corbis-Bettmann; page 47, © 1991 Bob Gruen/Star File Photo Agency, Inc.; pages 50 and 54, Courtesy of Jon Langford; page 56, © Roger Dong, Courtesy Outline; pages 70–71, Photograph by Edy Ferguson, courtesy of the artist; page 72, Photograph by David Ellis/Redfern's/Retna; pages 78, 134, 222, Courtesy of Photofest; page 88, Courtesy of the artists; page 98, Courtesy Reuters/Kimimasa Mayama/Archive Photos; page 122, Courtesy of Kathleen Hanna; page 127, Courtesy of the artist; page 144, Courtesy Tim Boxer/Archive Photos; pages 150–151, 244, © Chuck Pulin/Star File Photo Agency, Inc.; page 152, Courtesy Novosti/Corbis-Bettmann; page 176, Courtesy of the artists; page 192, Courtesy Archive Photos; page 196, Photo by Ed Ruiz; page 206, Courtesy Michel Aphesboro; page 230, Courtesy of the artist; page 233, Courtesy of the artist; page 236, Courtesy of the Rock and Roll Hall of Fame and Museum, Collection of Larry Lund and Bonnie Lund; page 238, Courtesy of the Rock and Roll Hall of Fame and Museum, Collection of the Bee Gees; page 239, Courtesy of the Rock and Roll Hall of Fame and Museum, Collection of Joe Walsh; page 240, Courtesy of the Rock and Roll Hall of Fame and Museum,

Collection of Tom Petty; page 241, Courtesy of the Rock and Roll Hall of Fame and Museum, Gift of Michelle Phillips; page 252, Courtesy MTV; page 260, Courtesy of the artist; page 266, Courtesy of the artist.

Portions of "Love Only Knows" were originally published as "Unbreak My Heart, An Overture" in Dave Hickey's *Air Guitar: Essays on Art and Democracy*, published by Art issues Press in Los Angeles, California. © 1997 The Foundation for Advanced Critical Studies, Inc. Reprinted by permission.

Excerpts from "Our Music Lesson #2, Or How We Appropriated You: An Imaginary Short Starring Elvis Chang, Rocky Rivera, and Jimi Hendrix" from *The Gangster of Love*. Copyright © 1996 by Jessica Hagedorn. Reprinted by permission of Houghton Mifflin Company and the author All rights reserved.

Also in this series:

Discussions in Contemporary Culture
Edited by Hal Foster

Vision and Visuality
Edited by Hal Foster

The Work of Andy Warhol
Edited by Gary Garrels

Remaking History
Edited by Barbara Kruger
and Philomena Mariani

Democracy:
A Project by Group Material
Edited by Brian Wallis

If You Lived Here: The City in Art,
Theory, and Social Activism
A Project by Martha Rosler
Edited by Brian Wallis

Critical Fictions:
The Politics of Imaginative Writing
Edited by Philomena Mariani

Black Popular Culture:
A Project by Michele Wallace
Edited by Gina Dent

Culture on the Brink:
Ideologies of Technology
Edited by Gretchen Bender
and Timothy Druckrey

Visual Display:
Culture Beyond Appearances
Edited by Lynne Cooke
and Peter Wollen

Constructing Masculinity
Edited by Maurice Berger,
Brian Wallis, and Simon Watson